GW00535554

GEORGIA

Georgia

Pawn in the New Great Game

Per Gahrton

PlutoPress
www.plutobooks.com

First published 2010 by Pluto Press
345 Archway Road, London N6 5AA and
175 Fifth Avenue, New York, NY 10010

Distributed in the United States of America exclusively by
Palgrave Macmillan, a division of St. Martin's Press LLC,
175 Fifth Avenue, New York, NY 10010

www.plutobooks.com

British Library Cataloguing in Publication Data
A catalogue record for this book is available from the British Library

ISBN   978 0 7453 2860 7   Hardback
ISBN   978 0 7453 2859 1   Paperback

Library of Congress Cataloging in Publication Data applied for

This book is printed on paper suitable for recycling and made from fully
managed and sustained forest sources. Logging, pulping and manufactur-
ing processes are expected to conform to the environmental standards of
the country of origin.

10 9 8 7 6 5 4 3 2 1

Designed and produced for Pluto Press by
Curran Publishing Services, Norwich

Printed and bound in the European Union by
CPI Antony Rowe, Chippenham and Eastbourne

CONTENTS

    Russia's whiplashes   205
    Escalation   207
    No anti-Russian feelings   210
    Russians against anti-Georgian policy   212
    Is a Russian carrot impossible?   213
    Notes   215

15 **Georgia's future: Caucasian, European and nonaligned**   216
    NATO: no solution   216
    Why not a Finnish option?   218
    Cyprus repeated in the Caucasus?   220
    What carrot for Russia?   222
    Russian neocolonialism – or just globalization?   225
    Options for Georgia   227
    The need for alternative policy   229
    Notes   232

    Bibliography   *237*
    Index   *243*

PHOTOS

ACRONYMS

AFP	Agence France-Presse
AO	autonomous oblast (region)
ASSR	autonomous Soviet socialist republic
BBC	British Broadcasting Corporation
BTC	Baku–Tbilisi–Ceyhan pipeline
BTE	Baku–Tbilisi–Erzerum pipeline
BTS	Baku–Tbilisi–Supsa pipeline
CE	Council of Europe
CEC	Central Election Commission
CEO	Caucasus Environment Outlook
CEPS	Center for European Policy Studies
CIA	Central Intelligence Agency (USA)
CIS	Commonwealth of Independent States
CISPFK	CIS Peacekeeping Force
CMPC	Confederation of Mountain Peoples of Caucasus
CSTO	Collective Security Treaty Organization
CUG	Citizens Union of Georgia
EAEC	Euroasian Economic Community
EBRD	European Bank for Reconstruction and Development
ECFR	European Council on Foreign Relations
EU	European Union
EUMM	European Union Monitoring Mission
FBI	Federal Bureau of Investigation
FSB	Federalnaya Sluzhba Bezopasnosti (Federal Security Service, Russia)
GECF	Gas Exporting Countries Forum
GNP	Gross National Product
GPB	Georgian Public Broadcasting
GUAM	Georgia, Ukraine, Azerbaijan, Moldova (previously GUUAM, but changed name when Uzbekistan withdrew from the organization)
GYLA	Georgian Young Lawyers' Association
HRIC	Human Rights Information Center
ICG	International Crisis Group

IMF	International Monetary Fund
INOGATE	Interstate Oil and Gas Transport to Europe
IEOM	International Election Observation mission
ISAB	International Security Advisory Board
ISFED	International Society for Fair Elections and Democracy
IWPR	Institute for War and Peace Reporting
KGB	Komitet gosudarstvennoj bezapastnosti (committee for state security, the FBI of the Soviet Union)
NATO	North Atlantic Treaty Organization
NDP	National Democratic Party
NEP	New Economic Policy
NGO	nongovernment organization
OCAC	Organization of Central Asian Cooperation
ODHIR	Office for Democratic Institutions and Human Rights (of OSCE)
OECD	Organization for Economic Cooperation and Development
OPEC	Organization of Petroleum Exporting Countries
OSCE	Organization for Security and Cooperation in Europe
SCO	Shanghai Cooperation Organization
SSR	Soviet socialist republic
TRACECA	Transport Corridor Europe–Caucasus–Asia
UAV	unmanned aerial vehicle
UNDP	United Nations Development Programme
UNEP	United Nations Environment Programme
UNHCR	United Nations High Commissioner for Refugees
UNM	United National Movement
UNOMIG	United Nations Observer Mission in Georgia
USSR	Union of Soviet Socialist Republics
WTO	World Trade Organization

PREFACE

My relation to Georgia started through contacts with the founder of the Georgian Green party, Zurab Zhvania, in the early 1990s. My first visit was during the stormy year of 1993. During my second and last period as Member of the European Parliament from 1999 to 2004 I was rapporteur for South Caucasus. I have for several years been a member of the Advisory Council of the Regional Environmental Centre in Tbilisi. I have also been an official election observer at several elections and visited the country as an accredited journalist. Thus, my relations to Georgia are personal, political and professional. This is reflected in this book, which is not a scientific treatise. I am clearly and openly biased in favour of the Georgian people, but very critical of several Georgian phenomena.

It will be obvious to the reader that I consider the death of Zurab Zhvania a major catastrophe for Georgia, and am convinced that, alive and politically active, he would have made an important difference. My thoughts go to his family members, who have contributed to my knowledge of Zurab and his work – his wife Nino, his brother Giorgi and his mother Mariam. I want to dedicate the book to his children, Elizabeth, 16, Bessarion, 14 and Anna, 11, who should know that although their loss is much worse, the premature and mysterious death of their father is a great loss to all Georgians and friends of Georgia, indeed to humankind.

I have a working knowledge of Russian, but not of Georgian. Several Georgian friends have helped and guided me in Georgia, and also followed the Georgian-language media for me and reported articles and items of interest for the book.

Two persons have played a special role in assisting me, including by commenting on the manuscript: Sofia Sakhanberidze, spokesperson for the Georgian Greens and Nato Kirvalidze, the first director of the Regional Environmental Centre in Tbilisi.

Also thanks to the general secretary of the Georgian Greens, Gia Gachechiladze, and other members of the Georgian Greens for invaluable support, as well as to the experts and personnel at the office of the Regional Environmental Center and the EU representation in Tbilisi. The list of all Georgians who have directly or indirectly contributed could fill a book, so let me send my gratitude to everybody. Without the help of all these persons the book could not have been completed. However I am of course fully responsible for the final version, especially for the conclusions and recommendations.

I am also grateful to Liz Egebäck-Foxbrook for checking and correcting my imperfect English and to Martin Axkull for improving my amateur photos into publishable quality. Finally I am indebted to David Castle at Pluto for several years of fruitful cooperation, as well as to his colleagues who have made my manuscript into a book.

The situation in the Caucasus region is extremely volatile, and changes occur rapidly and unexpectedly. Conventional printed books inevitably suffer from the risk of being partly outdated when they reach the readers. Those interested in my up-to-date opinion about Caucasus and Georgia could check my homepage www.gahrton.dinstudio.se or send me an e-mail, to pgahrton@swipnet.se.

Per Gahrton
Bessinge, Hörby, Sweden
November 2009

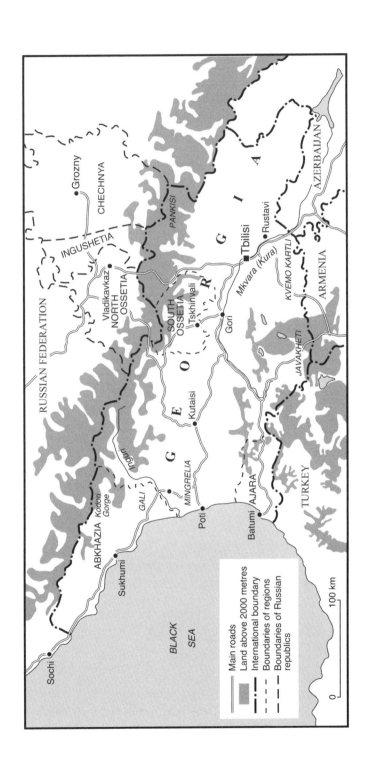

1

THE GEOPOLITICAL SETTING – A RENEWED GREAT GAME

The expression 'the Great Game' usually refers to the clash between British and Russian interests in Central Asia in the nineteenth century. Although the centre of the conflict was Afghanistan, British fear was also caused by the Russian expansion into South Caucasus, where the tsarist empire replaced Persia through the treaties of Gulistan (1813) and Turkmanchai (1826), by which most of Azerbaijan and Georgia came under the control of St Petersburg. During the Soviet period, Central Asia, the Caspian region and the Caucasus were firmly under the control of Moscow. After the breakdown of the Soviet Union in 1991, the resumption of the Great Game was postponed by a honeymoon period between the Yeltsin regime and the West. In 1997, however, US intentions were made clear by the former presidential adviser, Zbigniew Brzezinski, when he launched a 'geostrategy for Eurasia', asserting that 'What happens with the distribution of power on the Eurasian landmass will be of decisive importance to America's global primacy.'[1]

A dozen years later it has become clear how a modern and expanded version of the Great Game is developing rapidly, in which the Western aim is to transform South Caucasus into a two-way transport route: westbound for the fossil fuels of the Caspian region, eastbound for military personnel and material to Central Asia and further. As one commentator observed in the spring of 2009, 'South Caucasus is uniquely situated to become the nucleus of an international geostrategic campaign by the major Western powers to achieve domination of Europe, Asia, the Middle East and Africa and as such the world.'[2]

A TROUBLED AREA

Since ancient times the Caucasus area has been a frontier and link between Europe and Asia, where cultures, empires and religions have met, fought or cooperated. Waves of armies, explorers and traders have passed along the Silk Road between China and the West. At the end of the nineteenth century the centre of the emerging oil industry was situated in Baku, capital of Azerbaijan.

In a narrow sense the Caucasus region comprises the southern parts of the Russian Federation and the independent states of Azerbaijan, Armenia and Georgia. Some writers also include northern parts of Iran and eastern parts of Turkey. Armenia, Azerbaijan and Georgia have traditionally been bound together by economic, social and cultural ties. Today, the region is fragmented by border blockades, disconnected rail links, ethnic conflicts and the formation of breakaway territories.

The Soviet planned economy has only partly been replaced by a normal market economy. The Caucasian economies, like many other post-Soviet economies, suffer from what the Georgian economist Vladimir Papava has labelled 'necroeconomics', that is, those parts of the Soviet economy that lacked real customers and were virtually dead.[3] Such remnants of Soviet times are nothing but piles of scrap metal. It is symbolic that one of the major export goods of Georgia over several years was precisely that – scrap metal!

Another problem has been the methods used, often after recommendation from Western economists, to switch from a Soviet economy to a market economy – which could be described as 'shock therapy'. A decade after the liberation from the Soviet Union several politicians in the Caucasus area told this author that the transfer strategy was a catastrophe. Gagik Aslanyan, vice speaker of the Armenian parliament, was of the opinion that 'during 1991–1996 the privatizations were implemented blindly'. Artashes Geramyan, of the opposition party Law and Order, thought that Armenia should start a judicial process against the World Bank and the International Monetary Foundation (IMF) because of their catastrophic advice to liberalize rapidly. In Georgia the leader of the Industrial Party, Gogi Topadze, said that 'blind obeisance to the IMF will make us sink like the Titanic'.

A study by the Centre for European Policy Studies described the disastrous economic situation in the three countries during the 1990s as 'partly a result of liberalization' and 'caused by transition to a free market system'.[4] Together, necroeconomics and shock therapy had a catastrophic effect for all parts of the former Soviet Union. In 2000 the gross national product (GNP) of the twelve CIS states did not even reach 50 per cent of 1991 levels.[5]

All three South Caucasus countries suffer from unresolved conflicts. Armenia won a war (in the early 1990s against Azerbaijan over the territory of Nagorno-Karabakh), but during many years seemed to be in the process of losing the ceasefire, owing to the blockade imposed by Turkey and Azerbaijan. However, a visit by the president of Turkey to the Armenian capital of Yerevan in September 2008, and other bilateral contacts between Turkey and Armenia, have implied that a thaw in relations may be emerging. Georgia is in dispute with Russia on several fronts, as will be treated at length in this book: energy supplies, trade relations, the breakaway regions of Abkhazia and South Ossetia, and the border with Chechnya.

All three countries are formally multi-party democracies, but everywhere governments are accused, by opposition parties and nongovernment organizations (NGOs), of electoral fraud and human rights violations. The entire region is characterized by traditional male domination, which means that women cannot occupy their legitimate place in society.

The Russian influence is obvious, especially because of the close geographical, economic, cultural, ethnic and historical links between South Caucasus and adjacent parts of the Russian Federation. Russian is still used as a lingua franca in the region and understood by most inhabitants. Geographical, economic and cultural factors also make Iran and Turkey important actors of the area.

The environmental situation is alarming, with consequences for regions and countries beyond the South Caucasus itself, such as water pollution in the Caspian and Black seas. Some years ago the Caucasus Environment Outlook (CEO) looked at how to build environmental security for the region.[6] The approach was deeply pessimistic. The CEO chose to discard the option of 'sustainable development' as totally unrealistic for South Caucasus. Instead three other options were outlined:

- The status quo, based on peace, conflict resolution, return of refugees to their homes, internal stability and low economic growth. For the environment this would mean an inefficient environmental policy, more traffic corridors, too many cars and more hazardous chemicals used in agriculture.
- Chaos, with armed gangs roaming and anarchy. Paradoxically this was supposed to be partially positive for the environment, because the countryside and wildlife would get the chance to recover because of lack of human activity. However, anarchy would leave forests at the mercy of illegal logging, drinking water would be contaminated, and so on.

- A functioning market economy, with foreign investments and privatizations. This would create economic growth, but the result for the environment would be problematic, with more polluting emissions from industry, energy, traffic and the like, and more exploitation of scarce resources, such as clean water.

The fact that all three scenarios estimated as realistic predicted deterioration of the environmental situation is of course because none of the Caucasus states, according to the study, was believed to be capable of introducing strong environmental legislation and policies in the foreseeable future. A decade after the study was made, this forecast has come true, which is confirmed in several reports, for example on the homepage of the UN Development Programme (UNDP), where numerous examples of serious environmental problems in South Caucasus are given. Amongst others is widespread water pollution: 'due to the discharge of insufficiently treated waste water, heavy metals from mining and industry, and ammonia and nitrates from the fertilizer industry; large amounts of untreated waste water is discharged into water courses as many treatment plants are no longer operational (around 80 percent in Georgia)'. To improve the situation, the UNDP urges the South Caucasus countries 'to cope with current lack of political commitment for environmental mainstreaming and public involvement in policy making, lack of understanding of its benefits, lack of technical, administrative and financial capacity and lack of coordination among relevant national authorities.'[7]

THE NEW SILK ROAD

The Caspian region – Azerbaijan, Kazakhstan, Turkmenistan, Iran, Uzbekistan and Russia – is believed to have about 10 per cent of the oil reserves of the world. By 2010 Caspian countries are expected to produce between 2.9 and 3.8 million barrels of oil per day, which would exceed the annual production from South America's largest oil producer, Venezuela. While the United States is the number one net importer of oil, followed by Japan and the major EU countries (Germany, France, Italy and Spain), two of the top net exporters are Russia and Kazakhstan. The United States, because of the enormous amount of oil required to maintain the famous 'American way of life', imports 58 per cent of the oil it consumes.

The importance of the Caspian area, especially the Russian part, as a producer and exporter is even more gigantic for gas than for oil. Russia is estimated to be in possession of the largest quantity of world natural gas reserves, almost a third of the total, with Iran as number two. As has been shown by some well-publicized breakdowns of the delivery system, many European countries are highly dependent on gas from Russia.

To construct a new 'Silk Road' was a pet project of Edward Shevardnadze. He published a book about it in 1999, where he claims that he launched the idea back when he was minister of Foreign Affairs of the Soviet Union, in September 1990. He had a very grand approach, mentioning an 11,000 kilometres long railway from 'coast to coast' – Lianyungang to Rotterdam. In his book, written when he was president of independent Georgia, he maintains that the Silk Road project must include Russia and lead to 'a reinforcement of Russian–Georgian relations and a harmonization of their interests – those who think otherwise are wrong'.[8]

However, the ambition of Shevardnadze to use a new Silk Road as a method to strengthen East–West cooperation has not been accepted by all players in the Great Game. The US Department of Energy on its home page, with obvious delight, exclaims that 'thanks to the Soviet Union's collapse, the world has gained the opportunity to share in one of the planet's greatest supplies of natural resources.'[9] Neither the United States nor the European states are prepared to let the Russian Federation retain control over what was once a Soviet prerogative. That is why the whole area of Central Asia, the Caspian Sea region and South Caucasus, has been the object of a fierce battle for influence, since the beginning of the 1990s; a new Great Game.

Russia has a strategic position in the new Great Game not only because of its own huge reserves and actual production and export, but also because of its control over transport routes from the other producers in the region. The Russian political, social and economic influence in the Central Asian and South Caucasus states, all being former Soviet republics, has also been significant after the fall of the Soviet Union, despite nationalistic and other apprehensions about Moscow from within the newly independent states. The links and connections between the former partners in the thoroughly organized and centrally planned Soviet system were so complex that after 20 years of independence they are still strong enough to affect the situation in the whole region. Thus, there has been and still is a struggle between two countervailing trends. One is the ambition of the United States and, to a lesser degree, the European Union, to break the Russian semi-monopoly over the energy resources and the means of their delivery westwards, and to secure access routes to the Caspian oil and gas that are outside Russian influence. This trend is supported by the natural wish of the Central Asian and South Caucasian states to improve their political independence by diminishing their social and economic dependence on Russia. Set against this is the ambition of Russia to preserve as many advantages as possible by its control over energy resources and their transport routes, and to maintain some influence over its near neighbourhood, not only for economic but also for security reasons. This trend is supported by fears from ethnic minorities in several of the newly independent states about new nationalisms, against which Russia has been seen as a security guarantee.

THE WESTERN OFFENSIVE

The Western offensive in the area started in the early 1990s, although during the first period it was designed to not unduly offend Russia. The Caucasus states were included in NATO's Partnership for Peace in 1994 and the Euroatlantic Partnership Council in 1997, both of which have all non-NATO former Soviet Republics, including Russia, as members, as well as several non-aligned Western states, such as Sweden. In 1999 the Partnership and Cooperation Agreements between the European Union and the South Caucasus states, signed three years earlier, went into force, which according to one observer meant that the 'EU integrates South Caucasus in its sphere of influence'.[10] The same year Georgia became a member of the Council of Europe, followed two years later by Armenia and Azerbaijan. However Russia is also a member of the Council of Europe and has a partnership agreement with the European Union.

At the beginning of 1999 US President Bill Clinton, in connection with the NATO bombings of Serbia, made statements that have been called 'the Clinton doctrine'. They have been interpreted by an American commentator[11] as the starting point for a 'US effort to convert NATO from a defensive alliance in Western Europe into a regional police force governed by Washington', and by a French analyst as a sign that the United States aspires to control post-Soviet states.[12] One tangible result was the choice in November of the same year by the president of Azerbaijan, Heydar Aliyev, in favour of the pipelines Baku–Tbilisi–Supsa (BTS), Baku–Tbilisi–Ceyhan

(BTC) and Baku–Tbilisi–Erzerum (BTE), rather than alternatives passing through Armenia, thereby avoiding the territory of a close ally of Russia. Another Western victory in 1999 was the decision by Georgia and Azerbaijan, as well as Uzbekistan, to withdraw from the collective security organization of the former Soviet republics, the Collective Security Treaty Organization (CSTO).

Significant steps in a pro-US direction were taken when the three South Caucasian states sent troops to Iraq in 2003 and in 2004–05 were adopted as members of NATO's Individual Partnership Action Plans, which has a rather narrow membership, including only seven former communist states, and notably not Russia. What could be expected in the future was revealed in early 2008 by five former top-ranking American military leaders in a study called 'Towards a grand strategy for an uncertain world – renewing transatlantic partnership', where they presented a 'long-term vision of an alliance of democracies ranging from Finland to Alaska' – which of course excludes Russia. They also proposed 'the establishment of a directorate consisting of the United States, the EU and NATO,' which would 'coordinate all cooperation in the common transatlantic sphere of interest'.[13] Exit the United Nations, and exit all non-Western nations, from the rule of the world of tomorrow!

A major step towards Western access to the fossil fuels around the Caspian was the so-called 'Contract of the century', concluded in 1994, by which Azerbaijan sold extensive rights of exploitation to Western oil companies.[14] According to one analyst this contract meant that the United States 'obtains from Baku the control of several offshore Caspian oil wells'.[15] The European Union launched two projects for access to the Caspian resources, TRACECA – Transport Corridor Europe Caucasus Asia (1993) – and INOGATE – Interstate Oil and Gas Transport to Europe (1995). In the United States a Silk Road Act was adopted in 1999 to support more or less the same type of links as TRACECA and INOGATE.

TRACECA is described on its homepage as 'the renaissance of the Great Silk Road', and has as its aim to create a transport corridor on road and rail that starts in Eastern Europe, crosses Turkey and the Black Sea to the ports of Poti and Batumi in Georgia, further using the transport network of the Southern Caucasus, and by means of the Caspian ferries, reaches the railway networks of the Central Asian states and the borders of China and Afghanistan. From 1996 till 2006 more than 70 projects were supported by the TRACECA programme, for a total amount of €160 million. Thirteen countries have been beneficiaries of the TRACECA programme, including all former non-EU Soviet republics, except Russia and Belarus.

According to its homepage INOGATE is concerned with 'the broad energy security strategies of both the Partner Countries and the EU'. Turkey and all non-EU former Soviet republics, except Russia, are listed as members. Russia is listed only as an observer.

Because of the complicated situation in the region, with several unresolved internal conflicts and the obvious superpower competition for influence, almost every project, which under other circumstances would have been greeted with almost unanimous applause, is met with a storm of criticism and protests from governments and NGOs. One of the most disputed projects of the Silk Road concept has been the BTC pipeline, which was begun in 2002 and inaugurated on May 25, 2005. BTC is 1,762 km long and cost some US$3.6 billion. Arguments against the project included environmental concern, worries about the costs compared with possible gains, and geostrategic apprehensions.

According to the Swedish-American Central Asia-Caucasus Institute, the BTC pipeline was 'the culmination of a work, begun with the collapse of the USSR in 1991', which opened an 'oil window to the West'.[16] According to the same institute the BTC pipeline is 'a first step toward providing the lands east of the Caspian Sea with a direct connection to Europe that does not depend on former colonial overlords'.[17] A similar picture of the BTC, as a geostrategic US-sponsored, anti-Russian project, is supported from an opposite perspective by a fierce critic who states that the BTC is part of a strategy that includes 'overt and covert Washington backing and financing (of) new US-friendly regimes ... in former Soviet states which are in a strategic relation to possible pipeline routes from the Caspian Sea'.[18]

It is a fact that during a period of a few years before the inauguration of the BTC pipeline, so-called colour revolutions took place in several former communist states, from Serbia and Ukraine, via Georgia and Kyrgystan. International media speculated on a continued domino process taking revolutions to countries like Azerbaijan and even Russia. While most Western commentators and governments saw these regime changes as results of spontaneous popular and democratic revolts against authoritarian rulers, others, not only in Moscow, believed that even if the colour revolutions could not be reduced to simple machinations of the US Central Intelligence Agency (CIA), they had at least been supported by and rapidly taken over and steered by Western intelligence and political forces whose aims had little in common with democracy, but were more aimed at securing Western control over the sites and transport routes of the Caspian energy resources.

A REGIONAL ALTERNATIVE?

An alternative for the South Caucasian states to the difficult choice between either the United States and NATO, or Russia, might be more regional cooperation. In such a way the region could become a bridge between East and West, South and North, instead of being a centre of disputes and clashes. Some authors even suggest that the region should be renamed Central Caucasus in order to emphasize its centrality between Northern Caucasus in Russia and Southern Caucasus in Turkey and Iran.[19] The fact that the three countries are very different ethnically, linguistically and in religious make-up should not be an obstacle, because all efforts to base regional cooperation in former Soviet republics upon ethnic-religious principles, such as the Slav, Turk or Orthodox, have failed. Their common history, although not without complications, should work in favour of regional cooperation, as should their socioeconomic relations and a common interest in safeguarding their new independence. But the reality has been different, very much as a result of the inability of the three states to resolve their internal conflicts.

Whoever is to blame, it is a fact that regional cooperation in South Caucasus has never worked very well or for very long. It has worked even less well if North Caucasus is included, despite numerous efforts, such as the struggle for a Caucasian Emirate in the nineteenth century and proclamations of similar projects in the twenty-first century. The Transcaucasian Federation that was established after the Russian Revolution on April 22, 1918 lasted for little more than a month, Georgia being the first to break ranks and proclaim its own independence on May 26, followed by Azerbaijan on May 27 and Armenia on May 28. None of these republics, however, survived more than a couple of years. They were all conquered by the Red Army: Azerbaijan in February 1920, Armenia in December of that year and finally Georgia in February 1921. During its first 15 years as part of the Soviet Union, South Caucasus was again united in a Transcaucasian Republic, but even the centralized rule by Moscow was insufficient to keep the states together, and in 1936 they were split into three separate Soviet socialist republics.[20]

This has created an absurd situation where instead of a common and open South Caucasus area, two diverging alliances have emerged. One links Turkey to Georgia and Azerbaijan, and is supported by the United States and to some degree the European Union. Another links Russia with Armenia and has an extension towards Iran. As tragic as this pattern is for the regional situation, it is interesting from another point of view; it invalidates the famous Huntington theory of a clash of ethnic-religious 'civilizations', because both alliances contain very orthodox Christians and more or less fundamentalist Muslims.

RUSSIA'S COMEBACK

The Russian dominance of Central Asia, the Caspian Region and Caucasus has its origin before the Great Game against Great Britain, in the eighteenth century when the tsarist empire won several battles against the main regional competitors of that time, the Iranian shahs and the Ottoman sultans. This long history of Russian dominance is one of several reasons put forward by Russian authors to emphasize that 'the West must understand that Russia remains the major power in the area and will not accept a Yugoslavian solution'.[21] Already before the formal dissolution of the USSR, in December 1991, Russia, Ukraine and Belarus, by establishing the Commonwealth of Independent States (CIS), announced an ambition to re-establish some form of practical cooperation between the former Soviet Republics in order to counter the devastating effects of the introduction of border controls, customs and other symbols of independence, into an area which had since long been highly integrated. While the Baltic States immediately manifested their intention to cut every link to the Russian 'occupiers' and headed for integration into Nordic, European and transatlantic structures, the rest of the former Soviet republics, in some cases after considerable hesitation, were reunited in the framework of CIS in 1994 and have remained so. However after the South Ossetia War of 2008 Georgia decided to leave CIS.

The Eurasian Economic Community (EAEC) was founded in 2000 on the basis of an earlier customs union between Russia, Belarus and Kazakhstan, by six CIS states, with another three as observers. Outside are, for different reasons, Azerbaijan, Georgia and Turkmenistan. The declared ambition is to develop the EAEC, after the EU model, into a Common Economic Space in the near future. In 2006 another organization for cooperation between CIS states, the Organization of Central Asian Cooperation (OCAC), was merged with the EAEC.

The CSTO is the military branch of the CIS, although it has only seven members, Turkmenistan preferring to remain outside most regional organizations in order to maintain 'neutrality'. There is also GUAM – an anti-Russian cooperation between Georgia, Ukraine, Azerbaijan and Moldova which has so far mostly functioned as a faction inside CIS. The GUAM states either have never been CSTO members (Ukraine and Moldova) or have withdrawn (Georgia and Azerbaijan).

The Shanghai Cooperation Organization (SCO) is mainly busy with security matters. It was founded in 1996 and today has Russia, China and the Central Asian states, except Turkmenistan, as members, and India, Iran, Mongolia and Pakistan as observers.

During the two decades since the fall of the USSR there have been some changes in the membership of these organizations, and ups and downs in their development. While at the beginning they were mostly dismissed by Western observers, later there was a reversal in their estimations, despite the decision by Georgia to leave the CIS. A major turn-about has been the switch by Uzbekistan from the pro-Western GUAM to the Russian-supported structures. Kazakhstan became a strategic partner to the United States in 1997, but in 1998 it signed a treaty of 'eternal friendship' with Russia. Turkmenistan did not accept shock therapy and declared permanent neutrality, accepted by the United Nations in 1995.

For many years there was a conflict around the legal aspects of the Caspian Sea. Russia preferred common exploitation, and declared that the 1994 'Contract of the century' was illegal. Russia wanted something like the European Coal and Steel Union for the Caspian resources, which would have led to 'strengthening the Russian positions in the area'.[22] However in 1999 Russia admitted that its Caspian policy had been wrong. Since then the former Soviet republics around the Caspian have more or less agreed on the legal aspects, and the remaining conflicts are with Iran.

The mighty Russian megacompany Gazprom is planning several pipelines to Europe, among others the North Stream in the Baltic Sea and the South Stream from the Caspian Sea through Russia and the Black Sea to Bulgaria and Italy. The European Union would, however, prefer its own project, Nabucco, which would lead the gas through Georgia and Turkey. Some EU states, not least Germany, seem keen to make a deal with Russia, while others are vehemently protesting. One element in the gas delivery is the possibility – or threat – that the Gas Exporting Countries Forum (GECF), which was established in 2001, will be developed into an OPEC-like cartel of gas-exporting countries. If so, Russia, with its enormous gas reserves, would have an even more central position than it has today. That the weight of money is at least as powerful as strategic containment philosophies is shown by the fact that countries as far from Russian dependence as Qatar and Norway have shown interest in such a cartel.[23]

In the summer of 2008 it was reported that the role of Gazprom remains pivotal in Central Asia: 'Although Tashkent is trying to drive a hard bargain with Russian gas company Gazprom, it has little alternative to working with the firm to develop and export its oil and gas.'[24] Some observers claim that the visible and sometimes turbulent Western, mainly American, offensive into the Central Asian, Caspian and Caucasus region has backfired. Especially the 'coloured revolutions' have pushed the rulers of other states back to the Russian fold, because they have seen themselves as the next possible victim. In November 2005, the United States was asked to leave its base at Karshi-Khanabad, a symbol of Tashkent's strategic turnaround back towards Moscow and China. Not even in the few cases where the regime changes seemingly have succeeded are the long-term effects certain. A case to bear in mind is Kyrgystan, whose 'Tulip' Revolution in 2005 was considered to have turned the country into a clear-cut pro-Western bastion. But the new regime has remained rather 'Russophile', and early in 2009 it decided to terminate its unique position as the only country in the world hosting both a Russian and a US military base. On February 3 the Kyrgystani president, a child of the Tulip Revolution, announced that the US Ganci base at Manas airport must be closed, the Kyrgyz parliament confirmed this by 78 votes to 1, and on February 20 the US Embassy in Bishkek was ordered to vacate the base within 180 days. Even before the closure of the Ganci base, a pro-Western think tank summarized the situation by stating that 'the five Central Asian states, especially Uzbekistan, [are] returning back into Russia's fold after many years of rapprochement with the West, whose influence is in decline throughout the region'.[25] However, as a proof of the extremely volatile conditions in the area, in June 2009 the United States and Kyrgyzstan agreed that the Manas base would be transformed into a Transit Centre fulfilling almost the same functions, with a maintained presence of US forces. At the same time it was reported that Russia is establishing a second military base in Kyrgystan.

In a comprehensive study, sponsored by the Swedish Ministry of Foreign Affairs, the Central Asia-Caucasus Institute rang alarm bells against a possible Russian comeback on the scene. According to the summary, oil and gas resources in the Caspian Region constitute the most accessible energy alternatives for Europe, which makes it 'imperative that access routes to Caspian resources are secured, which are not under Russian influence'. But, it maintained, since the only infrastructure bringing Caspian energy to Europe outside Russian control so far comprises the BTC oil pipeline and the BTE gas pipeline, it is important that EU- and US-sponsored projects such as the Nabucco and Trans-Caspian pipelines are successfully implemented. 'There is, however, a clear risk that these projects will fail to materialize, especially as an effect of the so far rather successful Russian strategies for counteracting them.' According to the study the Russians work in several ways: first, by securing long-term contracts with Kazakhstan and Turkmenistan through Gazprom; second, by trying to form an intergovernmental gas cartel; third, by seeking to provide new infrastructure for energy transit to Europe from the Caspian – such as the Burgas–Alexandroupolis pipeline, the Blue Stream gas pipeline, and the South Stream, planned to run under the Black Sea from Russia to Bulgaria, which all are aimed at reducing the rationale for projects such as Nabucco and the Trans-Caspian pipeline; and fourth, by exploiting the European Union's inability to unite around a common energy strategy, thereby allowing Russia and Gazprom to buy majority shares in European energy companies, and strike bilateral deals with individual EU states.[26]

At the same time many reports give the impression that the producer states around the Caspian are keen to diversify their export routes in all possible directions, including southwards through Iran and eastwards to China. While the leaders of Azerbaijan and six other former Soviet republics met in Kiev in the summer of 2008, to launch a new initiative to transport Caspian oil through Ukraine without traversing Russian territory, and announced ambitious plans to send oil from Azerbaijan and Kazakhstan through Georgia to Ukraine, and through Poland onward to Gdansk, the governments of Turkmenistan and Kazakhstan reaffirmed their intention to expand their deliveries of oil and gas northward through Russian-controlled pipelines connecting Central Asia with European markets.[27]

CHECHNYA – ALL ABOUT OIL?

The crucial and often destructive role of fossil fuels in the life of Caucasus is tragically exemplified by the case of Chechnya. The refusal by Moscow to accept the de facto independence of this small Caucasian republic, which was established in 1995 after the First Chechen War, is often explained by a fear of a domino effect that might break up the Russian Federation, with its 26 more or less autonomous republics and areas, in the same way as the Soviet Union disintegrated. Another reason given by Russian politicians is that Chechnya had deteriorated into a gangster regime, infamous for kidnappings and drug trafficking, and a centre for Islamic terrorism. While these reasons for the Russian decision to start the Second Chechen War in autumn 1999 contain some truth, few observers seem to have dug very deeply to explain the fact that the single event that triggered the renewed Russian assault was a militarily minor incursion by Chechen-Muslim guerrillas into Dagestan. Several sources claim that the aim of this action was not just to spread the revolt against Russia into a neighbouring Caucasian republic, but that it was part of a far more ingenious plan, hatched not in Grozny but in the offices of Western Big Capital, to take control over large parts of Russian oil and gas and some of its transportation routes.

A short time before his death in 1997 the British-French financial tycoon James Goldsmith established the Caucasus-American Chamber of Commerce, the aim of which was to create a Caucasus Common Market, which Chechnya was supposed to join as an independent member. After the death of Goldsmith in the summer of 1997 the responsibility for the project was taken over by his close collaborator, Lord McAlpine, who visited Grozny in October 1997 with a delegation of high-ranking businessmen for talks with the Chechen president Aslan Maskhadov. Among other well-known figures involved in the project were Jacques Attali, former director of the European Bank for Reconstruction and Development (EBRD), Tsezar Shevardnadze and Altai Khazanov, the latter two being nephews of the presidents of Georgia and Azerbaijan. A Western think tank late in 1997 concluded that 'it seems quite possible that Russia, when transporting Caspian oil to the Black Sea port at Novorossiysk for onward transmission to western markets, will have to deal not only with Grozny but also, and even more unpleasantly for the Kremlin, western capital'.[28] But the risk of having to deal with Grozny and western money about transportation of Caspian oil was not the only problem for Moscow. The ambition of the Chechen leaders, McAlpine and others, was to achieve a merger of Chechnya with Dagestan into an independent federation, which would then become a riverain state of the Caspian Sea with legal control over two-thirds of the Russian part of the continental shelf – that is, over large parts of the Russian oil and gas resources.

For Western capitalists it was of course crucial that no reconciliation should occur between Russia and Chechnya. According to an article in the respected Russian newspaper *Kommersant* early in 1998, a peace agreement between Moscow and Grozny was imminent in autumn 1997, when McAlpine came to Grozny on October 13. Then suddenly the Chechens withdrew from their commitments to Russia, obviously after an internal power struggle.[29] In December that year the infamous rebel leader Shamil Basayev publicly threatened to 'liberate' Dagestan. When he put action to his words in August 1999 together with 1,400 Islamist fighters, the new Russian prime minister, Vladimir Putin, struck back mercilessly, and the Second Chechen War was a fact, with all its disastrous effects for the civilian population, elaborately described by the assassinated Russian journalist, Anna Politkovskaya.[30] The Caucasus-American Chamber of Commerce and its project to create a Caucasus Common Market are mentioned on the official homepage of FSB, the Russian security service, as an example of all the threats that have been directed against Russia since the fall of the USSR, and a proof that 'United States has not lost the hope of turning Russia into a zone under American influence'.[31]

NEW RUSSIAN STRATEGY

On May 13, 2009, Russia officially launched a new National Security strategy for the period until 2020, replacing the 1997 version, which was established during very different circumstances. Then, NATO membership of Russia was still considered a serious possibility. Now Russia officially accuses NATO of 'creating threats to international security'.

Are the Russian apprehensions about US and Western intentions in its 'close neighbourhood' nothing but a brainchild of Russian authoritarian minds? It is not only Western anti-Russian commentators who allege that that is the case. Some Russian democratic critics of the Putin–Medvedev regime seem to agree, for example the political scientist Lilia Shevtsova, who in 2009 published a book on Russian–Western relations in which she claims that the notion of

Western efforts to surround and contain Russia is just an invention by the 'ruling rentier class' to 'divert the attention of the population from internal problems'.[32]

While I agree with all the liberal and democratic criticism of the authoritarian abuses of the present rulers in the Kremlin, I find it naïve to deny that the West, or more correctly the United States, intends to prevent any Russian comeback as a strong and independent player in world politics, irrespective of Russia's political system. After all, Putin did not usurp power by a coup, but was picked for the job by Boris Yeltsin, usually praised in the West as a beacon of Russian democracy. In his autobiography Yeltsin describes how most of his presidency was characterized by a fear for a Russian 'variant of Yugoslavia', with total chaos, dissolution of the Federation, and a split into a myriad of warring ministates.[33]

A sincerely democratic Russian leadership would of course have acted differently in many ways. But not even the most liberal democrat in Kremlin would have remained inactive against the obvious ambitions by the West to control some of Russia's closest neighbours. That the Russian apprehensions cannot be discarded as mere fantasy was once more highlighted by the Jamestown Foundation in the beginning of 2009 in a report on the impact of the Ossetia War upon the transport routes for oil and gas through Georgia. It concluded that 'Georgia or Azerbaijan independently cannot guarantee the security of the transit lines. Only a strong European and American presence would prevent disruptive actions that sabotage the transit infrastructure.'[34]

From this perspective it was logical that the United States and Georgia in January 2009 agreed on a charter of strategic partnership, which held its first meeting in Washington in June the same year. In July 2009 minister Gia Baramidze told me that he saw this arrangement as almost the same as the coveted Membership Action Plan, and an important step towards NATO membership for Georgia.[35]

WILL OBAMA MAKE A DIFFERENCE?

However, the situation may change. On July 7, 2009, in a speech in Moscow, US President Barack Obama asserted that 'America wants a strong, peaceful, and prosperous Russia.' In September he abolished the US plans to deploy launching sites for missiles in Poland and the Czech Republic. Russia replied by scrapping similar plans for the Kaliningrad area. According to Pavel Felgengauer of

The author (right) with vice premier Gia Baramidze, former Green activist, who
considers the strategic partnership agreement concluded with the United States
in January 2009 as almost equivalent to a Membership Action Plan and an
important step towards NATO membership for Georgia

Novaya Gazeta, who is very critical of the Putin–Medvedev regime,
the United States and Russia have made a deal according to which
the United States will give Russia a more or less free hand in its
'close neighbourhood', including Georgia, in exchange for Russian
permission for the United States to use Russian air space for 4,500
military transport flights a year to Afghanistan.[36] The logic is of
course that the United States and Russia have a common interest
in defeating all kinds of Islamic insurgency, a theory that gains in
credibility by the frequent reports of growing dissatisfaction and
anti-Russian violence all over North Caucasus.[37]

The renewed Great Game is on. Even if it may change character,
even if the new Cold War between the traditional enemies of the
second half of the twentieth century is postponed in order to make
way for a Northern/Christian alliance against the Islamic South, the
result would be similar for the South Caucasus region, which is situated on the fault line not only between the classical East and West,
but also between major religious-cultural civilizations. As always,
the most vulnerable victims of the clashes between superpowers are

not the active players or combatants, but all those who happen to stand in the way, those who suffer collateral damage. One example is Georgia and its people.

NOTES

1   Zbigniew Brzesinski, 'A geostrategy for Europe', *Foreign Affairs*, September/October 1997.
2   Rick Rozoff, 'Eurasian crossroads: the Caucasus in US-NATO war plans', *Global Research*, 8 April 2009 <www.globalresearch.ca/index.php?context=va&aid=13101>.
3   Vladimer Papava, *Necroeconomics: The political economy of post-communist capitalism*, iUniverse.com, Tbilisi, 2005.
4   'Annex A: Background on the economies of the Caucasus', in M. Emerson and N. Tocci, *A Stability Pact for the Caucasus*, CEPS Task Force for the Caucasus, CEPS, Brussels, 4 May 2000.
5   S. S. Zhyltsov, *Geopolitika kaspijskogo regiona* (The geopolitics of the Caspian region), Mezhdunarodniye Otnosheniya, Moscow, 2002.
6   UN Environment Programme (UNEP) *Caucasus Environment Outlook*, UNEP, Geneva, 2002 <http://www.grid.unep.ch/activities/assessment/geo/ceo.php>.
7   <http://europeandcis.undp.org/environment/show/21D5FBC3-F203-1EE9-BC889A630978B873>.
8   Eduard Schewardnadze, *Die neue Seidenstrasse – Verkehrweg in die 21. Jahrhundert* (The new Silk Road: a communication route of the twenty-first century), Econ Verlag, Munich, 1999.
9   <http://www.energy.gov>.
10 Gaidz Minassian, *Caucase du Sud, la nouvelle guerrre froide* (South Caucasus, the new cold war), Éditions Autrement, Paris 2007.
11 Michael Klare in *The Nation*, 19 April 1999.
12 Minassian, *Caucase du Sud*, p. 20.
13 Written by General (ret.) Klaus Naumann, former chief of the Defence Staff Germany, former chairman of the Military Committee NATO; General (ret.) John Shalikashvili, former chairman of the US Joint Chiefs of Staff , former NATO Supreme Allied Commander in Europe; Field Marshal the Lord Inge, former chief of the UK Defence Staff; Admiral (ret.) Jacques Lanxade, former chief of the Defence Staff France, former ambassador; and General (ret.) Henk van den Breemen, former chief of the Netherlands Defence Staff, in a World Security Network report from Munich, Germany,16 January 2008.
14 *Azerbaijan International*, Winter 1994 (2.4), <http://azer.com/aiweb/categories/magazine/24_folder/24_articles/24_aioc.html>.
15 Minassian, *Caucase du Sud*.
16 S. Frederick Starr and Svante E. Cornell, *The Baku–Tbilisi–Ceyhan pipeline: oil window to the West*, Central Asia-Caucasus Institute and Silk Road Studies Program, Johns Hopkins University, Baltimore, Md., 2005.

17 Svante E. Cornell, Mamuka Tsereteli and Vladimir Socor, 'Geostrategic implications of the Baku–Tbilisi–Ceyhan pipeline', in Starr and Cornell, *The Baku–Tbilisi–Ceyhan pipeline.*

18 F. William Engdahl, 'Color revolutions, geopolitics and the Baku pipeline', *Global Research,* June 25, 2005.

19 Eldar Ismailov and Vladimer Papava, *Tsentralnyj Kavkaz ot geopolitike k geoekonomike* (Central Caucasus, from geopolitics to geoeconomics), CA&CC Press, Stockholm, 2006.

20 Siliva Serrano, *Géorgie – sortie d'empire* (Georgia – exit from the Empire), CNRS Éditions, Paris, 2007.

21 Zhyltsov, *Geopolitika.*

22 Zhyltsov, *Geopolitika.*

23 Qatar: *Der Spiegel,* April 2008; Norway: News Agency <realtid.se>, August 15, 2008.

24 NBCentralAsia, 15 June 2008.

25 Marlène Laruelle, 'Russia's Central Asia policy and the role of Russian nationalism', Central Asia-Caucasus Institute and Silk Road Studies Program <www.silkroadstudies.org>, April 2008.

26 Svante E. Cornell and Niklas Nilsson (eds), *Europe's Energy Security: Gazprom's dominance and Caspian supply alternatives,* Central Asia-Caucasus Institute and Silk Road Studies Program, 2008.

27 Richard Weitz, 'Caspian energy game heats up', *CACI Analyst,* June 11, 2008 <www.silkroadstudies.org>.

28 'Grozny is lobbying for a Caucasus Common Market hoping that the profit motive will force the world community to recognize Chechnya's independence', *Prism,* vol. 3, issue 20, December 5, 1997, Jamestown Foundation.

29 *KommersantVlast,* no. 4 (256), February 10, 1998.

30 Anna Politkovskaya, *Tjetjenien – sanningen om kriget* (Chechnya: the truth about the war), Ordfront, Stockholm 2003.

31 Jurij Ivanovitj Drozdov, 'Kto stoit za terrorizmom v Rossiya?'(Who is behind terrorism in Russia?), <www.fsb.ru>.

32 *Novaya Gazeta,* June 22, 2009.

33 Boris Yeltsin, *Presidentskij Marafon* (The presidential marathon), AST, Moscow 2000.

34 Mamuka Tsereteli, 'The impact of the Russia–Georgia war on the South Caucasus transportation corridor', Jamestown Foundation, <http://www.jamestown.org>, 2009.

35 A Membership Action Plan (MAP) is usually the last preparatory step for a candidate member before formal accession as a full member of NATO.

36 *Novaya Gazeta* no, 74, July 13, 2009.

37 For example in *Sydsvenska Dagbladet* (Sweden), August 21, 2009, 'Islamistgrupper stärks i kaoset' (Islamic groups are strengthened by the chaos) about fights in Dagestan; and *Der Spiegel* (Germany) no. 32/2009, 'Kult der Stärke' (The cult of strength) about 'the explosive situation between the Caspian and the Black Sea, which is a threat towards the leadership in Moscow'.

2

PUPPET OR BUFFER?

Many countries, nations and cultures boast of having hospitality as their special characteristic. This applies more to Georgia than to most of the many other countries I have visited. If it were only for the friendship, helpfulness and consideration I have encountered from Georgians, if the destiny of a nation could be decided by the personal qualities of its inhabitants, Georgia would be a haven of peace and cooperation. If the country had been situated, like my own home country of Sweden, in some calm corner of the world, outside major fault lines and hot spots and spheres of interests of superpowers, a lot would have been different, and perhaps easier. However Georgia is not outside, but right in the middle of everything.

PARADOXES

Georgia lies squeezed between the Greater Caucasus and the Lesser Caucasus mountain ranges, only some 100 kilometres apart. On a satellite picture its area of 70,000 square kilometres, the same size as the Republic of Ireland, looks like a narrow valley. When you travel along the main road from Tbilisi to the Black Sea coast the mountains hover under the sky on both sides as if watching or standing guard.

However, for much of the route there are vast plains with plenty of agricultural fields. But it is virtually impossible to get out of the country on land without crossing a mountain range. The paradox is that despite the fact that Georgia has been, and to a large extent still is, an agricultural country, the mountainous impression is so strong that it even has determined the title of a well-known guidebook, *Georgia: In the mountains of poetry*.[1] This is not the only paradox.

Another paradox has to do with the contradiction between Georgia's geographic and historical reality, and the conception most

Georgians have of their own identity. I still vividly remember a meeting in Kutaisi in western Georgia during my first visit to the country in 1993, with an elderly gentleman, who happened to be the father of the later minister of the environment, Nino Chkhobadze. I was warned that I would have to use my poor Russian to communicate with him, and painted for myself a prejudiced picture of a not very well educated, narrow-minded person, isolated from other cultures than his own, and possibly that of the latest foreign ruler. But when I entered his study I discovered that it was an enormous library stuffed with books not only in Georgian and Russian, but also in Persian and Turkish. There were few if any Latin letters on the spines, however. When we chatted I had to admit that this was a genuinely erudite scholar, with a vast international outlook, but not in the Western sense. In his cultural perception the major roles were played not by American and European cultures, but by other civilizations at least as old and full of wisdom as the Western ones.

However, things are changing. Today many Georgians are keen to convince everybody, including themselves, that they are not Asians, not from the East, but are Europeans, from the West. One commentator has observed that Georgia often seems to try 'to tear itself free from its geography'.[2] There was a noteworthy expression of this attitude when Zurab Zhvania, speaker of the Georgian parliament, in January 1999 exclaimed to the Parliamentary Assembly of the Council of Europe, 'I am Georgian, thus I am European.' Nevertheless, if hard facts are taken as indicators of the degree of the European character of a country, Georgia has still a long way to go. According to the latest figures (at the time of completion of this book in summer 2009), the GNP per capita is estimated to be US$3,060, compared with US$45,688 for the United Kingdom. The Human Development Index is 0.763, which gives Georgia a medium position (number 93) among the world's almost 200 states, while the United Kingdom has a high position (number 21), with an index of 0.942.

Although it can give the opposite impression, Georgia is also a very male society. During my contacts with political parties and NGOs I have met with high-ranking females just as often as with males. Georgia probably has more leading female politicians than any other former communist country: for example Nino Burjanadze, Salome Zurabishvili, Tina Khidasheli and Nino Chkhobadze, just to mention a few. However, the hard facts paint another picture. According to the Inter-Parliamentary Union, as of May 31, 2009, the Georgian parliament had only nine female deputies out of a total of 150: that is 6.0 per cent, which gives the country 160th position in a ranking list of 187 parliaments. The Georgian parliament has the lowest female membership of all former Soviet Republics; its female proportion is only a third of the average for Asia (18.4 per cent) and two-thirds of the average for Arab states (9.7 per cent). Azerbaijan and Armenia also have very low proportions of female parliamentarians, but their figures are higher than Georgia, at 11.4 and 8.4 per cent.[3]

To be blunt, according to basic indicators Georgia and the other two South Caucasus states are still more Asian than European.

At the same time it is a fact that politically the country has chosen a European option. That choice was made long before the Rose Revolution. As far back as September 1997 the Georgian parliament decided to harmonize its legislation with that of the European Union, but still the ambition was, according to Edward Shevardnadze, only to have 'Georgia embedded in the European traffic structure' – that is, it was seeking practical cooperation rather than total integration.[4] However, two years later the Georgian parliament officially declared its intention to join the European Union as a full member.

As a former member of the European Parliament who, as rapporteur for South Caucasus, has proposed that the European Union should make a clear commitment to receive Georgia (and the other South Caucasus states) as full members, I do of course appreciate the strong European aspiration of Georgia.[5] But at the same time I sometimes have doubts. What lies behind this denial of basic facts, so common among Georgian intellectuals and politicians? I have often been on the verge of shouting to Georgians, who have submerged me with overwhelming evidence of their genuine European identity, 'What's wrong with being Asian? Most people in the world are!' But so far I have managed to keep quiet. It would, of course, be impertinent of me, having an old nationality that has never seriously been questioned, to ridicule the widespread yearning among Georgians to get away, to leave a more or less sordid and violent and depressing reality, either individually by emigrating or collectively by moving the whole country to nicer company: the West, the European Union, NATO.

One writer has suggested that Georgians want to be Western to get away from Russia, not because of attachment to Western values.[6] Another one has described Georgia's complicated relationship to its reality as a Caucasian nation as follows: 'If Caucasus is not central to Georgian identity, Georgia perceives itself as central to Caucasus identity.'[7]

During history the feeling of being in the wrong place with the wrong company has had many effects – sometimes ridiculous, sometimes more tragic. Some Georgian nationalists, such as Merab Kostava, the collaborator of Zviad Gamsakhurdia, claimed that the Georgians have the right to be treated as 'an older brother' by other Caucasians because of the supposedly superiority of the Georgian culture.[8] And the theories of the linguist Nikolay Marr, active during the first three decades of the twentieth century, suggesting that all languages originate in one prototype, were interpreted by some nationalists to show that the Georgian language is not just one Caucasian language, but 'the mother of all languages'. The fact that Marr's theories, fiercely opposed by most serious linguists, after having been Soviet state doctrine for decades were finally discarded by Stalin personally in 1950 as 'unscientific', did not diminish their attractiveness for Gamsakhurdia and similar anti-Soviet Georgian nationalists.

They also took inspiration from a song by a medieval monk praising the Georgian language as a kind of holy sacrament. Zviad Gamsakhurdia and his followers claimed that on the Day of Judgement the Georgian language and nation would be a universal spiritual leader and judge humankind. It does not require very much imagination to understand what such aspects have meant for relations with the minorities speaking other languages, especially during the first years of independence.[9]

One more paradox is the name of the country. In Georgian it is *Sakartvelo*, which means 'the place where the Kartvelis live'. This originally was east Georgia, where two provinces are still called Shida (Inner) Kartli and Kvemo (Lower) Kartli. The Kartli kingdom was one of several Georgian principalities, which later gave its name to all Georgia. So why is it known as Georgia in English and other Western languages? The Russian name is *Gruzia*, which may originate in a Persian word for Georgians, *Gurzh*. According to one theory the Western word Georgia was developed from the Russian *Gruzia*, or maybe directly from *Gurzh*. Another theory, supported by Edward Shevardnadze, claims that the origin is the ancient Greek word for agriculture, '*georgia*'. One more 'theory' went into Georgian folklore during the visit of US President George W. Bush in 2005. As the story goes, Bush asked Saakashvili, 'Tell me, Misha, in whose honour did you baptize your country, in the honour of the US state or of me?'[10]

What about St George, the St George's cross which has featured on the Georgian flag since the Rose Revolution, the statue of St George on Freedom Square in Tbilisi, the innumerable children christened Giorgi or Gia, and the many churches in Georgia built to honour this mystic fourth-century soldier who is supposed to have defeated a dragon and died as a Christian martyr? Some believe that there is a connection between the enormous popularity for many centuries of St George in Georgia, and the name of the country. But why only in some Western languages; why not in Georgian? In Hebrew the official name of Georgia was based on the Russian *Gruzia*, but with improved relations between Israel and Georgia it has been changed into – no, not a Hebraized form of Sakartvelo, but *Gheorghia*. So maybe the Georgians are becoming the only people which cannot sense the connection between their country and St George directly in their language! Isn't that a magnificent Georgian paradox?

The list of similar paradoxes is endless. If some Georgians consider themselves victims of Russia, others, because of the behaviour of the Georgian nobles during the wars of the nineteenth century and some Georgian communists in the twentieth century, tend to consider Georgia as the 'gendarme of Russia'.[11]

And what about separatism? Both Georgia and Russia claim to be vehemently against it. However not only has Russia supported the separatists of Abkhazia and South Ossetia, Georgia has at least sometimes supported separatists in Chechnya, although much less than Russia has backed the Abkhaz and South Ossetian separatists. The alliance between Georgia and Chechnya was strongest during the rule of the most nationalist Georgian leader, Gamsakhurdia, who received asylum in Grozny. Still in the late 1990s the last leader of semi-independent Chechnya, Aslan Maskhadov, stated that the participation by some Chechen fighters on the Abkhaz side in the early 1990s had been wrong.[12] The explanation for this paradoxical alliance, which has not simplified Russian–Georgian relations, is of course the old rationale, 'my enemy's enemy is my friend'. The Chechens were separatists, but their desire was to secede not from Georgia but from Russia, thereby weakening the major supporter of the regions which wanted to break away from Georgia. This was far more important than theoretical principles, even to a staunch nationalist such as Gamsakhurdia. Today it is obvious that this 'pragmatism' has backfired. When Georgia has not been trustworthy about the territorial integrity of Russia, why should Russia be trustworthy about the same ambition of Georgia?

NATIONAL OR PRIVATE RELIGION?

Beside the language, a major symbol of Georgian identity has been the Orthodox faith. By the nineteenth century, the nationalist movement had coined the slogan *mamuli, ena, sartsmunoeba* (father-land, language, faith), which was taken over by the modern freedom fighters of the late twentieth century. Whether the Georgian relation to religion is a paradox or a mystery is difficult to judge. As a nonbe-liever in a secular country I may have difficulties in understanding the strong societal position of the Georgian Orthodox Church, which has more than two-thirds of the population as members. Interest in churches and religion is extremely high among Georgians. In connec-tion with the celebration in 2004 by Ilya II of his 27th anniversary as Patriarch it was reported that the number of churches during his time in office had increased from 48 to more than 800![13]

The Orthodox Church has obviously become a kind of national symbol, which to an outsider is very paradoxical because Christian-ity, as well as Islam, is supposed to be a universal religion. It is not like older creeds which were often closely linked to a special nation, with gods serving only that particular people: so the Romans had their gods, the Vikings theirs and so on. But when St Paul decided to convert not only Jews to the belief in Jesus, but anybody, Christian-ity became universal, a basic aspect that Islam took over. So how can a Christian church be part of a national identity? Without delving into a theological dispute, it is enough to observe that Christianity has split several times during its history, and especially in the Middle East. This has had the effect that many churches, for linguistic and other reasons, have developed very close links with one particular nation – such as the Ethiopian, the Coptic, the Maronite, the Syrian and other Eastern churches – in a way that has made national identity more or less equivalent to membership of a certain church. In South Caucasus this is most visible with the Armenian Church. Is it possi-ble to be Armenian without belonging to the Armenian Church? Is it possible to belong to the Armenian Church without being Armenian? The same questions could be put concerning the Georgian Church, although its separateness from the larger Orthodox community has been less distinct than that of the Armenian Church.

The independent, 'autocephalian', position of the Georgian Church was abolished by the Russian Empire in 1811, restored after the revolution in 1917 and finally recognized by the Patriarchate of Moscow in 1943. In the Georgian national discourse the ques-tion of the position of the Church has often taken proportions that are difficult for a secular outsider to grasp. Maybe a comparison with Poland is adequate. Most Poles belong to the most universal of all Christian congregations, the Roman Catholic Church. This has not prevented them from using their religion as a tool and a point of gathering in their national liberation struggle. During times of oppression such a link between politics and religion is probably beneficial for the survival of the national identity, and for mobilizing people in the freedom fight. But after liberation it becomes much more problematic, at least in an era where it is taken for granted that a state must be secular and treat all religions equally in order to be democratic, and where therefore religion must be eradicated from official manifestations and limited to the private sphere. It is, however, easy to note that not even the most developed democracies keep these rules completely.[14]

Nevertheless it is questionable whether the distinction between the private and public roles of religion in Georgia is compatible with European standards. Not only has the Georgian Church shied away from ecumenical relations, and in 1997 withdrawn from the World Council of Churches and the Conference of European Churches, it has also neglected, if not encouraged, the harassment of religious minorities by zealots. Such aggressions have usually not affected the faiths of the permanent minorities in the country, like Muslims or Catholics, but been directed against new imports from the West, like Baptists, Jehovah's Witnesses and Seventh Day Adventists. In 2005 international pressure forced Georgian authorities to take action against one of the worst of these fanatics, the priest Basil Mkalav-ishvili, who was sentenced to six years imprisonment for repeated attacks upon non-Orthodox individuals and installations.

The Georgian Constitution guarantees freedom of religion and equal treatment of all religions, but in 2002 the Georgian Ortho-dox Church was granted a privileged status, including exemption from taxes and exclusive authority over religion in education and the armed forces. Very often the Georgian Church and its Patriarch denounce the invasion of immoral mores and depraved life styles from the West into the pure Georgian culture. This, however, does not prevent most Georgians from venerating the Patriarch more than any other public person, and they regularly pray in one of the many churches, at the same time as they continue to yearn for a rapid integration into this immoral and depraved West!

GEORGIANIZATION

From an ethnic point of view Georgia since independence has moved from being considerably multicultural to being more one-dimensional. Its population has shrunk and is still shrinking because of a low birth rate and high emigration. According to some estimates the number of inhabitants will decrease to less than 4 million in the coming decades. As an effect of this trend the country has become more 'pure' Georgian. While the number of inhabitants increased during the Soviet period and continued to do so during the first years of independence, until it reached a peak in 1993 with 5.6 million, it has since decreased by about 1 million, and in 2008 was estimated to be 4.6 million, the breakaway republics included.

According to the 1989 census non-Georgians made up 29.9 per cent of the population of Georgia, a proportion that had dropped to 16.2 at the census of 2003. Today the percentages in Georgia proper – that is, excluding the two breakaway regions of Abkhazia and South Ossetia – are Azeris 6.5, Armenians 5.7, Russians 1.5, Ossetians 0.9, Yezids 0.4, Greek 0.3 and Jews 0.1. In 2009 some of these figures decreased, especially for Armenians, many of whom have expressed worries since the Russian military base in Akhalkalaki was closed in 2007, and for Ossetians after the 2008 war. Thus, emigration among the minorities has been very high. This may have been partly caused by discrimination against non-Georgians, although this is usually denied by representatives of the Georgian state. Outside observers are less sure.

According to Johanna Popjanevski of the Central Asia-Caucasus Institute, the Georgian government has often found itself squeezed between, on one hand, its ambition to abide by international conventions and standards in order to be accepted by Western institutions, and on the other hand its worry that by promoting minority rights it might equip 'national minority groups with tools for secession'.[15] While the Georgian parliament in 2005 ratified the 'Framework convention for the protection of national minorities', it added that it could not ensure full implementation until the territorial integrity of the country was restored. The International Crisis Group in 2005 concluded: 'Georgia is a multinational state, building democratic institutions and forging civic identity. However, it has made little progress towards integrating Armenian and Azeri minorities, who constitute over 12 percent of the population.'[16] In October 2007 the UN Human Rights Committee expressed concern over 'the obstacles faced by minorities (in Georgia) in the enjoyment of their cultural rights, as well as at the low level of political representation of minorities'.[17]

The Swedish Caucasus expert Svante Cornell, who has studied nine minority cases in South Caucasus (Abkhazia, South Ossetia, Nagorno-Karabakh, Adjara, Armenians and Azeris in Georgia, Talysh and Lesgins in Azerbaijan), draws the conclusion that there is a close relationship between the level of open conflict and the degree of minority self-rule. In the case of Georgia it is clear that severe clashes and even warfare have occurred around the three autonomies, Abkhazia, South Ossetia and Adjara, but not among the more numerous Armenian and Azeri minorities.[18]

Ethnic Georgians are over-represented and the minorities under-represented in most areas of Georgian society, such as politics and higher education. This may partly be explained as a leftover from the Soviet period, when the nationality policy deliberately gave privileges to the titular nations of all autonomies. Thus, if Georgians were over-represented in Georgia proper, Abkhazians and South Ossetians were over-represented in their respective autonomous areas. Another explanation, at least concerning higher education, is that during Soviet times it was easy for minorities who belonged to nationalities with their own titular autonomy in some other part of the Union – for example Russians, Ukrainians, Armenians and Azeris – to go to that republic for studies in their own language. To some extent this is still the case. Why should Armenians from Akhalkalaki or Azeris from Bolnisi struggle with the Georgian language test to be accepted at a university in Tbilisi, when they could go to Yerevan or Baku and study in their own language?

From one perspective, common among the minorities and some foreign observers, all minority problems are caused by Georgian political nationalism. From another, not less complicated, Georgian perspective, all problems have one common cause: Russia and its neo-imperial refusal to accept Georgia's independence. The truth is more complicated.

JAVAKHETI – FAR FROM TBILISI

The distance from Tbilisi to Akhaltsikhe, the capital of the Samtskhe-Javakheti region, is only some 300 kilometres. To Akhalkalaki, the centre of Javakheti, the area densely inhabited by Armenians, it is even shorter, although the journey may take some eight hours because of the poor roads. When the preface of a photobook on Javakheti that I received at one of my recent visits to Georgia describes the region as 'remote' and the life of the predominantly Armenian population as 'one of profound isolation', it is a verdict more based upon a psychological conception than on hard geographical facts. One of the major projects of the TRACECA is a railway from Kars to Baku, via Akhalkalaki and Tbilisi, which will connect Javakheti with the West as well as with Tbilisi and the Caspian Sea area. In addition, the above-mentioned book was published to celebrate a project initiated by the late Premier Zurab Zhvania, to construct a modern 245 kilometre road to Tbilisi, which will 'mean that for the first time since the Czarist period, Tbilisi and Samtskhe-Javakheti would be linked'.[19]

Historically Armenians have always made up a considerable part of the population in Georgia, especially in the towns and cities. In the beginning of nineteenth century Tbilisi was a predominantly Armenian city, with Armenian dominance of business and urban professions. Later, persecution of Armenians in the Ottoman Empire provoked a stream of immigrants to Georgia, and the Armenian population increased until it reached 450,000 at the end of the Soviet period. Since then it has decreased considerably, down to 249,000 according to the latest census, with 83,000 residing in Tbilisi. In Samtskhe-Javakheti Armenians make up 55 per cent of the population. In some communities their dominance is almost complete, with more than 90 per cent. The visible problems have been few, but in 2005 and 2006 protests erupted against alleged discrimination by the Georgian authorities.

When I visited the region in 2007 and met with local Armenian officials and schoolteachers, the complaints I heard had little to do with Georgian–Armenian ethnic strife, at least on the surface. However, there was a widespread feeling of being neglected by the central government. Some headlines in the local bilingual Georgian-Armenian newspaper *Samkhretis-Karibche* were reflections of that.[20] Above a picture of peasants ploughing with an ox could be read, 'Peasants return to old methods because the price of petrol is too high.' Other examples: 'Minister of Finance says that the governor of the province is responsible for the development of the region.' 'Old water distribution system and unused money – the money is spent on other things than reducing the water fees.' Several articles were about the bad economic situation and problems with young people. A young woman in a café told me that the only thing people could do was to drink. In sum, I met all the signs of a marginal region in the outskirts of a country, with problems which were not ethnic, but might very well be described as such if nothing is done to change the situation.

Concerning Georgian–Armenian relations numerous stories are told, just like Swedes tell stories about Norwegians, French about Belgians, English about Scots and vice versa. One of these stories, told with an Armenian outlook, goes like this: Armenian archaeologists are digging at a site from the millennia before Christ.

They find telephone cables; they conclude that even then Armenians knew about telephones! Georgian archaeologists start digging at another site of the same age. They find nothing. So they conclude: at that time Georgians already knew about mobile telephones!

While Armenians, as coreligionists and clever businessmen, have usually been met with respect from Georgians, the attitude towards Azeris has sometimes been different. Today the Azeris constitute the most numerous minority, some 285,000, with a concentration in the southern province of Kvemo Kartli, where they constitute 46 per cent of the population. In some communities they make up an overwhelming majority, such as Marneuli, 83 per cent, and Bolnisi, 66 per cent. The Azeris have sometimes been regarded as the most submissive minority. (See my account from a visit to the area in Chapter 11, 'Presidential election, January 5, 2008'). But maybe this situation is changing. In February 2008 a news agency reported that twelve organizations of Georgian Azeris had decided to join ranks in order to promote the position of the Azeris in Georgia.[21]

On of the most concealed minority problems of Georgia is that of the 'absent friends', the 100,000 Meskhetian Turks who used to reside in Javakheti, but were deported by the Stalin regime on 1944. In connection with Georgia's accession to the Council of Europe, the state had to undertake a commitment to create a legal framework for the integration of the Meskhetian Turks within two years of accession, but less than a thousand have been repatriated. When Gamsakhurdia was a powerless dissident in the Soviet Union he pleaded for the Meskhetian Turks, but as nationalist president of Georgia he displayed less interest in their cause. The few who have managed to return to Georgia have had difficulties in obtaining Georgian citizenship, and thus have not had access to all rights and privileges guaranteed to Georgian citizens.

After two decades of independence, Georgia's general policy towards its minorities is still considerably flawed. A recent study draws the rather alarming conclusion that 'efforts at promoting the national integration of ethnic minorities [are] lacking the necessary mechanisms for achieving successful results'.[22]

A TRANSIT COUNTRY

As several commentators have observed, Georgia is the only country that can break the Russian dominance over transport routes for Caspian energy. The only way towards the West outside Russia and Georgia would be via Azerbaijan and Armenia to Turkey, but because of the unresolved conflict over Nagorno-Karabakh that path is closed. Theoretically there are of course routes to both the South and the East, but from a European point of view they constitute more or less long detours, and more important, they would move control from authoritarian Russia to even more problematic or outright rogue states, like Iran and China. This is why Georgia's geostrategic importance has increased with the growing need for Caspian oil and gas. This trend was given a strong push after the failure in 1998 of the US oil company Unocal to establish a gas pipeline through Afghanistan.[23]

Despite all indications of Western support for Georgia, some observers are not satisfied: for example Mamuka Tsereteli, president of the Georgian Association in the United States, who has claimed that 'unfortunately, not everyone in the US or Europe realizes the strategic importance of Georgia for long-term Western security interests' and demanded a 'NATO Membership Action Plan for Georgia and Ukraine' in order to 'ensure stability in those countries, and thus keep alternative access routes to Eurasia alive'.[24]

Another method to guarantee security for the energy transportation routes through Georgia rather than bringing the country into NATO was proposed even before the Rose Revolution. In March 2002 a news report alleged that 'the proposed deployment of 200 US Special Operations forces to the former Soviet Republic of Georgia is about more than pursuing al-Qaeda terrorists around the globe – it's also about oil'. At that time the United States had recently stationed 1,000 soldiers in Uzbekistan and 300 in Kyrgyzstan as part of a new 'pipeline politics with military support', which had begun under President Clinton, 'but received a boost with Defense Secretary Donald Rumsfeld's visit to the region' in December 2001.[25] Thus, Georgia's position in the Great Game is of crucial importance not only to Georgia itself and its neighbours but to all players, not least the United States and the European Union. If Georgia is the object of special Western interest it may be neither because the Rose Revolution in 2003 made the country into a haven of democracy, nor because of the South Ossetia War in 2008, which by many was interpreted as proof of renewed Russian aggressiveness. As shown in this and the previous chapter there is an additional factor that has existed and affected the situation long before these dramatic events – the oil and gas of the Caspian.

PUPPET OR BUFFER?

There are several obvious similarities between Georgia and Cuba. Both have very close geographic, historic and economic relations to a superpower next door. Both have an ambition to liberate themselves from that dependence, and are rallying the support of another, distant superpower to achieve that goal. That this comparison is not only theoretical but a reality in the minds of major players is corroborated by a writer who quotes a source close to Vladimir Putin, who has revealed that 'Saakashvili stirs in Putin roughly the same animus that Fidel Castro does for US politicians'.[26] A strategic question is then, is Georgia able to leave its position as satellite or puppet state of Russia and move into real independence, or is it inevitably sliding into a satellite or puppet state relation to the United States? An alternative possibility would be to head for a position as buffer state, defined by several dictionaries as 'a neutral state lying between two rival or potentially hostile states and serving to prevent conflict between them'.[27] It is no coincidence that one of the most comprehensive recent treatises on the concept of buffer states has been written by a Georgian, on the background of Georgia's experience of that role as a buffer between the Persian, Ottoman and Russian empires earlier in its history.[28] Will Georgia exploit its strategic position to develop into a real, strong buffer state, serving to prevent conflict in the region, or will it be satisfied with shifting allegiance and switch the holder of its puppet strings from Moscow to Washington?

NOTES

1   Peter Nasmyth, *Georgia: In the mountains of poetry*, Curzon Caucasus World, 2001.
2   Silvia Serrano, *Géorgie – sortie d'empire* (Georgia – exit from an empire), Paris, 2007.
3   <www.ipu.org/wmn-e/classif.htm>.
4   Eduard Schewardnadze, *Die neue Seidenstrasse – Verkehrsweg in die 21. Jahrhundert* (The new Silk Road: a communication route of the 21st century), Econ Verlag, Munich, 1999, p. 51.
5   Per Gahrton, *Report on the Communication from the Commission to the Council and the European Parliament on the European Union's Relations with the South Caucasus, under the Partnership and Cooperation Agreements*, Committee on Foreign Affairs, Human Rights, Common Security and Defence Policy, February 28, 2002, A5-0028/2002.
6   Bruno Coppetier and Robert Legvold (eds), *Statehood and Security:*

     Georgia after the Rose Revolution, MIT Press, Cambridge, Mass., 2005, p. 10.
7   Serrano, *Géorgie.*
8   Ibid., p. 200, note 97.
9   Ibid., p. 199, note 88.
10 There is a US state called Georgia, and the Christian name of the US President 2001–09 was George.
11 Serrano, *Géorgie*, p 203.
12 Ibid., p. 190.
13 *Svobodnaya Gruzia*, December 25, 2004.
14 Secular Sweden had a state church until 2000 and according to the Swedish Constitution the monarch must still belong to the Lutheran creed.
15 Johanna Popjanevski, 'Minorities and the state in the South Caucasus: assessing the protection of national minorities in Georgia and Azerbaijan', Central Asia-Caucasus Institute and Silk Road Studies Program, Johns Hopkins University, Baltimore, Md., 2006.
16 International Crisis Group, 'Georgia's Armenian and Azeri minorities', Europe Report no. 178, November 22, 2006.
17 CCPR/C/GEO/CO/3/CRP.1, 19 October 2007.
18 Svante Cornell, *Autonomy and Conflict: Ethnoterritoriality and separatism in the South Caucasus – cases in Georgia, Uppsala University*, Uppsala, Sweden, 2002.
19 Daniel Kunin, 'Silence about Javakheti – in memory of Zurab Zhvania', in Daniel Kunin (ed.), *Javakheti*, Millennium Challenge Georgia Fund, Tbilisi, 2006.
20 <www.samkhretis-karibche.ge>.
21 *Regnum*, February 7, 2008.
22 Niklas Nilsson, Johanna Popjanevski, Ekaterine Metreveli and Temuri Yakobashvili, *State Approaches to National Integration in Georgia: Two perspectives*, Central Asia-Caucasus Institute and Silk Road Studies Program, 2009.
23 Peter Dale Scott, 'Pipeline politics: oil behind plan for U.S. troops in Georgia', <news.ncmonline.com/news/view_article.html?article_id>, web posted March 19, 2002.
24 Mamuka Tsereteli, 'Beyond Georgia: Russia's strategic interest in Eurasia', *CACI Analyst*, November 6, 2008.
25 Peter Dale Scott, 'Pipeline politics'.
26 Coppetier and Leghold, *Statehood and Security*, p. 19.
27 <http://www.thefreedictionary.com/buffer+state>.
28 Turnike Turmanidze, *Buffer States: Power policies, foreign policies and concepts,* Nova Science, Hauppauge, N.Y., 2009.

3

A HISTORY OF FAILED INDEPENDENCE

During the civil war of the 1990s in former Yugoslavia, a Swedish radio reporter once sighed during a direct radio transmission, 'Here most people seem to suffer from history bulimia!' The situation is similar in Georgia. Like most other peoples the Georgians have their own creation myth, which goes like this: 'When God created the world, he gave the merry Georgians the chosen land that he had reserved for himself.' It is also said that the dramatic adventures of the ancient Greek myth of Jason, the Argonauts and the golden fleece took place partly in Georgia. Such efforts to link the destiny and history of one's own nation with well-known ancient events are common to most peoples. And it must be admitted that compared with the attempt by a Swedish seventeenth-century historian to place the Argonauts in Sweden, the Georgian version is more plausible, as the western part of Georgia, which was called Colchis in ancient times, was undeniably in the sphere of influence of the Hellenistic civilisation.[1]

In a book published in 1999 Edward Shevardnadze with obvious pride claimed that the Georgian script was invented around 300 BC and that Christianity came to Georgia by the first century AD. He also declared that in the year 2000 Georgia would celebrate 3,000 years of statehood, 2,000 years of Christianity and 1,600 years with Christianity as its state religion.[2] According to the head of Tbilisi State University, Roin Metreveli, the Georgians are 'one of the oldest peoples of the world'.[3] Another Georgian historian pretends that Georgian tribes had 'reached the threshold of creating the country' by around 1000 BC.[4] The implication of such statements is of course that it is of special value for a state to be old and have a long national history. This is an outlook that is not uncommon.

I remember the time when as a journalist I followed the festivities of the shah of Iran in 1972 in Persepolis to celebrate the 2,500th anniversary of his kingdom. One of his guests was the president of Egypt, Anwar Sadat, who caught the headlines by delivering a greeting 'from a 5,000 years old civilisation'! It was undeniably a skilful PR gimmick – but for what purpose? Do modern Egyptians have a better life than inhabitants of younger nations? A rapid look at indexes of the standard of living and development gives another impression. There is absolutely no correlation between being an 'old nation' and being a happy one in the twenty-first century. Rather, it is easy to get the impression that in some countries the assumed great past is used as a sedative to make people forget their sordid present. However, as sociologists know, 'if a situation is defined as real by people, it is real in its consequences for them'. Thus, when trying to understand the Georgian paradoxes a brief dive into the history of the country is necessary.

LONG BEFORE CHRIST

Most historians agree that some type of Georgian kingdom existed during the fourth and fifth centuries BC. Christianity was made the 'state religion' when it was adopted in 337 AD by King Mirian of Kartli, who was converted by St Nino, a Cappadocian nun who is also supposed to have been a relative of Saint George. One of the first venerated, distinct personalities in Georgian history was Vakhtang Gorgasali (449–502), the founder of Tbilisi. At the end of the first millennium AD Bagrat III Bagrationi (975–1014) ruled a united kingdom of East and West Georgia with its capital in Kutaisi. Wars with Byzantines and Seljuk Turks were common and intermittent. David IV Ashmashenbeli, the Rebuilder (1089–1125), defeated the Seljuks and declared Tbilisi to be the capital. He is also said to have pressured Ossetians into submission. On August 12, 1121, he won a battle against Muslims at Didgori, the 887th anniversary of which in 2008 was used by a Georgian newspaper to claim that the South Ossetian War was a Didgori-style Georgian victory.[5]

Later in the twelfth century followed the famous 'Golden Age' with a queen as head of state, Tamar (1184–1213), who divorced a Russian husband and wed an Ossetian, a fact that is sometimes used as an argument in modern debates about the Georgian relations with Russians and Ossetians. This was the time when the national poet Shota Rustaveli, who worked at the court of Queen Tamar, wrote his famous national poem about chivalry, love, courage and similar virtues, 'The knight in the panther's skin'.[6] It is noteworthy that this impressive work of art, consisting of 1,587 four-line verses, which is still honoured as the major classical masterpiece of Georgian literature, has as its main heroes not Georgian personalities, but an Arab nobleman and an Indian prince. Maybe this is yet another of the Georgian paradoxes.

After the Golden Age the Georgians had fateful encounters with the Mongols, as did many other peoples in Eurasia: first Djingis Khan in 1220, then Tamerlane around 1400. During the sixteenth and seventeenth centuries the region was dominated by Muslim rulers, and not until the beginning of the eighteenth century did Georgia re-emerge as a visible unit into history, with the confirmation in 1716 of Vakhtang VI as Georgian king by the Persian shah. According to the Georgian historian George Anchabadze, 'Vakhtang hoped that Russia, which was of one religion, would help Georgia to revive independence.'[7]

GEORGIEVSK 1783 – OCCUPATION OR PROTECTION?

After three-quarters of a century of fighting with Iranians and Turks, during which the eastern provinces of Kartli and Kakheti became independent from Iran, the time had come for the controversial 1783 Treaty of Georgievsk, which placed East Georgia under Russian protection. While many Georgians today consider the treaty as the beginning of a long Russian occupation, Roin Metreveli characterizes it as 'a triumph of the forces that fought for the liberation of Georgia from the domination of Iran and Turkey'.[8] Anyhow, the promised tsarist shield was not implemented against an Iranian onslaught in 1795, which destroyed Tbilisi. The Russians did not intervene. This 'treason' created much animosity among Georgians, and is still today often taken as an argument when Georgians refuse to consider the integration of Georgia into the Russian empire from the beginning of the nineteenth century as anything but an occupation. And it is true that protests and even revolts erupted from the first moment after the entry of Russian troops in 1799 and the abolishment of the Kartli and Kakheti kingdoms in 1801, followed by their formal annexation and transformation into Russian governorates. Despite the repeated movements of resistance, the integration of Georgia into Russia was pursued stepwise during most of the nineteenth century.

The crucial question is, what did the Russian rule entail for Georgia, its culture and development? Was it only negative? One major analysis of the 'making of the Georgian nation' maintains that 'with the integration of Transcaucasia into the Russian Empire Western influences both cultural and material penetrated Georgia rapidly'.[9] At the beginning of the nineteenth century the Georgian population dominated the countryside, as nobles or peasants. The town-dwellers and traders were mostly Armenians and Muslims, and many of the soldiers were Cherkess, Ossetian and Kalmuk mercenaries.

The Russian authors Mikhail Leontiev and Andrei Zhukov, in a book which was published after the South Ossetia War (in 2008) with the provocative title *Independent Georgia: A bandit in a tiger's hide*, claim that until the eighteenth century Georgia often stood on the side of Muslim rulers and was not 'really Christian'.[10] The authors, one close to the ruling party, United Russia (Leontiev), the other a former KGB officer and member of parliament for the nationalist Rodina (Fatherland) faction, are obviously making a joke of the classical poem by Rustaveli. But despite their anti-Georgian approach they admit that the intention behind making Georgia into a Russian protectorate by the tsarist regime was not primarily to protect Georgia against Muslims, but to make the country into a bridgehead for Russian expansion throughout South Caucasus. One of the first Russian actions was to start building the Georgian 'military highway' which is still one of very few paths crossing the Caucasus Mountains. At the same time, Leontiev and Zhukov suggest, the Georgian King Erekly planned to exploit Russian protection not only for defence but also as a means to expand his rule through war with Iran and Turkey.

For a long time most of the protests against Russia came from the peasants and some intellectuals. Several anti-Russian groups emerged among Georgians in St Petersburg. Some moved to Tbilisi in 1827–29. One conspiracy had the slogan 'Georgia to Georgians'. The ruling social class, the nobles, was treated leniently by the tsarist regime. The nobles got their privileges restored, but in 1840 the Georgian language was replaced by Russian for official use, although most Georgians did not understand Russian. In 1859 30,000 Georgians got their status as nobles recognized. During the Crimean War (1853–56) Georgians overwhelmingly 'rallied to the Russian banner'.[11] According to one historian the Georgian nobles were extremely conservative and archaic, and lacked an entrepreneurial attitude. Surplus production was considered counterproductive because it would only inspire thieves! The relation between nobles and peasants was paternalistic; nobles had the right to kill their serfs and often used to give away serfs as gifts.[12] At the end of the

eighteenth century it is estimated that 78 per cent of the population
were serfs, 16 per cent free producers and 7 per cent nobles. At the
same time 75 per cent of the inhabitants of Tbilisi were Armenian.
When Russia in 1861 abolished serfdom, the Georgian nobles were
alarmed. A commission of Georgian nobles frankly admitted that
'the peasants have always fed us; we have existed because of them'.
Finally even Georgian serfdom was abolished, but it was a process
that took many years, and the result was that the serfs received
personal liberation, but remained economically and legally dependent on their masters. Nobody was satisfied, which was a starting
point for national revolts. By the last decade of the nineteenth
century 'Georgia had developed into a nationality for itself'.[13]

Several intellectuals emerged at the end of the nineteenth century
as spokespersons for Georgian national liberation, such as the tradi-
tionalist Ilia Chavchavadze, the liberal reformers Giorgi Tsereteli
and Niko Nikoladze, and Marxists such as Noe Zhordania and
Pilipe Makharadze. The rapid development of the liberation movement can be understood from the increase in the number of strikes.
They were 19 during the 30 years from 1870 to 1900, and 17 in the
year 1900. In 1901 there were 15 strikes during the first two months
alone. The paradoxical situation is, as one historian puts it, that 'the
road to West lay through Russia'.[14]

Nobody knows of course what would have happened to Georgia
if there had been no Treaty of Georgievsk and no Russian occupation, if there had been an independent Georgian kingdom during the
nineteenth century. But this option is very hypothetical. The likely
alternatives to Russian dominance, an insight that was the explicit
reason for King Erekly to seek Russian protection, were submission
under Iran or inclusion in the Ottoman Empire.

THE FIRST MODERN INDEPENDENCE

Early on, the leading Georgian Marxist Noe Zhordania became a
leading representative for the 'minority' – Mensheviks – in the Russian
socialist movement. After the failed Russian revolution of 1905, when
the tsar for some time made experiments with limited democracy,
elections, a parliament and so on, the Georgian delegations to the
Duma in St Petersburg were dominated by Mensheviks.

One point of conflict between the two Georgian socialists Noe
Zhordania and Josef Dzhugashvili, alias Stalin, was the definition of
national autonomy in the framework of a socialist society. In 1913
Stalin published 'The national question and social democracy', where

he took a position against national autonomy, in favour of regional autonomy. This may seem like a very theoretical distinction, but it is crucial. While national autonomy in principle applies to everybody of a certain ethnic-linguistic origin, regional autonomy, although it may include some national aspects, applies to everybody in a certain geographical region. This distinction between national and regional autonomy has some similarity to the difference between the classical French revolutionary concept of citizenship, which gave ethnic and linguistic minorities equal individual rights as citizens but neglected their special collective needs, and the traditional German concept of 'Deutschtum', which gave special rights to every 'ethnic' German all over the world (Volksdeutsche) but tended to discriminate against non-German citizens of Germany. It is of interest that both France and Germany have had to modify their legislation lately, in order to comply with European rules, which have the intention of finding a reasonable balance between equal citizens' rights for everybody and special consideration for the cultural and linguistic rights of every nationality.

It was a variety of the Stalinist (or French Revolutionary) principle which was later applied in the Soviet Union, where autonomy was given to geographical units, but with some cultural and linguistic privileges to a 'titular nation', whose part of the population, however, was often less than the majority. Unfortunately this type of autonomy was of course completely distorted when implemented under a dictatorial regime. But the fact that the classical Georgian concept of autonomy, as pursued by Zhordania, was based upon nationality and ethnicity, not region, has undeniably had serious repercussions for the relations between independent Georgia and its minorities.

The clash between the Georgian Mensheviks and the Russian Bolsheviks continued during and after the First World War. Some Georgians wanted to support Germany from the outset, hoping that this would simplify Georgian liberation. After the beginning of the war the committee for 'Georgian independence' moved to Berlin.

The Georgian Mensheviks did not support the Bolshevik October Revolution. The Brest–Litovsk separate peace treaty between the Bolsheviks and Germany and the other Axis states gave to Turkey Batumi and some southwestern Georgian territory, which the Georgian leaders refused to accept. Under some pressure from the Ottomans a Transcaucasian Federation – Georgia, Armenia and Azerbaijan – declared its independence on April 22, 1918. However, the same type of split as can be seen today was present between the South Caucasian states even then. While Armenia, just after the genocide of 1915, refused to link its fate with the Ottoman–German side, Azerbaijan was for cultural reasons close to the Turks, and Georgia wanted to rally German support against Russia. On May 26, 1918, Georgia declared independence with German support, and on June 10 German troops arrived in the country and Georgia became virtually a German protectorate.[15] While formal recognition came from Germany almost immediately, Great Britain, France, Italy, Japan and the Soviet Union waited until 1920.

In November 1918 the World War ended with a German defeat and 'Georgia's German orientation was now bankrupt'.[16] There was land reform, but unlike in Bolshevik Russia the nobles were allowed to preserve some land and peasants could own privately, not only collectively. Industry was hurt by the isolation from Russia, Azerbaijan and the West. Despite this it has been said that independent Georgia 'exemplified the social democratic ideal'.[17] In December 1918 a short war with Armenia disturbed Armenian–Georgian relations. When the Red Army had defeated the antirevolutionary armies in Russia and had time to cope with South Caucasus, the West did not intervene. In February 1921 Georgia was invaded by the Red Army. On March 18 the Georgian government left Tbilisi and later the country. The British Foreign Secretary Balfour explained the British priorities frankly: 'We will protect Batumi, Baku, the railroad between them and the pipeline,' but not the independence of the Georgian state.[18]

After the defeat and flight of Zhordania's Menshevik government, power was taken by the Caucasian Bureau of the Central Committee of the Russian Communist Bolshevik Party under the leadership of Sergo Ordzhonikidze, a Georgian. Several other persons responsible for establishing Bolshevik power in Georgia were also Georgians, among them Pilipe Makharadze. Abkhazia became part of Georgia 1921 by a treaty, Adjara 1922 became an autonomous Soviet socialist republic, and South Ossetia in 1922 an autonomous oblast. The first anti-Soviet action occurred as early as 1921 in the northwestern mountain province of Svaneti. In 1923 several Georgian nationalists were executed. Another revolt in August 1924 all over Georgia was crushed and the leaders sent to Siberia.

According to Leontiev and Zhukov, the Menshevik regime was a total 'bankruptcy' and to define 'Georgia 1918–21 as independent and democratic is possible only formally and legally'. This is an argument that is not very strong because the same applies to quite a lot of the present sovereign members of the United Nations. A more apt observation was made by the historian Ronald Suny when he stated that the short Georgian independence of 1918–21 was possible only because of the 'power vacuum left when neither Bolshevik Russia nor Turkey was able to impose its traditional authority over the region'.[19]

SOVIET GEORGIA = OCCUPIED TERRITORY?

On March 12, 1922, the Federal Union of the SSR of Transcaucasia was established, which became a member of the newly formed USSR on December 30 of the same year. From the beginning there were conflicts between Tbilisi and Moscow. Leaders of the Soviet Bolsheviks, like Stalin and Ordzhonikidze, accused the local leaders, Makharadze and others, of nationalist activities, such as not cancelling checkpoints at the frontiers, and closing the borders to hungry Russian refugees from the north. After years of disputes the Stalinists took over in Georgia, as in the whole of the Soviet Union. From 1931 to 1938 the later infamous Lavrentij Beria, a Georgian, was first secretary of the Georgian Communist Party.

Was the period of Soviet Communist rule in Georgia equivalent to a Russian occupation? The fact is that the Soviet period did not destroy Georgian culture or the Georgian identity. The paradox is that the Soviet regime, through the spread of literacy, 'nativization' (that is, Georgianization) of administrative and cultural institutions, and sponsorship of Georgian art, language and learning, in many ways promoted the Georgian identity. At the same time a profound social and economic transformation of the country was carried out. The collectivization of Georgia's peasant farms was the most radical transformation of land tenure and village life in Georgia's history. During the Stalinist period from 1928 to 1953 'Georgia was transformed more fundamentally than in any comparable period in its three thousand year history'.[20] The population grew from 2.7 million in 1926 to 4 million in 1956. The proportion of rural population decreased from 78 to 58 per cent. The number of inhabitants of Tbilisi grew from 294,000 to 703,000. Georgia became more urban, more industrial and more proletarian. In 1937 the Transcaucasian Federation was abolished and Georgia received the status of a Soviet socialist republic in its own right. One symbol of the Georgian integration into the Soviet Union is of course the fact that the dictator himself, Stalin, was a Georgian. Another one, more often mentioned by Russians than by Georgians, is that of the two soldiers who raised the red flag on the Berlin Reichstag in May 1945, one was a Georgian.

Leontiev and Zhukov devote a whole 60-page chapter to 'Georgia under the swastika', where they delve into detailed recapitulations of Georgians fighting in the ranks of the Wehrmacht during the Second World War. It is obvious that this is meant to be a decisive argument against the Georgian 'bandits' for an audience of the Russian public. But that was not unique for Georgians. As a matter of fact nationals from all over Europe fought in Nazi armies, not only in the regular army (the Wehrmacht) but also in the criminal SS forces. This is true not only for all German-occupied nations, such as the Danes, but even for neutral Swedes. And not least, the Russians formed a whole pro-German army under General Vlasov. Some of these mercenaries may have been ideologically attracted by Nazism, some were primarily anticommunist, but many were simply nationalists who hoped to gain freedom for their nations by supporting the enemy of their oppressors.

In hindsight it is easy to conclude that it was naïve to believe that a racist regime could become a serious supporter of any national liberation movement. Leontiev and Zhukov of course make an easy point when they recall that the leader of the Georgian committee in exile, Georgi Magalashvili, announced as a great victory that the Third Reich after years of reluctance had finally listened to his pleas and recognized the independence of Georgia – in April 1945! Interestingly enough Leontiev and Zhukov themselves indirectly contradict the claim that the presence of some Georgians on the Nazi side could be used as a proof that all Georgians are 'bandits', by correctly observing that Georgia lost 307.000 out of its 3.5 million population in the fight against Hitler, which is a higher percentage than most Soviet nationalities.

The lowest percentage of Georgians in Georgia in modern times was registered in 1939: 61.4 per cent. That proportion grew during the rest of the Soviet period to reach 74 per cent around the time of the dissolution of the USSR (and in 2008 about 84 per cent). If there was ever any Soviet aggressive intention against the Georgian nation as such, it failed utterly.

The heritage of Stalin is a complicated aspect for many Georgians. Some non-Georgian anti-Stalinists maintain that Stalin's repressive actions were conditioned by his Georgian origin. And some Georgians have undoubtedly felt some pride. The 'de-Stalinization' campaign launched by Nikita Khrushchev at the Twentieth Communist Party Congress at the beginning of 1956 was not welcomed by everybody in Georgia. On March 5 that year demonstrators in Tbilisi required the rehabilitation of Stalin and criticized the CPSU resolutions, and on March 9 Soviet troops opened fire, killing some 80 persons and wounding some 300.

There is still a huge Stalin statue in his town of birth, Gori. The little cottage where he was born is part of a Stalin museum on the central square. When I visited the museum in the summer of 2009 the guide orally told about the Stalinist terror, but very little such information could be seen among the considerable amount of documents and pictures, which presented Stalin as a revolutionary hero and victor of the Great Fatherland War. Maybe that bias is a reason why, apart from me and my company, the museum had no visitors at all. Only a short time before my visit a demonstration was staged around the statue, demanding its removal. New generations of Georgians are realizing that even if Stalin was a native of Georgia, he was primarily a ruthless dictator who oppressed his own peoples, including Georgians.

On September 29, 1972, Edward Shevardnadze became first secretary of the Georgian Communist Party. His main tasks were declared to be to fight against corruption and nationalism. Until he was brought

to Moscow by Gorbachev to become minister of foreign affairs of the Soviet Union in the mid-1980s, he was a very loyal party worker. At the Twenty-Sixth Party Congress in Moscow he made his infamous statement that for Georgians the sun does not rise in the east but in the north. Despite the profound changes in the Georgian social structure,

The heritage of Stalin is a complicated aspect for many Georgians. There is still a huge statue of him in his town of birth, Gori.

one observer claims that during the last decades of the Soviet Union it still 'remained a network in which family and kinship ties, ideas of honour and trust, nepotism and patron client alliances provided informal links within the population and prevented penetration from outsiders, whether members of other nationalities or representatives of the state power'.[21]

In November 1988 a demonstration in Tbilisi with 100,000 participants under the old flag from the independence of 1918–21 demanded an end to discrimination against Georgians by Abkhaz, Azerbaijanis, Adjars and Ossetians. On March 18, 1989, Abkhazia demanded separation from Georgia, and on April 9 Soviet troops killed 19 students at a rally in Tbilisi. In March 1990 Georgia officially declared itself to be occupied and annexed.[22] And on October 28, 1990, the Round Table won the elections and Zviad Gamsakhurdia declared that 'Ossetians who don't want to live with us should leave'.[23] The nationalists had won, the 'occupier' was falling to pieces – but so was Georgia itself.

NOTES

1   Olof Rudbeck, *Atland eller Manheim*, curio, Uppsala 1679–1702 <http://www.britannica.com/EBchecked/topic/41051/Atland-eller-Manheim>.
2   Eduard Schewardnadze, *Die neue Seidenstrasse – Verkehrsweg in die 21. Jahrhundert* (The new Silk Road – a communication route of the twenty-first century), Econ Verlag, Munich, 1999.
3   Roin Metreveli, *Georgia*, Publishers International, Nashville, Tenn., 1995.
4   George Anchabadze, *History of Georgia: A short sketch*, Caucasian House, Tbilisi, 2005.
5   *Asaval-Davasali*, August 11–17, 2008.
6   Shota Rustaveli, 'Vitjas v tigrovoj shkure' (The knight in the panther's skin), Merani, Tbilisi, 1984.
7   Anchabadze, *History of Georgia*, p. 24.
8   Metreveli, *Georgia*.
9   Ronald Grigor Suny, *The Making of the Georgian Nation*, 2nd edn, Indiana University Press, Bloomington, Ind., 1994, p. xiv.
10 Mikhail Leontiev and Dmitrij Zhukov, *Nezavisimaya' Gruzia - bandit v tigrovoj shkure* ('Independent' Georgia – a bandit in a tiger's hide), Yauza Press, Moscow, 2008, p. 79.
11 *Suny, The Making*, p 75.
12 Ibid., p. 86.
13 Ibid., p. 115.
14 Ibid., p. 122.
15 Ibid., p. 192.

16 Ibid., p. 193.
17 Ibid., p. 202.
18 Ibid., p. 204.
19 Ibid., p. 208.
20 Ibid., p. 280.
21 Ibid., p. 316.
22 Christoph Zürcher, 'Georgia's time of troubles 1989–93', in Bruno
    Coppetier and Robert Legvold (eds), *Statehood and Security: Georgia
    after the Rose Revolution,* MIT Press, Cambridge, Mass., 2005.
23 Suny, *The Making,* p. 325.

4

THE DISSOLUTION OF THE SOVIET UNION – BLESSING OR DISASTER?

When Vladimir Putin once stated that the dissolution of the USSR had been a major catastrophe, he was ridiculed in the West, or worse, the remark was taken as a proof that he was dreaming of restoring a large Russian empire. I am of course no fan of his policies. I rather tend to agree with the devastating judgement of both Putin and his policies made by Anna Politkovskaya, a remarkable woman I had the privilege to meet when she visited the European Parliament in Strasbourg.[1]

Nevertheless Putin had a point that most outside observers refuse to accept, or even understand, despite the fact that his statement contains important explanations for much of Russian behaviour since the early 1990s. Let us assume that the European Union broke up. Would Western politicians not consider that to be a major disaster? And would such a collapse of a political union not have incalculable repercussions? When the United States broke up about 150 years ago this led to a civil war to reunite it by force. When Yugoslavia fell to pieces we all know the disastrous consequences. So why should the *raspad* of the USSR not affect the behaviour of the former constituent elements, including the official successor state, the Russian Federation?[2]

One of many indications that the West has not been able, or rather willing, to understand the extent of the trauma that shook the former Soviet Union, and especially Russia, during the 1990s was the fate of a book by the venerated Nobel Prize laureate Alexander Solzhenitsyn, published in 1998. Here the author gave a vivid description of the humiliating situation he found during his extensive travels all over Russia after his return from his long exile in the United States.[3] However, in contrast to the unlimited praise Solzhenitsyn had been used to receiving from all kind of Western commentators during his decades of literary crusade against the 'evil' Soviet system, I have not been able to detect any translation of that book into any Western language. I doubt that the main reason for this is the author's bias in favour of rather ambiguous nationalist and slavophil solutions to Russia's problems, which of course cannot be accepted by any sincere democrat. Rather the West did not want to know that the hero of anticommunism had mercilessly exposed the neoliberal shock therapy as a cruel and antihuman attempt to eliminate Russia as a global player for ages to come.

From this perspective the well-known fact that the USSR was no democracy, but during most of its lifetime a repressive one-party dictatorship, is not enough to discard Putin's statement as preposterous. The USSR was more than gulags and lack of freedom. It was also, among other things, a common economic and social area, based upon the famous 'four freedoms', which are also usually seen as the foundation for the European Union. One of my Georgian friends told me that her mother, during Soviet times, used to fly from Tbilisi on a morning flight to Moscow to meet friends or go to the theatre. Usually she came back the same day on a late-night flight.

This is not a book about Russia. This chapter will not attempt to give anything approaching a full analysis of Russia's history after the fall of the USSR. Nevertheless it is my conviction that it is impossible to understand the last 20 years of troublesome Georgian–Russian relations without having at least a rudimentary knowledge, or rather a sense, of the trauma of the dramatic first years of independent Russia after the fall of the USSR. Thus, compared with other parts of this book, this chapter contains fewer hard facts and more personal experiences and impressions from Russia before and after the resignation of Mikhail Gorbachev in late December 1991.

I have of course not the faintest intention of defending the Communist system. The old pre-*perestroika* USSR was an unsustainable and deeply undemocratic society. I will give only one symbolic example from a visit I made in 1984 as a sociologist to study the workings of the Supreme Soviet. The system was something between a joke and a tragedy. Heydar Aliyev, later president of independent Azerbaijan, was chairing a session of the Soviet 'parliament'. He was a cynical actor. For every proposed 'decision' he asked, formally correct, 'Approval, rejection or abstention?' In every case there was 100 per cent approval, but Aliyev managed to sound highly surprised every time he asked 'rejections' or 'abstentions' and got zero replies, as if it was a great sensation or totally unexpected that not a single one of the thousands of delegates even once raised a hand against the proposal by the leadership. 'No rejections? Really?' was Aliyev's recurrent comment!

PERESTROIKA

Five years later, at the height of *perestroika*, something was clearly happening. I met with Vadim Zagladin, secretary of the Foreign Policy Committee of the Supreme Soviet. He replied reluctantly to my question about the possibility of spreading *perestroika* and *glasnost* to the rest of the Soviet bloc:

> We try to give examples, but concerning export, the history shows that the best way of creating conflict is that one country tries to teach another. We have tried this and we have not reached far with it. We have shown our opinions but our friends have been insulted, they have to learn from life.

One evening I saw *Zoikina kvartira* by the famous and earlier banned author of *The Master and Margarita*, Mikhail Bulgakov (who died in 1940), a chaotic piece concerning dreams about going to Paris in Moscow of the 1920s. However, more interesting than the play was a review some days later in *Pravda* which asked:

> We just saw with somewhat distanced interest the residents and guests of the happy apartment of Zoikin, who relaxed and amused themselves as they could do and did, greedily inhaling the poisonous gas of NEP [the New Economic Policy of the 1920s], which only yesterday was unthinkable and already today is almost underground – and tomorrow?[4]

The NEP of course was compared to *perestroika*, which created similar hopes, and unfortunately met with a similar fate.

Despite all this, and despite the fact that Gorbachev later became very unpopular in Russia, there was, at least until the ill-fated attempted coup by reactionary communist nostalgics in August 1991, a great hope that *perestroika* and *glasnost* were a workable method to achieve a measured transformation of the USSR into a democratic union, at a tempo that would not generate misery and suffering for large parts of the population, and without destroying those aspects of unity between the participating states that the ideologues of the European Union are so proud of concerning their own union.

Maybe the hopes for a reformed union between the peoples of the USSR through *perestroika* and *glasnost* were never realistic. Freedom movements were already strong in several of the constituent republics, and I must confess to having supported this trend actively by leading a campaign in the Swedish parliament to officially recognize Lithuanian independence at the beginning of 1990. As a Swedish member of parliament I even delivered a supporting speech in the besieged parliament in Vilnius in January 1991.

Thus, there were different hopes. Some hoped for a peaceful transformation of the Soviet Union into something like the European Union, but at the same time a political and economic alternative with independent status. Others hoped for the total dissolution of the 'evil' Communist empire and rapid incorporation of the remaining pieces into the Western capitalist hemisphere. In hindsight it is clear that the West was never prepared to accept a strong, democratic and competing Eastern union.

SOCIAL COLLAPSE, POLITICAL PLURALISM

I got my first impressions of the human reality of the drama only a few weeks after the end of the USSR. When one evening in February 1992 I stepped out from a subway station in central Moscow, I had an awkward experience, which at first almost scared me to death. Hundreds of women and some men formed a long passageway, and I had to run the gauntlet between them. As soon as I found a breach in the human wall I hurried to escape out of this frightening passage, which reminded me of medieval methods of punishment I had learned about from films and books when I was a teenager.

But I had misunderstood the situation. These well-dressed, silent, middle-class Russians had no intention whatsoever of hurting me. They just wanted to sell some petty commodities they stretched forward, like a flask of perfume, a bottle of Stolichnaya vodka or Armenian brandy, some tablecloths, a couple of statuettes, some jewellery. After about 100 metres the human alleyway thinned out, but in another 50 metres it returned to its previous thickness outside a restaurant. Probably the amateur salespeople hoped that some of the nouveaux riches might be interested customers when they left their tables, sated and in good humour. I thought this scene showed that there were no pawnbrokers in Moscow. Anyway, a pawnbroker would not have paid much, even in devalued roubles, for most of the small things that were being offered for sale. Last in the long human line stood two elderly women, chatting away. Each had a carton of milk in her hand. I didn't ask how much they wanted for their milk – maybe ten roubles, I guessed. Less than two months earlier, in December 1991, a litre of milk had cost 36 kopeks. Now it cost 18 roubles in the shops, 50 times as much!

Such was the result of the switch from the communist-controlled state economy through the famous 'shock therapy', which was introduced by the Gajdar government after recommendations from neoliberal economic advisors, the American Jeffrey Sachs and the Swede Anders Åslund, who were more interested in their own doctrines than in the welfare of human beings. Maybe the two ladies had hoarded frozen milk before the price shock – although refrigerators were rare luxuries in the USSR. But it is cold in Russia in the middle of the winter, so they might have stored a few litres in plastic bags outside their kitchen windows, a method that was pretty common in Soviet Russia. If they were lucky they could make a little profit, provided they found customers before the hyperinflation made the rouble even more worthless.

In the USSR most people had savings because it was difficult to find anything to spend money on. And when some popular commodity became available the distribution was determined not by the price but by who had the patience to stand in line to get a chance to buy it for a low and fixed price. This was a popular duty for the *babushka* (grandmother) of the family. There were extremely few shops for *produkty*, the Russian variant of grocery stores, and anyhow they often did not have much to sell. In the cities there was nothing private, not even a newspaper stand or small café. Thus, people had money that they could not use.

This system was of course not sustainable. Nothing new happened without a decision by the party. I remember from my visits in the USSR in the 1980s that I regretted the enormous hidden potential for initiative that I took for granted was concealed beneath this totally stifling system. In the long run a change was inevitable if the whole society was not to come to a standstill. The declared ambition by Khrushchev to overtake the GNP of the West in a limited number of years was of course both unrealistic and bizarre.

Nevertheless the system gave some social and economic security. The question was how, and how rapidly, the transformation should take place without creating human misery. There were many different theories, but the one that won the day was 'shock therapy'. Russia was to be transformed into a Western-style free market in 500 days. This was of course madness. Price controls were abolished, state property was 'given' to the citizens via vouchers which were bought by the future oligarchs, and an enormous inflation followed at the same time as a minority became super-rich. The result was not a normal market economy ruled by law, but a mafia economy ruled by armed gangs. Most Russians became totally broke, their savings became worthless, and their standard of living deteriorated many times over at the same time as the super-rich 'new Russians' started to lead an ostensibly luxurious life, which was very visible to all the poor. One effect was the sordid and depressing scenes outside the metro stations in Moscow and similar places all over the country.

If the loss of about 100 million people in the other, now independent 14 former Soviet republics, the introduction of borders and customs between former 'provinces' in a very integrated, even if inefficient, economic common market, and many other problematic effects of the disintegration of a former superpower are taken into account, nobody should be astonished that this development, during the first period of 'freedom', created a gigantic frustration and nostalgia, but also split the population and the political establishment about how to proceed further. Some wanted to go on faster with 'reforms', supported by the West, while others wanted to take it more slowly in order not to exacerbate the human misery. Some even wanted to turn the tide and more or less revert to some kind of a socialist system. A few dreamed of restoring the USSR. Most could unite around the conviction that the alcoholic and heartsick Yeltsin ought to be removed in one way or another.

An interesting aspect of all this was of course that the one-party system had been replaced by a multitude of political movements. When one day in early 1992 I passed the Lenin Museum, I felt as if I was back in the days of the student revolt in 1968 in my university town of Lund in southern Sweden. There were red flags, posters, innumerable street vendors of radical and left-wing news papers and magazines. I counted 34 different opposition newspapers with names such as *Molnja* (Lightning), which accused international capitalists of having destroyed the USSR; *Borba* (Struggle), which warned that the socialist fatherland was in danger; *Glasnost* (Openness) which criticized social inequalities; and *Narodnaya Pravda* (People's truth), which demanded that Gorbachev's pension should be paid by the United States.

There were also nationalist groups like *Russkij puls* (Russian pulse), *Russkij put* (Russian road), *Nasha Rossija* (Our Russia), and Zhirinovsky's 'liberals', which had more right-wing nationalist programmes, including restoring the borders of 1913, which would not only return all seceded Soviet republics, but also remake Poland and Finland into Russian provinces.

Very visible on the public scene was the vice president and acknowledged war hero Alexander Rutskoj, who was actively campaigning against the regime in which he himself was number two. One example of his contribution to the public debate was an article he published in *Izvestia* where he criticized those Russians who stood in line to get into McDonald's, a phenomenon that had continued unabatedly for two years since the opening of its first shop in Moscow by the American hamburger company. 'These people don't want something to eat but just want to feel part of a Western lifestyle,' he wrote. 'But what do we have to offer?' he asked, and then made a covert attack on his own boss, President Yeltsin.[5] The editors of *Izvestia* wrote an unusual reply, and stated that in fact people wanted a decent meal for a reasonable price. They wondered where Rutskoj was heading. Rutskoj gave his reply on two full pages in *Pravda*, where he demanded an economic state of emergency and threatened those who resisted such a policy with the loss of power and 'full responsibility'.[6]

Almost two years later, in September 1993 I had another experience, similar to the one outside the metro in Moscow in February 1992. I was going to take a night train together with my wife from Nizhny Novgorod to Kazan, capital of the autonomous republic of Tatarstan, but we almost missed it because it was impossible to get on the platform, which was congested with people approaching in the opposite direction from some local trains. It was a horde of old and young, men and women, rather shabbily dressed, everybody carrying or hauling something: potatoes, carrots, onions, apples, turnips. We watched dumbfounded. Were they heading for the local market to sell their products? Or were they going to join the mass of destitute housewives who stood selling petty commodities outside the station building, which we had just passed? 'We have become a country of peddlers,' a Russian friend had told us. But the timing was odd, eight o'clock in the evening. We asked and received the explanation: 'They are coming back from their *dachas*. They are going to eat these things themselves. The small cultivation plots are the basic means of survival for Russians today.' The neoliberal fanatics had not pushed Russia forward into a modern market system, but backwards several centuries to a pre-monetary subsistence economy!

According to the economist Alexander Buzgalin, 70 per cent of the population had experienced a deterioration in their standard of living since the 'liberation', for 20 per cent there had been no change, and for only 10 per cent had there been an improvement. The privatizations had a Russian nickname, '*prichvatisatia*', which implied that privatization in reality was a kind of theft, where a few people could often take over state property almost free of charge.

ON THE BRINK OF CIVIL WAR

Such were the material circumstances behind the clash and coup d'état in September–October 1993. Yeltsin had been elected president of Russia with 57.3 per cent of the votes in June 1991, but in September 1993 his popularity rating was lower than Rutskoj's.[7] Parliament was dominated by nationalist and revanchist groups under Rutskoj and the speaker of the parliament, Ruslan Khasbulatov, who exploited the general dissatisfaction. The political situation was characterized by deadlock and power struggles between the Supreme Soviet and the president.

In August *Komsomolskaya Pravda* reported that 'the president promises a hot autumn'.[8] In the beginning of September Yeltsin fired Rutskoj from his position as vice president. A list of the 100 most popular Russian politicians was published under the headline, 'The influence of the presidential team has diminished'.[9] Some days later a poll showed that Yeltsin was only number four.[10] The official, later banned, newspaper of the Supreme Soviet asked, 'Will Yeltsin carry out a coup d'etat?'[11] This he did on September 21 by dissolving the recalcitrant parliament, which he had no right to do according to the constitution. The result was an escalated crisis which I partly watched at close range outside the White House, the parliament building by the Moscow River.

Unfortunately the parliamentarians were not satisfied to resist by peaceful and constitutional means only. The protest demonstration in early October started as a peaceful march of mainly pensioners, but soon developed into something else, with young violent veterans from the disastrous Russian war in Afghanistan as the advance guard. When these hardcore guys occupied the TV tower Ostankino and it emerged that arms were being distributed inside the White House, Yeltsin got his excuse to call in the army and shell his own parliament in the centre of Moscow.

If the manoeuvre was intended to save Russia from a return to communism, it was probably unnecessary. A poll showed, after the coup but before the bloodshed, that only 18 per cent wanted a return to communism, while 58 per cent were against.[12] Despite the enormous frustration, humiliation and dissatisfaction with the shock therapy and the rule of Yeltsin, the Russians did not want to lose their relative political freedom.

The September–October events 1993 were a very tough struggle for power where Yeltsin, increasingly unpopular at home but supported by the West, fought for his political life against different groups, some democratic, others absolutely not, who wanted a less brutal shock therapy and less humiliating submission to the dictates of the West. After the intervention in favour of Yeltsin by the army, the Swedish Russia specialist Stefan Hedlund assumed that 'probably the military will require payment by Yeltsin'.[13] At least concerning Georgia, there is a strong indication that this was a well-founded assumption.

In December 1993 I was one of several international observers at the Russian parliamentary elections. My place of mission was Syktykvar, capital of the Komi autonomous republic in the far north, where the temperature was close to 40 degrees below zero. Several voters openly grunted that they considered it a shame that the West should observe a Russian election. Why was there not also Russian observation of elections in the West? The growing degradation of Yeltsin's Russia to a kind of colony under the guardianship of the West was widely felt.

Two episodes, or rather, letters, are worth mentioning. They were both delivered to me personally, as a representative not of a super-power but of neutral Sweden.

The first, handwritten letter was given me by L. A. Gamitin, who presented himself as 'minimal pensioner'. He wrote:

All earlier Russian generations must be called crippled by disaster: the Bolshevik revolution, the civil war, the dekulakization, the big repression in the 1930s, the Great Patriotic War, the reconstruction of the destroyed country, the harshness of communist life. But what have we got from the novelties of today? The impossibility of governing the country, an absence of fundamental laws and non-implementation of those that exist, enormous inflation, emission of unnecessary money coupons, corruption, mafia, lies, murders, violence, sales to foreigners of everything that the people have created by their own work.

The letter from Mikhail Ivanovich was typewritten and mainly related a long and complicated story of local power abuses. But he also wrote:

During two years Yeltsin has destroyed our economy no less than Hitler did in five years of war and Stalin during the repressions of the 1930s. For this the West is eulogizing him and praising him for the destruction and humiliation of a great people.

WESTERN INDIFFERENCE TO RUSSIAN SUFFERING

I believe these examples are enough to make my point about the Russian catastrophe after the breakdown of the USSR and its repercussions for Georgia – and for many other events in the area of the former USSR.

I shall give only one last example to illustrate the complete lack of compassion for Russians that has been so typical of many Westerners, not only politicians, but also 'experts' on Russia. In the summer of 1996 Anders Åslund, who from 1991 to 1994 had worked as official adviser to the architects of the shock therapy, Jegor Gajdar and Anatoly Tjubajs, published an article in a major Swedish daily under the headline 'Russian shock therapy was a success'.[14]

This was when poverty was widespread among the Russian masses and the health situation so bad that the Russian population had started to decrease. At the same time some super-rich oligarchs became more visible and arrogant day by day. And only two years later the whole Russian economy collapsed. In one of the best and most compassionate analyses of the Russian catastrophe I have read, the former editor of *Hindustan Times*, Prem Shankar Jha, wrote about the period and policy that Åslund defines as a 'success' under the significant headline 'The unmaking of Russia': 'As the effects of the crisis revealed themselves it became clear to the Russians that shock therapy and the opening to the West had devastated their country.'[15]

To consider a social and human collapse 'a success' is possible only from a perspective where Russians are regarded as *Untermenschen* without the same human value as others. I have never met such a disdainful attitude towards Russians in Georgia. But the fact that it is rather common in the West unfortunately even has an impact on Georgia.

NOTES

1   Anna Politkovskaya, *Putins Ryssland* (Putin's Russia), Ordfront, Stockholm, 2004.

2   *Raspad* (disintegration) is the usual Russian term for the collapse of the USSR.
3   Alexander Solzhenitsyn, *Rossia v obvale* (Russia at the brink of crumbling), Moscow, 1998.
4   *Pravda*, March 6, 1989.
5   *Izvestia*, January 31, 1992.
6   *Pravda*, February 8, 1992.
7   Oleg Moroz, *1996 – Kak Ziuganov ne stal presidentom* (1996 – how Ziuganov did not become president), Raduga, Moscow, 2006.
8   *Komsomolskaya Pravda*, August 20, 1993.
9   *Nezavisimaya Gazeta*, September 2, 1993.
10 *Moskovskie Novosti*, September 12, 1993.
11 *Rossiskaya Gazeta*, September 11, 1993.
12 *Sevodnja*, October 8, 1993.
13 *Svenska Dagbladet*, October 8, 1993.
14 *Dagens Nyheter*, July 28, 1996.
15 Prem Shankar Jha, *The Perilous Road to the Market*, Pluto Press, London, 2002.

5

THE BREAKAWAY REGIONS – RUSSIAN STOOGES OR FREEDOM SEEKERS?

Are the two Georgian regions, Abkhazia and South Ossetia, that broke away from Georgia when the USSR crumbled, just Russian stooges or genuine freedom seekers? No issue connected with Georgia is so hot and controversial, and so full of emotions and prejudices.

SOUTH OSSETIA

The Ossetians are a Christian people, speaking an Indo-European language, which is related to Persian. They live on both sides of the Caucasus mountain range, in the autonomous republic of North Ossetia in the Russian Federation and in South Ossetia in Georgia. According to the 1989 census South Ossetia had 100,000 inhabitants on an area a little larger than Cornwall, out of which 66.2 per cent were Ossetians and 29 per cent Georgians. During the bloodshed in the early 1990s thousands of Georgians left South Ossetia, and tens of thousands of Ossetians left Georgia outside South Ossetia.

Before the 2008 war, the population of South Ossetia was about 60,000 Ossetians and 10,000 Georgians. There also remained thousands of Ossetians in other parts of Georgia. However, since the war in the beginning of the 1990s their position was vulnerable. A report about a year before the 2008 Ossetia War from a purely Ossetian village in Kakheti province gave a sad picture: 'Among the hundred inhabited houses stands about the same number of abandoned, derelict buildings whose owners fled during the Georgian–Ossetian conflict and have never come back.'[1]

Some Georgians like to interpret Queen Tamar's marriage in 1189 with the Ossetian prince David Soslan, after having divorced her

Russian husband, as a symbol that shows Georgian–Ossetian relations are basically friendly, provided they are relieved of Russian
interference. Russian and Ossetian critics tend to take a more pessimistic view, one author describing the Georgian–Ossetian relations as a history of 'age-old attempts by Georgian lords to strip
the Ossetians of their will and land'.[2] Ossetians claim that South
Ossetia became a part of Russia decades earlier (1774) than Georgia (1801). The South Ossetians reacted negatively against the first
Georgian independence, and started an uprising in 1918 which was
'crushed by the Menshevik government'.[3] Two years later the Ossetians made another attempt, this time with a pro-Bolshevik political
touch, which was routed with brutal force. Ossetians claim they lost
5,000 dead, and refer to this period as 'the first genocide' committed by Georgians against them. Georgians, on the other hand, take
the Bolshevik colour of the Ossetian revolt as foreshadowing later
Russian exploitation of Ossetian dissatisfaction.

The South Ossetian Autonomous Oblast was established in 1922
in the framework of Georgia. Delegations from South Ossetia in
1925 twice demanded union with North Ossetia, but Stalin replied
with oppression, and finally had all the members of these delegations
executed, a fact that many Ossetians and Russians recall to validate
their argument that Georgians enjoyed a lot of privileges during the
Soviet period because of the over-representation of Georgians in top
positions in Moscow: Stalin, Ordzhonikidze and Beria.[4]

Abolishing the autonomy

The modern crisis started after the bloodbath in Tbilisi on April 9,
1989. In Georgia signatures were collected in support of a demand to
abolish the South Ossetian autonomy. As a response to this and the
Georgian aspirations for independence, the Supreme Soviet of South
Ossetia on November 10, 1989 transformed itself from an autonomous oblast into an autonomous Soviet socialist republic, a decision
that was cancelled the next day by the Georgian Supreme Soviet. On
November 23 some 20,000 Georgian nationalists organized a march
on Tskhinvali, the capital of the region, which was prevented by
Soviet internal forces from entering the city. In September 1990 South
Ossetia proclaimed itself a Soviet socialist republic, which meant its
split from Georgia and its acquisition of the right of secession (just as
Georgia had seceded, according to the Soviet constitution). Immediately after his election victory in October Gamsakhurdia struck back
by reducing the region to a common Georgian administrative unit,

Shida Kartli or Samacheblo (after the feudal family who used to own the area), which are the names for the area used by Georgians, if they do not say just Tskhinvali.

On December 9, 1990, elections were held in South Ossetia and Torez Kulumbekov was elected president. A state of emergency was declared in the region by the Georgian government. These events were followed by fighting and bloodshed. According to the French specialist on the Caucasus, Silvia Serrano, 'Georgian paramilitary as well as official militias committed atrocities in Tskhinvali.'[5] The chief doctor in Tskhinvali reported on January 5, 1991 that his hospital had received 289 wounded, out of which 39 had died.[6]

Kulumbekov was arrested. In February 1991 the Supreme Soviet of North Ossetia demanded that Gorbachev should stop 'the genocide' upon their southern compatriots, but the Soviet leader thought he could lure Gamsakhurdia into a new Moscow-led union if the Georgians were given free hands in South Ossetia. On March 17 South Ossetia voted to join the new union. Some weeks later the Georgians overwhelmingly voted in favour of independence. It must of course be observed that at elections now and later in South Ossetia, the Georgian minority usually did not participate, just as South Ossetians did not vote in Georgian elections.

On March 21 the leader of the Russian Soviet Republic, Boris Yeltsin, who already had his mind set on the dissolution of the Soviet Union, met with Gamsakhurdia in Kazbegi, just south of the Russian–Georgian border. They agreed on the establishment of a joint Russian–Georgian committee, and that some Soviet troops should leave the region. South Ossetia was called 'a former autonomy'. When, on April 1, the Supreme Soviet of USSR demanded a state of emergency in South Ossetia, Gorbachev was still not ready. But later in April Soviet troops entered and created some law and order.[7] Gamsakhurdia proclaimed victory and exclaimed, 'We have restored historical justice to Shida Kartli and returned Tskhinvali to the Gori region.'[8]

The conflict was not settled, however. The year 1991 saw the failed coup in Moscow in August, which was supported by both North and South Ossetians, which may be understood as a reaction against the reluctance of Gorbachev to intervene against the Georgian assault. At the end of the year the Soviet Union was dissolved, and on January 22, 1992, 99 per cent of the voters of South Ossetia (but without the participation of the Georgian minority) demanded to join the Russian Federation. On June 10, the new leaders of Georgia, Shevardnadze and Kitovani, met in Kazbegi with North

Ossetian leaders. Shevardnadze admitted there had been Georgian faults, and made excuses to the Ossetians. On June 24, Shevardnadze met with the new number one in Moscow, Boris Yeltsin, in Dagomys and agreed on a ceasefire and a system for deploying peacekeeping forces from Russia, Georgia, and North and South Ossetia under the umbrella of Organization for Security and Cooperation in Europe (OSCE) observers. This has been interpreted as a political victory for Russia, which showed that it was able to avoid full scale war in 'its area', in contrast to the chaotic and rapid deterioration of the situation in Yugoslavia at the same time.[9]

Years of relative calm

Despite the fact that the conflict was not resolved, for more than a decade after the Dagomys treaty the situation was relatively calm, but hardly normal. South Ossetia, with no natural resources or unique skills, developed into a paradise for smugglers. At Ergneti, just at the border between the self-proclaimed republic and Georgia, an enormous market for contraband was established. The border between North and South Ossetia was not guarded by either Ossetians or Russians, and the Georgians considered it legally impossible to establish border and customs control between two parts of their own territory. Thus, everything could cross unchecked between Georgia and Russia through South Ossetia, which gave some people enormous chances to make a profit.

When I visited South Ossetia in 2000 I had the feeling of entering a part of Russia. Nothing Georgian was visible, but also not very much Ossetian. When I was invited for dinner by President Ludvig Chibirov he served typical Russian food (*borchkh* and *zakuzky*) and Russian beverages (beer and vodka), and talked in Russian. However, the Russia I encountered in Tskhinvali was not the one I had known in Moscow, St Petersburg, Nizhny Novgorod and other places in the Russian Federation during the 1990s; it was more like the country I had visited in the 1980s. South Ossetia smelled of the Soviet Union! At the same time the apparatchik-type Chibirov proved to be more international than I had expected. He had been named after a Bavarian celebrity his parents had admired, and he had himself visited South Tyrol to study a functioning autonomy. He could not imagine being put under the authority of Tbilisi politicians, but it seemed that some type of wide autonomy might be acceptable.

Chibirov and his staff vividly described how, from the Ossetian point of view, Georgian independence was a catastrophe. It meant that the border between the two parts of Ossetia, which for ages had been just an administrative line on the map, was suddenly transformed into an international barrier. One effect of the dissolution of the USSR was that the partition of Ossetia has not always been taken seriously by Georgians.

A member of the Georgian government once told me that North and South Ossetians have absolutely nothing in common, being linked 'only by a tunnel' – the Roki Tunnel through the mountains, which became world-famous during the 2008 war.[10] However history has proved that North and South Ossetians have often acted as one nation, even if divided. This has been demonstrated by the frequent demands for reunification of North and South Ossetia into one administrative unit. It was also shown during the Ossetian War of 2008.

Attempts at reconquest

During the Shevardnadze period the Ossetians did not consider Georgia to be an imminent threat, although no final solution was found despite numerous efforts. The situation changed, however, with the Rose Revolution. In the beginning of the summer of 2004 – after the successful reintegration of Adjara under Tbilisi authority (see Chapter 10) – the new rulers decided to close down the Ergneti market. The Ossetians protested, with Russian support. The situation deteriorated. In June the wife of the Georgian president was denied entry into Tskhinvali and was forced to return to Tbilisi by helicopter, which according to her own account the Ossetians threatened to shoot down.[11] In August Prime Minister Zhvania was shot at when he was visiting Georgian villages in the region. Then violent fighting erupted. Georgian troops entered South Ossetia. At the same time an opinion poll showed that 98.8 per cent of the South Ossetians rejected Georgian supremacy. This might of course have had many causes, including some mundane ones. For example while a Georgian pension was equivalent to US$7 a month, a Russian pension, which most South Ossetians were entitled to after having adopted Russian citizenship, was ten times higher, US$70.

According to the Georgian Embassy in Brussels, 26 Georgians were killed and only seven Ossetians. The situation however had not improved when the Georgian forces withdrew on August 19; instead the opposite happened. Several years later Gia Khukhashvili of the *Resonansi* newspaper told me that 'it was after the closure of the market that everything started to deteriorate, the situation fell ten years backwards.' He thought the closure was a serious mistake, because 'it was a point of contact and tens of thousands of people made their living from it, there should have been established a legal free zone'. Nevertheless, Mikheil Saakashvili proclaimed victory.

In 2005 President Saakashvili presented a peace initiative in Strasbourg and to the UN General Assembly, which was supported by the OSCE in December. The plan outlined comprehensive autonomy for South Ossetia inside Georgia, including a number of linguistic, educational and other rights. On my printed copy I made a note, 'Seems generous.'[12] The South Ossetian President Eduard Kokoity presented similar ideas at about the same time, but with the crucial difference that the decision about the eventual reintegration of South Ossetia into Georgia would be postponed. A refugee from an Ossetian village, Zenta Bestajev, was made Georgian minister of integration, and some well-publicized efforts were made to convince Ossetians to return from North Ossetia to Georgia proper, but with little effect. There are a number of reasons given for the reluctance of Ossetians to return to Georgia proper, including that those who have opted for Russian citizenship have no Georgian citizenship; they believe they would have slight possibilities of getting a job, especially if they originate from the tight Ossetian communities where Georgian has been little used; they do not feel secure; they fear that in Georgia they will not be able to retain their Ossetian language and culture, or even the Russian language and culture; and they believe it is difficult for Ossetians to get their rights in Georgian courts.[13]

After a period of relative calm, tension rose in South Ossetia when in November 2006 President Saakashvili established a special administration for the Georgian villages of the breakaway region, headed by an 'alternative president', Dmitry Sanakoyev, an Ossetian defector from the secessionist government, in which he had served as minister of defence. In May 2007 South Ossetia closed the road from the most isolated Georgian villages to Tskhinvali and blocked passage for anybody who did not have a South Ossetian or Russian passport. On May 11 Sanakoyev delivered a speech to the Georgian parliament, symbolically in Ossetian, where he stated that the future of South Ossetia lay inside Georgia. South Ossetia dismantled the checkpoints after only a few days, reportedly on request by Russia, but the chain of events provoked a confrontational climate.[14]

After the failed attempt to reconquer South Ossetia in 2004 President Saakashvili ordered the minister of defence, Irakli Okruashvili, to prepare for a another try, a *blitzkrieg*, which was intended to integrate the seceded region into Georgia before the end of 2006. When experienced generals claimed that the mission was impossible, they were replaced by more optimistic officers. Saakashvili was prevented from his *blitzkrieg* only by intervention by Javier Solana, responsible for the foreign policy of the European Union. The cancellation of the *blitzkrieg* was the main reason behind the split between Saakashvili and Okruashvili at the end of that year.[15]

In April 2007, Saakashvili proposed an amended version of his peace plan of 2005, which included the creation of a temporary administration for South Ossetia. Unfortunately this was not credible enough, either for the South Ossetians, or for the Russians, who had been far more involved than was justified by their role as peacekeepers, mandated by the OSCE. Thus, the stage was set for the developments that brought about the 2008 war (see Chapter 12).

ABKHAZIA

Abkhazia is a region of about the size of Cyprus in the far northwest corner of Georgia, bordering on Russia and the Black Sea. The Abkhazians speak a Caucasian language, related to Circassian and Adygean and other languages of North Caucasus. Most of the Abkhazians have been Muslims since the sixteenth century. For several centuries Abkhazia had its own princely rulers. The region was affiliated to Russia as an autonomous region in 1810, but in 1864 the autonomy was abolished and it was completely integrated into the Russian empire, which provoked a large part of the population to take refuge in the Ottoman empire in a wave of emigration that became known as *Mohajirstvo*. This profoundly changed the composition of the population and made the Abkhazians into a minority in their own country. Their number stagnated around 56,000 from 1897 to 1926, while during the same time the number of Georgians more than doubled – from 26,000 to 67,000. The Abkhazian proportion of the population decreased from 42 per cent in 1886 to 27 per cent in 1926 and 15 per cent in 1959.

According to the Abkhazian discourse, Stalin and Beria tried to 'Georgianize' the region, through the immigration of ethnic Georgians, the introduction of the Georgian script to write Abkhazian, Georgian schools and so on. The nationalistic Russian writers Leontiev and Zhukov maintain that in '1937–53 there were undertaken measures in Abkhazia that were criminal'.[16] This judgement is partly corroborated by the Swedish writer Svante Cornell, who observes that 'after 1953 things changed', a fact that gives some 'credence to a certain anti-Abkhaz policy during the Stalin era'.[17] The Russian, anticommunist and pro-Georgian observer Svetlana Chervonnaya concurs but emphasizes that 'if in Stalin's time advantages and privileges were artificially conferred on the Georgians, after 1956 the situation went to another extreme and now the ethnic Abkhazians began to supplant the Georgians'.[18] During the last years of the Soviet period, 37 per cent of local party secretaries and 45.5 per cent of provincial party secretaries in Abkhazia were ethnic Abkhazians.

Before the civil war and the mass flight of some 250,000 Georgians in 1993, the total population was estimated to be 525,000, out of which Abkhazians made up only 18 per cent, while 46 per cent were Georgians, the remainder being Russians, Armenians, Ukrainians, Greeks or those having other Soviet nationalities. During the Soviet period Abkhazia was an example of 'Soviet cosmopolitism' with many ethnic and national groups.[19] With its sunny climate it was a coveted holiday paradise for people from all over the Soviet Union, dotted with seaside resorts and sanatoria along its 250 kilometres of Black Sea coastline.

To Gamsakhurdia, however, 'the Abkhaz have never existed, they just fight against Georgia and Georgians for the sake of russification'.[20] Unsurprisingly the Abkhazians have been of another opinion. Abkhazian intellectuals asked for a merger with the Russian Soviet Federative Socialist Republic in 1957, 1967, 1978 and 1988. Abkhazians maintain that Abkhazia was almost independent from 1921 to 1931, in the form of a Soviet socialist republic. But Georgians reply that Abkhazia had already in December 1921 signed a treaty that delegated some competence to Georgia. In the 1924 USSR Constitution Abkhazia is described as an autonomous republic within Georgia, and in 1931 Abkhazia was formally degraded from SSR to ASSR.

Abkhaz authorities allege that some 700,000 ethnic Abkhazians and their descendants live in Turkey; others are in Syria, Jordan, Germany and Israel. The leader of the Abkhaz liberation movement, Vladislav Ardzinba, who was an anthropologist by profession, was convinced that many Abkhazians in exile would return to an independent Abkhazia.[21] The American journalist Thomas Goltz asserts that 'a significant number did indeed return', even if not at all as many as Ardzinba had hoped.[22] According to another estimation 'no more than 1,000 are believed to have permanently resettled from Turkey'.[23]

Countdown towards war

The final countdown started with a large rally in Lychny, on March 18, 1989, organized by the Abkhazian nationalist association

Aidgylara. On March 24 the Lychny Appeal for the restoration of the Abkhaz SSR of 1921–31 was published. This provoked Georgian protest rallies in the southernmost part of Abkhazia, Gali, where more than 95 per cent of the population was Georgian. The pivotal Tbilisi manifestations of early April were also at least partly a reaction against the Lychny Appeal. In May 1989 a decision was taken to establish a branch of the Tbilisi State University in Sukhumi. In the tense situation, this was interpreted by Abkhazians as an assault, and protest rallies were organized. However, for some time tensions calmed down and the focus was transferred to South Ossetia. According to Chervonnaya the pause in the confrontation in Abkhazia was a result of intervention by mafia bosses who feared for their profits![24]

However, after the fall of the Soviet Union the focus soon returned to Abkhazia. On December 29, 1991, the Abkhazian leader Ardzinba gave orders to his militia to take over police stations, a move that Chervonnaya interprets as a coup d'état. However, this happened at the same time as the Soviet Union ceased to exist. Was it not logical that responsible leaders all over the dissolved union feared a power vacuum and chaos? Another similar contradiction in Chervonnaya's argument refers to the Confederation of Mountain Peoples of Caucasus (CMPC), which intervened to support Abkhazia in the conflict with Georgia. According to Chervonnaya and most Georgian commentators, this body was nothing but an instrument for Russian *siloviki* (security institutions). At the same time, she admits that the stated goal of the CMPC was that all the Caucasus autonomies 'would first secede from Russia and Georgia and then unite with each other'. How could that be acceptable for the most imperialist forces in Russia, who feared nothing more than the dissolution of the Russian Federation? In a similar way, most arguments that are intended to reduce the Abkhazians and Ossetians to nothing but Russian stooges, without any sincere ambition of their own for national liberation, collide with disturbing facts. This of course does not exclude the possibility that such ambitions may have been exploited and distorted by Russian machinations. Nevertheless, that is quite another thing.

When Shevardnadze returned to Georgia in March 1992 the train was already rolling with full speed towards the clash. It did not help that his record in Abkhazia from his time as leader of Soviet Georgia was fairly good, as he recalls in a foreword to the English edition of Chervonnaya's book. He started a 'peaceful dialogue, resulting in the expansion of Abkhazian autonomy ... an Abkhazian University was opened, as were an Abkhazian TV channel and Abkhazian literary journals'.

Chervonnaya maintains that the ceasefire in South Ossetia in June 1992 was a signal for the 'redbrown army of imperial revenge' to act in Abkhazia. It is true that the decision by the Abkhazian Supreme Soviet to restore the 1925 constitution of the Abkhazian SSR came after the Dagomys agreement. It was nullified by the Georgian government on July 25, and on August 4 Georgia celebrated a Great Reconciliation. The state of emergency was lifted, and an amnesty was granted. Then there were attacks against a railway in Abkhazia, and it was decided to send in Georgian troops to defend the railway. On August 12 there was a rally in support of Shevardnadze in Tbilisi. Two days later war erupted in Abkhazia. What had happened? According to most Georgian observers the Abkhazians started it. Chervonnaya concurs: it was Ardzinba who 'started his long-planned war on August 14, 1992'.

Nevertheless, it was the Georgian militia leader Tengiz Kitovani who marched into Abkhazia with 3,000 soldiers who, as admitted by Chervonnaya, 'did not display angelic gentleness'. Another observer states unambiguously, 'It is the intrusion of Georgian troops into Abkhazia which is the start of the conflict.'[25] Goltz, who reported directly from the war, states that 'who started the killing remains a subject of bitter dispute', but maintains that the entry of Kitovani's forces entailed an 'orgy of violence'. Coppieter claims that the invasion of Abkhazia by Kitovani was 'the action of a private army out for plunder'. Leontiev and Zhukov refer to a meeting on August 8 with Shevardnadze, Sigua, Kitovani and Ioseliani where it was 'unanimously decided to send troops to Abkhazia'. They claim that some of the Georgian soldiers were released prisoners. The Georgian historian Anchabadze admits that 'the greatest mistake of the State Council was to enter the troops into Abkhazia,' and gives the following account. The Georgian forces entered Abkhazia, claiming that they were going to protect the railway:

> but the actions of the soldiers who invaded Sukhumi did not resemble the actions of the defenders of transport highways. One of their first actions was to throw the Abkhazian flag which was not recognized by Tbilisi from the roof of the Government House, and to fix a Georgian flag.

Shevardnadze in his memoirs claims that even in May he knew that two members of his government had 'secret intentions'. He puts the start of the escalation to July 9, when the Georgian vice premier was kidnapped in West Georgia. Two weeks later he was released after a visit by Shevardnadze to Mingrelia. Then the Abkhazian proclamation of the restoration of the 1925 constitution was announced, followed by the Georgian annulment of that decision. On August 11 Georgian negotiators were kidnapped by Zviadists (that is, Gamsakhurdia's forces), and on August 14 'the Army on order by Kitovani marched into Abkhazia ... that was in contradiction with my agreement with Ardzinba'. Abkhazia mobilized. Kitovani disobeyed, and the army entered Sukhumi 'out of control and started to rob and plunder'. Zviadist soldiers took part on the Georgian side until Gamsakhurdia returned from Chechnya and forbade his supporters to fight together with Georgian troops! Sukhumi was conquered by the Georgians. On September 2 Shevardnadze met with Yeltsin and formally terminated the war.

The fall of Sukhumi, and Georgian mass flight

The assumed stooges of Russia were apparently not integrated into the agreement. In the beginning of October, there were Abkhaz counterattacks and, Shevardnadze maintains, Russian air strikes. In the spring of 1993 occasional fighting erupted, and in March the Georgians shot down a Russian Su-27. Finally, on May 14 there was a ceasefire agreement, and in June 50 UN military observers arrived. However, the Zviadists were not included, and continued to harass the Georgian forces. According to Shevardnadze, Gamsakhurdia and Ardzinba were 'the closest soul mates and found themselves discussing joint plans for a war against their own peoples in the hospitable quiet and coolness of the private mansion in Grozny'.

In September 1993 the combined, if not coordinated, onslaughts by Zviadists and Abkhazians, supported by North Caucasians, including later well-known Chechen fighters such as Shamil Basayev, incited Shevardnadze to go to Sukhumi personally. There Goltz met him on September 18 together with 'two dozen enormous men dressed in black flat jackets and wearing black ski masks' armed with American Smith & Wesson revolvers and M-16s; 'they were Shevardnadze's personal guard, trained at Fort Bragg, North Carolina'. Goltz reports that the real enemies were professional Russian forces, and that many of the Georgian soldiers were military amateurs, who displayed 'utter chaos and drunkenness'. Shevardnadze declared to the world that this was revenge from the crumbling empire.

Sukhumi fell to the Abkhaz/Russian troops on September 27. Two days later Georgian newspapers published a declaration by

Shevardnadze that he had informed the Russian leadership he wanted
to join the CIS, and that he had accepted help from Russian troops
because 'Georgia is on its knees'.[26] In fact, the struggle was not only
about Abkhazia, it was just as much about the power in Georgia.

According to one Russian newspaper, Gamsakhurdia's forces, the
Zviadists, controlled seven out of eight *rayons* in West Georgia.[27]
Another report asserted that 'the conquest by Zviadists of three
towns threatens Georgia with complete chaos'.[28] And in a third
example a well-known Zviadist leader, Loti Kobaliya, was pictured
on a full first page, with a half-metre long black beard, claiming that
'I defend the legally elected president' (in other words, Gamsakhurdia).[29] All this was not Russian propaganda, but journalistic reporting of the harsh fact that Gamsakhurdia was not beaten and could
probably not be beaten by Georgian government forces alone. That
is why Shevardnadze asked for Russian help to beat the Zviadists
– which he got.

More than a decade later he alleges that it was all a 'war with
Russia in Abkhazia', accuses Abkhazia of ethnic cleansing, and
claims that 4,465 Georgian civilians were killed and 147 disappeared, a toll he calls 'a genocide'. It is not clear if the accusation of
'genocide' applies to Abkhazians, Russians or both.

It is true that some 250,000 Georgians fled from Abkhazia, many by
extremely difficult roads in the snowy mountain area of the Caucasus
slopes. But not all refugees had to go through that ordeal: a Georgian
newspaper reported about another possibility. Under the headline
'Refugees are saying', some refugees told the newspaper that:

a Russian embarkation ship took on board several thousand refugees. When we hurried towards it on the beach the separatists
shot at us and wounded two people. Then a Russian cruiser that
was covering the embarkation returned fire and the hostile guns
were silenced. The Russian ship brought us, more than 1,700
refugees, to Poti.[30]

Shevardnadze was flown out from Sukhumi to Batumi. On October 8 a Georgian delegation arrived in Moscow. Later that month
Georgia joined the CIS and a Russian embassy was opened in Tbilisi.

On February 3, 1994, Yeltsin visited Tbilisi and signed a Russian–
Georgian friendship treaty, and also an agreement that three of the
Russian military bases should remain for another 25 years. On May
14 a formal ceasefire agreement was concluded in Moscow, under
UN auspices. Three thousand peacekeepers from the Peacekeeping

Forces of the Commonwealth of Independent States (CISPFK), in reality all Russian, were deployed along a buffer zone, 12 kilometres deep on each side of the border river Inguri. According to a briefing document by the European Parliament, compiled in connection with my visit to the area in 2000, 'it is evident that the role of Russian peace-keepers in Abkhazia is not all clean – they are apparently involved in drugs and arms trafficking'. A UN observer mission was established, UNOMIG. The Geneva peace process was initiated.

Russia – culprit or scapegoat?

Does this mean that Russia had won and retaken control over Georgia? It is easily forgotten that the chaos in Russia at this time was no less than that in Georgia (see Chapter 4). So what role did Russia actually play?

Under the Tashkent Treaty of May 15, 1992, in which former Soviet republics shared arms and equipment from the common Red Army, Georgia received 100 tanks and 200 armoured combat vehicles.[31] The Russian Transcaucasian military district, which still had its headquarters in Tbilisi, next to the Georgian Ministry of Defence, declared that it was ready to defend Georgian sovereignty.[32]

Chervonnaya, who had earlier written a book sympathetic towards Crimean Tartar nationalists, visited Abkhazia from the middle of August to the end of October 1992 on the invitation of the Slav Home – Abkhazian Society of Russian Culture, which was the 'ideological headquarters of the powerful Abkhazian separatist movement'. She was implicitly expected to 'provide ideological "cover" for the separatism', but became convinced that the Abkhazian movement was led and supported by groups who hated the disintegration of the USSR and wanted to take revenge against Shevardnadze. At the same time she admits that before he came to power and during his reign, Zviad Gamsakhurdia put 'forward categorical demands for immediate and overall change to the Georgian language, telling the "newly come" peoples to leave the ancient Georgian land, and proclaiming the special mission of Christian Georgia as an advanced post of European civilization in the Muslim East'. There were calls for de-Armenianization, control of the birthrate of non-Georgians, abolition of autonomies, and so on.[33] But to Chervonnaya, as to many Georgian observers, it seems to be absolutely incomprehensible that the nationalist fanaticism of the first Georgian president could have seriously scared Abkhazians, Ossetians and other minorities.

Another 'defector', the Abkhazian economist and high-level functionary in Soviet Abkhazia, Lorik Marshania, agrees with

Chervonnaya in blaming the 'adventurous actions by the separatist clique that had formed a clan court around Ardzinba', a person to whom Marshania denies every morally acceptable intention and legitimacy as spokesperson for the Abkhaz people because he has lived for decades in Moscow and has a name that is not even of Abkhaz origin, but Adygean. For his service to Georgia, Marshania was in 1997 awarded the Gorgasali Prize.[34]

Nevertheless, not many impartial outside observers have been convinced by the one-sided pro-Georgian discourse. Oksana Antonenko claims that Russia supported both sides. The Russian Ministry of Foreign Affairs sent a letter to Georgia supporting its fight against terrorists, referring to Chechnya. The Russian behaviour was linked to the power struggle in Moscow. According to Antonenko, local commanders may have acted independently, but 'there is no documentary evidence to suggest that the conflict itself had been planned and executed by Moscow'.[35]

It is obvious, though, that some powerful groups in Russia ruthlessly exploited the apprehensions of the minorities. It is true that Russia tied the break-away regions to itself more and more, by granting most of the inhabitants Russian citizenship, exempting them when visa requirements were introduced for Georgians, and supporting them in practical terms. At the same time, it is often forgotten that despite several demands from Abkhazia and South Ossetia to be recognized as sovereign states, or alternatively be accepted as subjects of the Russian Federation, Russia did not comply until after the Ossetian War of 2008.

As a matter of fact Russia closed its borders to Abkhazia in December 1994, and participated in the sanctions against Abkhazia that were established by CIS in January 1996. Men of military age were not allowed into Russia, and all import and export of goods was illegal. Together with damages from the war, the sanctions are estimated to have cost Abkhazia a total of US$11 billion. Russia supported this policy of isolating Abkhazia until 1999. Only in 2002 was the traffic on the Sukhumi–Sochi railway resumed, and in 2006 Russia liberalized trade a little more and foreigners were allowed into Abkhazia. Nevertheless, not until the beginning of 2008 did Russia formally terminate its participation in the CIS sanctions, a fact that is rarely recalled when Russia is unilaterally blamed for the Abkhaz secession.

Thus, when Putin in December 2003 announced that 'we support the territorial integrity of Georgia', it was not only empty words.[36] There are many examples that show Russia's support for

Abkhazia was neither unanimous nor consistent, and that Abkhazia was not just a Russian stooge. One such example was the peace initiative in 2002 by the UN special envoy Dieter Boden, which proposed autonomy for Abkhazia as a 'sovereign entity' within Georgia, which Russia and Georgia accepted, but Abkhazia refused.

Renewed tension

After some years of relative stability in Abkhazia, in May 1998 nationalist Georgian guerrillas, such as the Forest Brethren and the White Legion, intruded into southern Abkhazia, raised the Georgian flag atop government buildings in the 'ghost town' of Gali, and tried to kill the local Abkhaz administrator. According to the former Russian prime minister Primakov, Shevardnadze was not informed before the Georgian onslaught.[37] Georgia demanded that international troops should replace the Russian peacekeepers, but both United Nations and OSCE declined. After some months of skirmishes the Abkhaz militias had forced tens of thousands of Georgian returnees (50,000 according to Georgia, 20,000 according to UN sources) to flee a second time back over the Inguri river.[38] Nevertheless, after the end of hostilities the movement of Georgians was reversed once more, and tens of thousands have come back to the Gali region, some on a part-time basis.

From the informal and scattered return of some tens of thousands of Georgians to Gali it is, however, a big step to complete repatriation of all the Georgian refugees to all parts of Abkhazia. Goltz quotes Oktay Chtizia, head of the Association of Diaspora Abhkaz, who had returned to Sukhumi from exile: 'We will let all innocent refugees return, not murderers.' Goltz asked, 'Does that mean all Georgians who picked up a gun to defend their homes?' Chtizia replied, 'And their families.'[39] This reminds me of a visit to Kosovo shortly after the 1999 war. I was shown around Prizren by the Kosovo-Albanian driver of the Swedish 'governor' of the district. I asked about reports that houses belonging to Serbs were set on fire every night. He replied, 'That happens only to Serbs who are guilty of having persecuted Albanians.' I asked, 'And how many are those Serbs?' He replied, 'All Serbs have persecuted Albanians.'

Most observers agree that not only ethnic Abkhaz participated in the Abkhaz militia, but a considerable number of Russian nationals, many from North Caucasus. At the same time, Abkhaz militias showed a helmet taken from Georgian guerrillas with script in Hebrew letters. In addition, many of the arms used by Georgians were of Ukrainian origin. Both parties were supported by outsiders, with their own interests and aims.

In 1999 the Abkhazians once again organized a referendum, which showed a majority in favour of independence. Shevardnadze and Putin met in Sochi, and agreed to open the Sochi–Sukhumi railway and create a UN police force. According to a Georgian newspaper, in March 2000 the Georgian government threatened the Abkhaz leader Ardzinba that he would be treated with 'Chechen medicine' if he did not accept autonomy inside Georgia. However, the paper asserted, the army of Georgia was not strong enough, so there might need to be an international Kosovo-type operation.[40] In September 2001 paramilitary Georgian units, supported by Chechen rebels, took to the offensive in the Kodori valley, the only territory of Abkhazia controlled by Georgia. This became one more Georgian military defeat. In March 2003 Shevardnadze and Putin met in Sochi and established three working groups: for the return of refugees, for the restoration of the Sochi–Tbilisi railway and for the renovation of the Inguri power station.

While the presidential elections in Abkhazia 1999 were Soviet-style, and Ardzinba won with 190,000 out of a total of 192,000 votes, the elections of 2004 became a contested drama between Russian-supported prime minister Raul Khajimba and Sergey Bagapsh from the opposition, whose wife is Georgian.[41] Finally, the Central Election Committee ruled that Bagapsh was the winner, which was contrary to Moscow's wish. Demonstrations and counter-demonstrations followed, and only hours before the planned inauguration of Bagapsh a compromise was announced, including a new election in January 2005 with Bagapsh as candidate for president and Khajimba for vice president. This model, which was motivated by the need for national cohesion in the troubled situation of the country, was accepted by 92 per cent of the voters. At the parliamentary elections of March 2007 the high-level compromise coalition split and there was a fierce struggle between Bagapsh loyalists and supporters of Khajimba. More than 100 candidates from twelve parties ran for the 35 seats. While the Bagapsh camp, supported by most minorities, not least the Armenians, came out clearly on top with 28 seats, observers claimed that the result by the 'pro-Russian' opposition were better than expected.[42]

Since 1995 there has been a government in exile for Abkhazia, installed by Georgia, which grew into an oversized bureaucracy, vulnerable to corruption. When Irakli Alasania became chairperson, he introduced reforms and cut down the staff to less than half its former size. The headquarters was moved from Tbilisi to the Kodori Gorge in order to be present on Abkhaz soil.

In the spring of 2008 tension rose once again in Abkhazia. In the middle of May Thomas de Waal revealed that 'the talk I heard in Tbilisi ten days ago was that some hotheads around the president are tempted to make a move on Abkhazia, perhaps as early as next week'.[43] The background was a couple of mysterious Russian rocket attacks in 2007, without victims, in remote parts of Georgia; a Russian threat to reinforce its peacekeeping forces by 500 soldiers; and paradoxically, a unilateral peace initiative by Saakashvili that backfired. Also, as a reaction against the Western-supported Kosovo declaration of independence on February 17 and the commitment by NATO at its Bucharest summit on April 2–4 that Georgia (and Ukraine) would eventually be admitted as members, Russia on March 6 formally withdrew from the Abkhazia sanctions. On April 16 Putin (who was still president) declared that Russia would strengthen its official links with Abkhazia and South Ossetia. On April 21 Saakashvili in a phone call asked Putin to rescind the official links with the breakaway regions, but 'Putin refused boorishly and the tone of the conversation was extremely hostile'.[44] Abkhazia downed several Georgian drones. Georgia denied any responsibility but a UN report confirmed, 'After the Mission's fact-finding team investigated the first downing of a UAV [unmanned aerial vehicle], on 18 March, UNOMIG informed the Georgian Ministry of Defence of its position that such flights constituted a violation of the ceasefire and separation-of-forces regime.'

The International Crisis Group observed that 'a number of powerful advisers and structures around President Mikheil Saakashvili appear increasingly convinced a military operation in Abkhazia is feasible and necessary.'[45]

Peace efforts

Even if there has been a strong Georgian tendency to blame Russia for all problems, there have also been occasional signs that a part of the public believes that Georgia should do more to facilitate an end to the conflict. In the beginning of 2005 a number of Georgian NGOs proposed that Abkhazia should be granted a very wide autonomy in order to achieve a peaceful solution. It was, among other things, suggested that the currency should be bilingual – Georgian/Abkhazian – and that the Abkhazians should be given double citizenship.[46] It should be noted that even a staunch supporter of the Saakashvili regime, Matthew Bryza, US deputy assistant secretary of state for European and Eurasian affairs, found it necessary to emphasise at a seminar on Russian–Georgian relations in April 2008, 'I hope our Georgian friends realize that the Abkhaz really want independence, they feel a certain threat.'[47]

In May 2009 the UN general secretary presented his report on Abkhazia, which could be interpreted as leaning towards the Russian/Abkhazian position by omitting the phrase 'de facto' when mentioning Abkhazian authorities, and 'Georgia' after Abkhazia when referring to the region.[48] Despite this, Russia vetoed a resolution to prolong the UN Mission in Georgia. Russia has also refused to accept the prolongation of the OSCE mission to South Ossetia. This has made the EU Monitoring Mission (EUMM) the only international monitoring group present in Georgia from the middle of 2009. The EUMM, however, has not been allowed to enter either Abkhazia or South Ossetia. In July 2009 the EU Council decided to prolong the EUMM for another year. Demands by Georgia to include observers from the United States and Turkey were rejected by the French minister of foreign affairs, Bernard Kouchner, who reckoned the arrival of American observers might be interpreted as 'a provocation'.[49]

Despite all the polemics and hostile rhetoric, it is as a matter of fact that talks between all parties in the secessionist conflicts, Russia, Georgia, Abkhazia and South Ossetia, are going on in Geneva, where the United States is also participating and the United Nations, OSCE and the European Union are involved.[50]

WAITING FOR A GEORGIAN DE GAULLE

One commentator concluded that all the major minority conflicts – South Ossetia, Abkhazia, and Javakheti – were explained by the oil and gas pipelines, because 'everybody knows that these conflicts are steered by Russia to prove to the West that the Western route is dangerous'.[51] Undoubtedly this is one aspect that cannot be discarded. At the same time the fact that Russia did not interfere with any of these transport routes during its brief invasion of parts of Georgia proper in August 2008 implies that any effort to reduce any or all of the minority conflicts in Georgia to one single cause is doomed to blur understanding and the possibility of finding solutions.

The accusation that freedom fighters do not sincerely want freedom but are only serving the dirty interests of somebody else has been directed at every freedom movement in human history. One of the most infamous examples is probably the refusal by French social-ists to accept that the Algerian liberation movement in the 1950s was not only an agent for the Egyptian president Gamal abd al-Nasir's pan-Arab ambitions, but an expression of a sincere and popular wish to achieve liberation from France. It cost one million lives and eight years of war until Charles de Gaulle, who understood the reality, could put an end to the suffering. The Americans saw the Vietnamese as agents of Mao's China, and many other liberation movements in the twentieth century were reduced by Western leaders to parts of a Communist effort to establish world power. So what about the East European, Baltic, Ukrainian and Georgian freedom movements in the 1980s – were they nothing but CIA-steered parts of Ronald Reagan's campaign to crush the 'evil empire', the USSR?

The sordid fact is of course that nothing is clean in politics. Just as probably every freedom movement has had a sincere intention, there is most likely no case where there have not been attempts by external forces to exploit such processes for quite other purposes. Abkhazia and South Ossetia are certainly no exceptions. Their situation has doubtless been exploited by outside forces; they have become victims of a political power play by Russia and other players in the Great Game. Only if such a multiple responsibility is acknowledged is there any possibility of finding compromise solutions acceptable to everybody.

In a progress report in April 2008, after Georgia's establishment of a state commission for defining the nature of autonomy in the separatist regions after their reunification with Georgia, the Euro-pean Union observed that 'these unilateral measures did however further fuel mistrust between the parties and have not yet produced substantial results for advancing the peace process'.[52] It is no exag-geration to assert that the inability of the rulers of independent Geor-gia to understand and handle the aspirations of the non-Georgian minorities has been fateful. So far they have acted too much like the French socialists in the 1950s. Georgia is still waiting for its Charles de Gaulle.

NOTES

1   *Caucasus Reporting Service*, no. 403, July 2007.
2   Mark Blijev, *Juzhnaya Ossetia v kolliziakh rossijsko–gruzinskikh otnosheniakh* (South Ossetia in the confrontation of Russian–Georgian relations), Evropa, Moscow, 2006.

3   Svante Cornell, *Autonomy and Conflict: Ethnoterritoriality and separatism in the South Caucasus – cases in Georgia*, Uppsala University, Uppsala, Sweden 2002.
4   Inga Kochieva and Alekesej Margiev, *Gruzia – etnicheskie chistki v otnoshenie osetin* (Georgia – ethnic cleansing against the Ossetians), Evropa, Moscow 2005, p. 11.
5   Silvia Serrano, *Géorgie – sortie d'empire* (Georgia – exit from the empire), CNRS Éditions, Paris, 2007.
6   Kochieva and Margiev, *Gruzia*, p. 31.
7   Serrano, *Géorgie*, p. 105.
8   Kochieva and Margiev, *Gruzia*, p. 38.
9   Serrano, *Géorgie*, p. 105.
10 Conversation with Gia Baramidze, vice premier of Georgia, 9 November, 2004.
11 Sandra Elisabeth Roelofs, *Die first lady of Georgië – het verhal van een idealiste* (The first lady of Georgia, the story of an idealist), Archipel, Amsterdam, 2005.
12 *Gruzia Online* <www.apsny.ge>, February 19, 2006.
13 Kochieva and Margiev, *Gruzia*.
14 *Caucasus Reporting Service*, no. 392, May 2007.
15 *Svobodnaya Gruzia*, October 3, 2007.
16 Mikhail Leontiev and Dmitrij Zhukov, *'Nezavisimaya' Gruzia – bandit v tigrovoj shkure* ('Independent' Georgia – a bandit in a tiger's hide), Yauza Press, Moscow, 2008, p. 274.
17 Cornell, *Autonomy*, p. 152.
18 Svetlana Chervonnaya, *Conflict in the Caucasus*, Gothic Image Publications, London, 1994.
19 Thomas Balivet, *Géopolitique de la Géorgie, souverainité et controle des territoires* (The geopolitics of Georgia, sovereignty and controle of territories), L'Harmattan, Paris, 2005.
20 According to Serrano, *Géorgie*, the remark was made on April 5, 1989.
21 Thomas Goltz, *Georgia Diary: A chronicle of war and political chaos in the post-Soviet Caucasus*, M. E. Sharpe, Armonk, N.Y., 2006, p. 62.
22 Ibid., p. 71, footnote 2.
23 International Crisis Group, 'Abkhazia today', Europe Report no. 176, September 15, 2006.
24 Chervonnaya, *Conflict,* p. 70.
25 Serrano, *Géorgie*, p. 106.
26 *Vechernaya Tbilisi*, September 29, 1993.
27 *Nezavisimaya Gazeta*, August 31, 1993.
28 *Izvestia*, August 31, 1993.
29 *Moskovskie Novosti*, September 5, 1993.
30 *Svobodnaya Gruzia*, October 1, 1993.
31 Bruno Coppetier, and Robert Legvold (eds), *Statehood and Security: Georgia after the Rose Revolution*, MIT Press, Cambridge, Mass., 2005.

32 Serrano, *Géorgie*, p. 119.
33 Chervonnaya, *Conflict*, p. 56.
34 Lorik Marshania, *Pravda o tragedii Abkhazii* (The truth about the Abkhazian tragedy), Samshoblo, Tbilisi, 1998.
35 Coppetier, *Statehood*, p. 208.
36 Antonenko, p. 231 in Coppetier, *Statehood*.
37 Evgenij Primakov, *Gody v bolshoi politiki* (The years in big politics), Molodaya Gvardiya, Moscow, 1999.
38 Goltz, *Georgia Diary*.
39 Ibid., p. 221.
40 *Georgian Times*, March 6,. 2000.
41 Just as in South Ossetia, the Georgian population usually has not participated in Abkhazian elections, one obvious reason being that most of the Georgians were evicted from Abkhazia in 1993. Some of the Georgian returnees to the Gali district have managed to participate in Georgian elections, by travelling to nearby towns in Georgia proper, such as Zugdidi.
42 Johanna Popjanevski, 'Parliamentary elections in Abkhazia: opposition on the rise?', *CACI Analyst*, February 5, 2007.
43 United Nations, *Report of the Secretary-General on the situation in Abkhazia, Georgia*, S/2008/480, Security Council, July 23, 2008.
44 International Crisis Group, 'Georgia and Russia: clashing over Abkhazia', Europe Report no. 193, June 5, 2008.
45 Ibid,
46 *Georgian Times*, January 5, 2005,
47 CACI Forum, Central Asia-Caucasus Institute, *Recent Russian Policies in Georgia: How should the West respond?*' Johns Hopkins University, Md., April 22, 2008.
48 United Nations, *Report of the Secretary-General pursuant to Security Council resolutions 1808 (2008), 1839 (2008) and 1866 (2009)*.
49 *Le Monde Hebdomadaire*, August 1, 2009.
50 Civil Georgia, *Fifth Round of Talks End in Geneva*, May 19, 2009.
51 Gaïdz Minassian, *Caucase du Sud, la nouvelle guerrre froide* (South Caucasus, the new cold war), Éditions Autrement, Paris, 2007, p. 1.
52 European Union, 'Implementation of the European Neighbourhood Policy in 2007', *Progress Report Georgia*, Brussels, April 3, 2008, SEC(2008) 393.

6

GAMSAKHURDIA, THE TACTICAL FANATIC

When I visited Tbilisi in 1993 I could not read the signs in the subway because all Latin and Cyrillic letters had been cleaned away. Only the Georgian script remained. This was but one indication that I had come to a country where strong nationalistic policies had recently been implemented. At the end of 1993 Georgia still suffered a lot from the brief but turbulent rule of Zviad Gamsakhurdia, a philologist and writer who was elected president of the newly declared independent republic on May 26, 1991, and after some weeks of civil war was toppled through a coup d'état on January 6, 1992. However, Zviad Gamsakhurdia's career as a fiercely anti-Russian Georgian nationalist started much earlier.

Born in Tbilisi in 1939 as a son of a venerated Georgian author, Constantine Gamsakhurdia, Zviad even as a teenager founded a protest group, the Gorgasliani, referring to the founder of Tbilisi. The Gorgasliani, of which Merab Kostava was also a leading member, tried to exploit the massive popular demonstrations in Georgia in March 1956, which opposed the de-Stalinization policy of Khrushchev. In 1957 some of them were arrested. A few years later Gamsakhurdia was confined to a mental hospital, which is often used by his critics as a proof of his insanity, but confinement to a mental asylum was an infamous method during the Soviet regime to cope with perfectly sane dissidents. In the 1970s Gamsakhurdia founded several human rights groups, the most well-known of which was the Helsinki Group, after the European Security Conference in Helsinki in 1975, where even the Soviet Union committed itself to some basic principles of human rights. He contributed articles to Georgian and Russian *samizdat* publications (underground 'self-publications'). At the same time he pursued a career as scholar and author.

However, in 1977 the Brezhnev regime in Moscow got fed up with dissidents. During the crackdown Gamsakhurdia and his fellow activist Kostava were arrested, sentenced to six years hard labour and exile, and sent away from Georgia. This happened when Edward Shevardnadze was first secretary of the Georgian Communist Party. In 1979 Gamsakhurdia suddenly reappeared as a free man, while Kostava remained in custody until 1987. The reason became evident when Gamsakhurdia made a public and televised declaration of repentance, with formulations which recalled the 'confessions' of Stalin's victims during the great purges of the 1930s. Later he maintained, with support from Kostava, that his recantation had been a tactical move to guarantee the survival of the nationalist movement in Georgia. It is a fact that soon after his release he restarted his activities as a dissident, and had another brief period in jail after a demonstration in 1981.

A typical example of events that could trigger vehement Georgian opposition and accusations that Moscow was trying to destroy the Georgian national identity was a proposal in 1978 to make Russian an official language in Georgia alongside Georgian. This was interpreted as a move in favour of 'Russification'. Russian commentators deny this, and call to memory that Georgia was the only republic of the Soviet Union where Russian, the uncontested lingua franca of the union, was not an official language together with that of the titular nation of the republic. However, the protests became so strong that Shevardnadze backed down and withdrew the proposal, a move that a Russian critic interprets as a revelation of his 'chauvinistic attitude'.[1]

APRIL 9, 1989

A pivotal date in modern Georgian liberation history is April 9, 1989. It was then that Soviet Special Forces violently dispersed a peaceful demonstration in central Tbilisi, an action which cost the lives of at least 19 Georgian protesters. Two years later this date was chosen for the declaration of independence, and in 2009 the growing opposition against the rule of Mikheil Saakashvili chose the same date for one of its major protest demonstrations. It is undeniable that the Soviet forces acted with an old-fashioned brutality that most people, in the Soviet Union as well as outside, believed had been thrown into the dustbin of history by Gorbachev's *perestroika* regime. Not all the victims were killed by spades, which is the dominant picture given by Georgians but denied by Soviet authorities. Some succumbed to asphyxiation during the chaos and stampede among the demonstrators that followed the assault by the troops. Nevertheless, the responsibility was without any doubt attributed to the Soviet Special Forces and the political leaders of Soviet Georgia, not only by international and liberal Soviet media and the Georgian opposition, but also by the investigation carried out by a committee from the Soviet Peoples' Congress under the leadership of the liberal mayor of Leningrad, Anatoly Sobchak.

However, it is rarely recalled why a demonstration took place at all. Of course, nationalistic and anti-Soviet public activities in Georgia had steadily increased in number and scope for a long time. But the demonstration that started on April 4 and was crushed on April 9 was somewhat special. Its main scapegoat was neither Moscow nor its stooges in Tbilisi. The direct arousing factor was the Assembly of Lychny on March 18, 1989, where thousands of Abkhazians demanded the restoration of Abkhazia's status as a union republic. Such a demand could of course be interpreted as a wish to secede from Georgia. Undoubtedly the people who were meeting in Lychny did not want to be part of an independent Georgia. But although the demands for independence by Georgian nationalists were known in March 1989, there was still more than half a year to go before the Berlin Wall came down, and more than two and a half years before the Soviet Union ceased to exist. If the Lychny demands are seen in the framework of a continued Soviet Union, they are not very dramatic. As one commentator observes, to demand a change of status 'contained nothing unconstitutional and was not exceptional during the latter years of *perestroika* when all AOs and ASSRs strove to have their status raised'.[2]

The tragedy of April 9 gave a push to the Georgian national movement, which grew, but also split. One faction decided to boycott the first multi-party Soviet elections of 1990 and organized their own election to a kind of national assembly. But despite his reputation as a fanatic, Gamsakhurdia was obviously a shrewd tactician, and understood that the Soviet election could be exploited to give him a legal platform. So his Round Table contested the election for the Supreme Soviet of October 30, 1990, and won a clear victory, gaining 64 per cent of the votes, compared with 27 per cent for the Communist Party. On November 14 Gamsakhurdia was elected chairman of the Supreme Soviet, almost equivalent to president. Events unfolded rapidly. In a referendum on March 31, 1991, an overwhelming majority of Georgians said yes to independence. The declaration of independence was made on April 9, but most foreign states awaited the dissolution of the Soviet Union before they recognized the new independent state. On May 26, 1991, 87 per cent of the voters made Gamsakhurdia president of the republic of Georgia, which was ethnically more Georgian than ever, virtually without control over the three autonomous regions, Abkhazia, South Ossetia and Adjara, and with only nine minority representatives out of 245 in the new parliament. Gamsakhurdia's campaign slogan 'Georgia for the Georgians' was coming true.

GOOD LIBERATOR, POOR ADMINISTRATOR

If Gamsakhurdia was an attractive and even efficient leader and symbol of a national liberation movement, he was a catastrophe as executive administrator and president. That he was an expert in criticizing the democratic flaws of others did not make him into an expert in implementing democracy. Even on December 27, 1991 Helsinki Watch could present a report including devastating criticism of the regime's abuses. By then the civil war to topple Gamsakhurdia had already started. His prime minister, Tengiz Sigua, resigned in August and joined the opposition. One reason was the ambiguous reaction of Gamsakhurdia towards the failed reactionary coup d'état in Moscow. He first tried to exploit the situation to convince the world to recognize the independence of Georgia, but then he accused Gorbachev of having staged the coup himself in order to gain sympathy. The most controversial element was, however, Gamsakhurdia's decision to obey a call from the 'State Committee for the State of Emergency', the ruling body of the putschists, to dissolve all military units outside the regular Soviet army. On August 23 he decided to place the National Guard under the Interior Ministry.

The National Guard, comprising some 12,000 soldiers, had been formed in November 1990 in order to be the core of a Georgian army. Its commander, Tengiz Kitovani, was an old friend of Gamsakhurdia until the decree on reorganization of the National Guard, which he interpreted as equivalent to its dissolution. Consequently Kitovani moved his troops out of reach. The National Guard was joined by the Mkhedrioni (knights), which was a nationalist militia, a 'loose union of criminal groups and juvenile gangs', according to one observer, founded in 1989 by Jaba Ioseliani, a professor of art and a former patron of the Soviet underworld.[3] They controlled the gasoline and tobacco trades. The Mkhedrioni hated Gamsakhurdia for his apology in the 1970s and was consequently banned.

Gamsakhurdia closed newspapers and television-stations, arrested some members of the opposition and proposed that 60 Communist deputies should be relieved of their seats. Fights broke out in the streets of Tbilisi, which on December 22, 1991 escalated into a virtual coup d'état. After a couple of weeks of heavy fighting, costing more than 100 lives, Gamsakhurdia and his collaborators fled Tbilisi, first to Azerbaijan, then through Armenia to Chechnya. Despite the fact that most of North Caucasus had sided with Abkhazia from the start of the conflict in the late 1980s, the charismatic leader of Chechnya, Dzhokhar Dudayev, broke ranks and granted Gamsakhurdia asylum in Grozny after his fall from power in Tbilisi.

During 1992 and 1993 clashes and bloody encounters between Gamsakhurdia's supporters and government forces flared up repeatedly, but not until the Abkhazian War in September 1993 seemed to turn against Georgia did the deposed president leave his refuge in Chechnya and come back to Georgia, via Mingrelia, his native province in the far west, bordering on Abkhazia. Here, in an undeclared and unholy alliance with the Abkhaz, he had some military success for a while. But not only was the Shevardnadze regime in Tbilisi his staunch enemy, the neighbouring countries, Armenia, Azerbaijan and Russia, feared that the military activities along the Black Sea coast would cut off their important links of communication. In a covert deal Russian forces gave Gamsakhurdia the final blow in exchange for Georgia's belated entry into the CIS.

This probably was too much for the psychological status of Gamsakhurdia. With all hopes of a return to power thwarted, according to most accounts, including that of his wife, he committed suicide on December 31, 1993. In 1994 Zelimkhan Yandarbiyev, who later took over as president in Chechnya when Dudayev was killed in April 1996 by a Russian laser-guided missile while using his satellite phone, went to Tbilisi to bring the ashes of Gamsakhurdia to a final rest in Grozny.

Since then the influence of Gamsakhurdia's politics has been declining in Georgia. However, he was officially rehabilitated in January 2004 by the newly elected president, Saakashvili. And in the spring of 2007 his remains were retrieved from under the rubble of Grozny and sent to Tbilisi for final burial.[4]

DARK LEGACY

Despite the obvious political failure of Gamsakhurdia as president of Georgia, he has left a dark legacy. He did not by himself create the type of Georgian nationalism that has made coexistence with the minorities so complicated. As one writer has observed, 'the large majority of Georgians shared the vision of Zviad Gamsakhurdia of an ethnic nationalism'.[5] But he was the leader who exploited such sentiments more than others, which also shaped a wave that brought him to power. At the same time, as has been exemplified by his recantation in the 1970s and his decision to contest the Soviet elections of 1990, rather than follow the nationalist dogma and abstain from participation, he sometimes showed a political shrewdness that is not usually associated with political fanaticism.

One more example is the mysterious election law for Abkhazia, which he supported in the summer of 1991. It was based on ethnicity, which might of course be seen as an element close to Gamsakhurdia's ideology. But it gave the Abkhazian minority, only 18 percent of the population, such an over-representation that it provoked strong protests. Critics, including Shevardnadze, have called it an 'apartheid' law, which paved the way for anti-Georgian legislation in Abkhazia. The system guaranteed the Abkhazians 28 seats in the regional parliament, which is equivalent to 43 per cent of the seats. The Georgians would get 26 seats (40 per cent), while making up 46 per cent of the population, and others (Russians, Armenians, Greeks and so on) were to get 11 seats (17 per cent), although they constituted some 36 per cent of the population. Even if the under-representation of the Georgians would have been considerably less than that of other non-Abkhazians, many observers have failed to understand how such a construction could be promoted by the major proponent of 'Georgia to the Georgians'. Was it a proof that the 'fanatic' was after all prepared to make a peace-friendly 'serious attempt at reaching a compromise' with the Abkhazians, as one commentator maintains?[6] Or was it just another of the Georgian paradoxes, a whim by an erratic and desperate psychopath?

Based on facts as these, it might be argued that Gamsakhurdia's nationalism was not different from nationalist trends in other parts of the former Soviet Union and even in Europe. That a political leader draws on nationalist sentiments to mobilize the people in times of social and economic stress is nothing unique. The American writer Stephen Jones has made an effort to defend and minimize the scope of Georgian nationalism in general, and that of Gamsakhurdia specifically. He claims that 'one cannot understand the Gamsakhurdia phenomena without going outside the national framework,' and states that 'Gamsakhurdia was an authoritarian populist who scapegoated not only the national minorities but

Georgian groups too, such as the "red intelligentsia" and university students'. All in all, Jones claims, Gamsakhurdia was an 'illiberal radical populist'.[7] It may be so, but at the same time it is undeniable that the attitude Gamsakhurdia publicly displayed against anybody who was not ethnically Georgian, spoke Georgian and was a true believer of the Georgian Orthodox Church, has nothing in common with the standards and principles of the United Nations, the Council of Europe and the European Union. If Russian accusations that Gamsakhurdia 'incited the masses to pogroms' in 1989 may be exaggerated, there is no doubt that his 'messianism, megalomania, paranoia and intolerance' served to alarm the minorities, and made it seem very logical for Abkhazians and Ossetians to seek protection from the Big Brother in the North.[8] It is noteworthy that he referred to minorities as 'guests'.[9] Maybe the writer who suggested that Gamsakhurdia was a 'modern Macbeth' hit the nail on the head.[10]

After the flight of Gamsakhurdia, power was taken over by a triumvirate consisting of the former premier, Tengiz Sigua, and the leaders of the two militias who had carried out the coup d'état, Ioseliani and Kitovani. This was not a sustainable regime, which the triumvirate understood. In this situation Edward Shevardnadze was brought back to Georgia from Moscow, where he had just lost his job as minister of foreign affairs because the state in which he had held this function had ceased to exist.

NOTES

1   Mikhail Leontiev and Dmitrij Zhukov, *'Nezavisimaya' Gruzia – bandit v tigrovoj shkure* ('Independent' Georgia – a bandit in a tiger's hide), Yauza Press, Moscow, 2008.
2   Christoph Zürcher, 'Georgia's time of troubles 1989-93', in Bruno Coppetier and Robert Legvold (eds), *Statehood and Security: Georgia after the Rose Revolution*, MIT Press, Cambridge, Mass., 2005.
3   Ibid.
4   Zaza Tsuladze in Tbilisi and Umalt Dudayev in Grozny, 'Special report: burial mystery of Georgian leader', Caucasus Reporting Service, 070125.
5   Silvia Serrano, *Géorgie – sortie d'empire* (Georgia – exit from the empire), CNRS Éditions, Paris, 2007.
6   Ibid.
7   Stephen Jones, 'Georgia – nationalism from under the rubble', in L. B. Barrington, *After Independence: Making and protecting the nation in postcolonial and postcommunist states*, University of Michigan Press, Ann Arbor, 2006.

8   Ronald Grigor Suny, *The making of the Georgian Nation*, 2nd edn, Indiana University Press, Bloomington, 1994, p. 326.
9   Ghia Nodia, 'Georgia - dimensions of insecurity', in Coppetier and Legvold, *Statehood*.
10 Suny, *The Making*, p. 327.

7

SHEVARDNADZE, THE
FAILED SAVIOUR

When I visited Georgia for the first time in my life, Edward Shevardnadze had been head of state for 18 months. I came directly from
Moscow, where post-Soviet Russia was close to civil war (see Chapter
4). However, in Georgia the situation was much worse, politically,
economically and socially. And Georgia was not merely 'close to'
civil war: there were in fact two different, but intertwined, civil wars
going on at full strength. Shevardnadze had been brought home from
Moscow in March 1992 in order to save the country from its mess. In
September 1993 I could see no signs that he was going to succeed.

CONTRADICTING MOODS

On one of my first days in Georgia I met with a friend whom I had
come to know at a Green conference in Stockholm a couple of years
earlier, Nato Kirvalidze, who was later to become the first general
director of the Regional Environmental Centre for Caucasus. She
gathered some of her friends to give me a touch of the mood in
Georgia. Most of them were critical of the effort by Shevardnadze to
regain Abkhazia and defeat Gamsakhurdia by military means.

The economic situation was a disaster. One illustration was
the cost of public transport. While a ride on a trolleybus cost five
coupons, a trip on a minibus cost 1,000 coupons. According to my
notes one coupon was equivalent to a hundredth of a eurocent, so
1,000 coupons roughly equalled 10 eurocents, and 18,000 coupons,
a common monthly salary, was equivalent to a little less than €2.
When working on this book I had difficulty in believing my own
notes, and suspected that I had mixed the figures up: that 1,000
coupons should be worth €10, and consequently a common salary
was €180 a month. I asked Nato, and she was adamant:

The monthly salary could not have been €180. That would have been a luxury. That was a crazy time. I remember once that my mother, who was a senior lecturer at the language university, went to get her salary on a day when she had no lectures. She came back very upset, and told me that she had allowed herself to take the minibus and had had to pay almost her whole salary for the ride! So, I am sure you noted down correctly.

This bleak minipicture of the socioeconomic situation in Georgia at the beginning of independence has been confirmed by professional economists. From 1991 to 1994 there was a triple decline in production, and inflation reached 50–60 per cent – a month! The interim currency, the coupons, lost value rapidly until almost nothing could be bought. According to Vladimer Papava, who was minister of the economy in the 1990s, the first years of Shevardnadze were characterized by 'disregarding economics', for lack of experience and skill or because of the chaotic situation.[1]

Another friend I met with several times during these weeks in September–October 1993 was Zurab Zhvania, founder of the Green Party in the late 1980s, but since 1992 a close collaborator of Shevardnadze. In Moscow I had read an interview with him in which he warned that a clan society was being created. He also emphasized that the Greens had protested on December 22, 1991 against the revolutionary way of changing power (the coup against Gamsakhurdia).[2] Nevertheless, now he confirmed that the supposedly pacifist Greens did not see any other way than violence to reconquer Sukhumi, which the Georgian troops had lost only a few days before my arrival. Zurab was very upset and talked about 'a world war because of Abkhazia'.

So how were the reconquest of Sukhumi and the final crushing of the Zviadists being prepared? On one of the first days of October Zurab brought me to the parliament building, to what was supposed to be the headquarters of the government military forces. In one room three men were gathered around some maps. It was said that the Zviadists had taken a little village north of Kutaisi. Probably they were planning to surround the city, one man assumed. A quarrel erupted. An elderly man in civilian clothes shouted to a general of the internal troops – in Russian. Obviously the furious man was a former officer of the Red Army. He was not satisfied with the level of mobilization. The general replied, 'To play chess one needs chessmen!' Another man, a former officer, yelled, 'Shevardnadze is the greatest enemy of the Georgian people! What do you think would

happen if the Zviadists arrive here?' Zurab rapidly replied, 'In any
case I will not survive.'

We continued and looked into several rooms, finding similar
scenes. Men were smoking, discussing, quarrelling, talking on the
telephone, but no purposeful activity could be discovered. And this
was supposed to be the centre of planning for struggle against at
least two enemies!

After this we went to Kutaisi, in the middle of the war zone. Zurab
told me that he had managed to get a parliamentary session cancelled
because the Nationalists intended to make a statement saying that
Abkhazia had been occupied by Russia. He was against such empty
rhetoric. 'Georgia cannot declare war against Russia. The Nationalists have no realism, just slogans, they don't understand that there is
a shortage of bread, oil, arms, everything.'

Outside the town hall in Kutaisi people were gathered to wait
for information about the refugees. It had been announced by the
UN High Commissioner for Refugees (UNHCR) that six Russian
(!) helicopters would start to bring Georgian refugees down from
the snowy mountain roads. A curfew was declared. It was reported
that the Zviadists were only 40 kilometres away. A bunch of men
with Kalashnikovs were lingering outside the town hall, but without
military order, rather more like people waiting for the bus. It was
obvious that their motivation to fight was low. These people did
not like Gamsakhurdia, but they also did not like civil war, and they
were not prepared to sacrifice their lives for Shevardnadze.

Zurab got more and more desperate: 'This is typically Georgian:
talk, talk, but no action!' He had been very proud at being Georgian
when we were still in Tbilisi, but now everything was crumbling.
Zurab scorned a woman outside the town hall: 'You supported
Gamsakhurdia!' She laughed, embarrassed. But she was not ready
to die to stop Gamsakhurdia. Zurab admitted that the motivation of
the Zviadists was much higher, they were fanatics, and they believed
that everything bad said about Gamsakhurdia was a lie, just as was
everything good said about Shevardnadze. They were convinced that
the television pictures from Shevardnadze's visit to Sukhumi were
faked.

In the evening I was told to sleep with my clothes and shoes on,
ready to leave in an instant. But in the morning there was general
relief. During the night government troops had retaken a strategic
village called Khori. The mood rose. General Kitovani appeared thoroughly rested, relaxed and neatly shaved. 'Now we will liberate all

Georgia from Gamsakhurdia, we don't need any Russian help!' But Zurab warned, 'We must have reasonable relations with Russia.'

In the evening we had dinner with Governor Shashiashvili, General Kitovani, who had been appointed commander-in-chief the same day, and some members of parliament. One represented the National Democratic Party (NDP). Kitovani's comment was, 'The NDP is Shevardnadze's Komsomol.' Kitovani was the guy who had set in motion the catastrophic process that had resulted in the Georgian defeat in Abkhazia. He did not try to conceal his utter contempt for Shevardnadze. And now he was commander-in-chief of the armed ragamuffins who were supposed to play the part of a Georgian state army, with the task of defending the rule of – Shevardnadze. It could have been an amusing Shakespearian play, except that those who were shot dead did not get up and laugh the next second, but remained very dead. It was deadly serious, cruel and devastating. But what I saw in Kutaisi gave the impression that the whole thing was a play. Maybe it was, to some of the participants. In Georgia you never know.

Back in Tbilisi we were met by a state of emergency. Worse, we could also read in the newspaper of the Russian Transcaucasian army, which still had its headquarters in Georgia, that Aslan Abashidze was being mentioned as a possible successor to Shevardnadze.[3] In that perspective the 'old fox' appeared as almost a saint, and lots of Georgians immediately turned into enthusiastic Shevardnadze fans. Whatever faults the former Soviet minister of foreign affairs might have, he was not a psychopathic lunatic and petty dictator, like Abashidze (see Chapter 10).

On October 5 Shevardnadze spoke on Radio Svoboda. He blamed the Russian support for Abkhazia totally on the Supreme Soviet, and relieved Yeltsin of guilt. He also announced that he was forming a new political party, which was to become the Citizens' Union of Georgia (CUG).

One of these tense days Nato's mother and her female friend were arrested and put in a cell with eleven other women. They were accused of being supporters of Gamsakhurdia, and asked to put down in writing whom they intended to vote for in a future presidential election. Zurab intervened to get them released, but he refused to take it seriously. He laughed at my uneasiness, and claimed that Georgia was a 'mad country', which could not become a police state. Seven years later he was less sure, and broke with Shevardnadze.

SHEVARDNADZE'S COMEBACK

Was Edward Shevardnadze a democrat when he restarted his carrier in Georgia in 1992? His reputation in the West was extremely good. He was known, together with Gorbachev, as a major architect of *perestroika* and *glasnost*, and responsible for the peaceful Soviet retreat from Eastern Europe from 1989 onwards. On December 20, 1990 he resigned, warning that 'a dictatorship is looming'. In his memoirs Shevardnadze quotes Gorbachev as agreeing with him, and declaring in early 1991 in Minsk, 'The danger of a dictatorship is real.' Shevardnadze rhetorically asks, 'So he said, but what did he do? He went to Crimea for a holiday.'[4]

During the failed coup in Moscow in August 1991 Shevardnadze supported Yeltsin. He is very critical of Gorbachev: 'Had he launched the idea of a confederation only three months earlier even the Baltic republics would have been satisfied.' But Gorbachev did not, and the secessionist activities all around the Soviet Union became stronger and provoked reactionary circles to strike back. Shevardnadze is adamant: 'I was and am of the opinion that Gorbachev and nobody else has the political and moral responsibility for the coup.'

So why did Shevardnadze return to the position of minister of foreign affairs on November 20, 1991? Did he really believe that the Soviet Union could still be saved? Did he want to save it? At the end of 1991 industrial production was down 40 per cent and agrarian production 25 per cent, as a result of the loss of economic links between the republics. The Baltic states and Georgia had already declared themselves independent. Even the Autonomous SSR of Tatarstan had proclaimed itself an independent state. And some days after Shevardnadze's return to office in Moscow 90 per cent of the voters in Ukraine said yes to independence. The Soviet 'saga' was at its end, and did not survive New Year's Eve 1991. On March 7, 1992, Shevardnadze was back at the top in Georgia, from where he had been brought to Moscow by Gorbachev in July 1985. There was of course a difference. Then Georgia had been a province of a superpower, relatively well off and peaceful. Now the country was a sovereign state – but neither well off nor peaceful.

Shevardnadze had considerable influence on Georgian affairs even before his final move from Moscow to Tbilisi. One example is the tragic events of April 9, 1989. According to Yegor Ligachev, who was number two in the Soviet Union from 1985 to 1990, Shevardnadze could have prevented the tragedy. He had already been ordered by Gorbachev to go to Tbilisi and try to sort things out peacefully when the demonstrations started, but claimed that the first secretary of the Georgian Communist Party, Dzhumber Patiashvili, was in control. When the massacre of April 9 proved that this was not the case, Shevardnadze rapidly went to Tbilisi and, together with the Nobel Peace Prize winner Andrei Sakharov, confirmed that not only spades, but also poisonous gas had been used by the security forces. By doing this Shevardnadze sealed his reputation among the Soviet military, especially the responsible commander during the Tbilisi events, General Igor Rodionov, who some years later would be promoted to minister of defence by Yeltsin. At the same time Shevardnadze was accused by left-wingers of not having intervened in time to stop the slaughter.[5]

Another example of his meddling in Georgian affairs before his return as its leader, mentioned in his memoirs, is the telephone talks he had with Zviad Gamsakhurdia about South Ossetia in the spring of 1991. Shevardnadze declares that he was against the annulment of South Ossetia's autonomy, and considered it to be a 'criminal decision' (by Gamsakhurdia) to start a war in the region.

So why did he return to Georgia? He received several petitions asking him to return, and maintains, 'My decision was correct, because my return saved the country from dissolution, hunger and other catastrophes.' He was received at Tbilisi airport by the militia commanders Tengiz Kitovani and Jaba Ioseliani. Then he went to Sioni Cathedral and was blessed by the Patriarch. He even boasts that he was baptized when he moved to the strongly religious Georgia. On March 10, 1992, the military committee resigned and Shevardnadze was elected head of state by the parliament. 'I could have become dictator, but refused,' he writes. When he took over there were war in Abkhazia, a conflict with South Ossetia, terror actions on streets and railways, kidnappings, bombs set on electricity supply lines and so on. What followed was '100 days of loneliness', but also success. Shevardnadze claims that he tried to establish good neighbourly relations with Russia. Foreign minister Kozyrev made a visit, 'but we had to restore our natural relations with the West, the European Union and the USA'. This ambition, to link Georgia to the West, gained rapid results. On March 23, 1992, the European Union recognized Georgia; on April 12 the German minister of foreign affairs, Hans Dietrich Genscher, made a visit; and on April 23 the United States opened an embassy in Tbilisi. And on May 25, James Baker – 'the American friend' – arrived. Eight years later James Baker would call Shevardnadze 'a hero' of peace.[6]

Several commentators emphasize that Shevardnadze was a man of 'great personal courage'[7] and that he 'took calculated risks throughout his career'.[8] Maybe this is substantiated by the fact that as head of state or president of Georgia he was the victim of three organized assassination attempts:

- October 3, 1992, in Abkhazia. Shevardnadze blamed 'Russian nationalists' who accused him of having destroyed the Soviet Union, and pointed directly at the Russian military and the Duma, which was then still led by Khasbulatov and Rutskoj, in opposition to Yeltsin.
- August 29, 1995, before signing the new constitution. The main culprit was the militia leader, Jaba Ioseliani, who was angry at having lost power. Security minister Igor Giorgadze was also involved and secretly extradited to Russia, from where, according to Georgian sources, he was later involved in several terror attempts against his native country.
- February 9, 1998, before the final seal on the decision to build the BTC pipeline. For this Shevardnadze blamed Russian military groups in Chechnya. Yeltsin called Shevardnadze and congratulated him on his survival, said that he did not want to discuss further whether and how Russia was involved, and suggested that the attack was part of international terrorism against modern civilization.[9]

SHEVARDNADZE'S FIRST 'REALISTIC' PHASE

The first years of Shevardnadze's rule were characterized by the civil wars, the conflicts with the secessionist regions and efforts to reinstall some state authority. Even before he formally took over, on March 9, 1992 he was met by a revolt in Zugdidi, a western town in the region where sympathies for the deposed president Gamsakhurdia were strong. In April Russian special units left South Ossetia, which was in principle good for Georgia, but in reality opened the way for rebels to act more freely. In May separatist activity increased in Abkhazia. Thus there were three separatist regions in all, Shevardnadze observes: South Ossetia (which in the Georgian style he calls Shida Kartli), Abkhazia and Mingrelia (the Zviadists).

On May 13 Rustaveli Avenue was blocked by refugees from the conflict areas. The ceasefire in South Ossetia was broken, and Shevardnadze admits that the shots came from the Georgian side.

Russia cut off gas deliveries, and vice president Rutskoj threatened to bomb Tbilisi. Georgia's application for membership of the United Nations was delayed by Russia. On June 24 Zviadists attempted a coup with the unholy support of Abkhazians when Shevardnadze was on his way to meet with President Yeltsin in Sochi. The Russian media claimed that the coup was staged by Shevardnadze himself in order to enforce national unity in Tbilisi, justify repressions against Zviadists and demonstrate threats against the Georgian democracy in the wake of the Georgian–Russian summit. Shevardnadze is convinced that he was up against an unholy alliance of Abkhazian separatists, South Ossetian rebels, Zviadists and 'reactionary Russian circles'. At the Sochi summit it was agreed that Russia and Georgia would recognize each other's sovereignty, and that Russia would support Georgia's application for membership of the United Nations. Russian troops should be withdrawn from South Ossetia. In reality, however, they were replaced by rebels with arms from Russia.

Shevardnadze was elected speaker of parliament on October 11, 1992, with an overwhelming majority. In March 1993 the Liberals, National Democrats and Greens formed a coalition to support him, and Kitovani was dismissed from his position as minister of defence. In 1995 a new constitution was adopted, and Shevardnadze was elected president of the republic on November 5 with 74 per cent of the votes. Both militia leaders, Kitovani and Ioseliani, were arrested. Formally Georgia was now a democracy, but a German analyst asserts that 'corrupted clan structures' were the real rulers.[10]

During this first 'realistic' phase of Shevardnadze's rule, decent working relations with Russia made possible international recognition of Georgia's independence, membership of the United Nations, a peace agreement about South Ossetia, and Russian support to defeat Gamsakhurdia. Despite Georgian accusations against Russia for the loss of Abkhazia, a treaty of cooperation and friendship with Russia was agreed in 1994. Georgia even asked to be incorporated into the rouble zone because of its exorbitant inflation, but Russia declined. The guarding of the border with Turkey was maintained in cooperation with Russia, until 1999. Shevardnadze's political power base was his newly created CUG, a 'catch-all' party formed on the initiative of, among others, a group of people who in the late 1980s had established the successful Green Party. The leader of this group was Zurab Zhvania, speaker of the parliament from 1996 to 2001, who also 'established himself as Shevardnadze's possible successor'.[11]

The social and economic breakdown of Georgian society was a

major issue in the Shevardnadze years. Emigration is estimated to
have reached more than one million from 1990 to 1997: that is,
around 134,000 people left the country every year. There was an
almost total collapse of infrastructure and unbridled corruption. The
International Monetary Fund (IMF) had a very disruptive impact,
one example of which was the requirement that Georgia should
liberalize all trade with metals as if it was a normal country. Under
Georgian circumstances the result was that every piece of metal that
could be found was stolen and sold. Electric wires were cut down
or dug up so that the copper could be marketed; functioning railway cars were sold as scrap metal to Turkey, and so on. As late as
2001–02 a common monthly salary was 30–100 lari (US$14–54),
while the minimum requirement for a four-person family was estimated at some 200 lari a month.[12] One writer has concluded that
Shevardnadze's problem was that he saved the state by tolerating 'a
deeply corrupt system'.[13]

2000: CRACKS IN THE WALL

According to the OSCE the parliamentary elections of October
31, 1999, were 'steps towards Georgia's compliance with OSCE
commitments although the election process failed to fully meet all
commitments'. The EU delegation in Tbilisi concluded: 'The Parliamentary Elections, though defective in some respects, were gener-
ally considered to be consistent with democratic norms except for
in Ajara.'[14] The Georgian opposition did not agree. Some 20 political parties characterized the elections as a 'complete falsification',
partly blamed the 'antidemocratic' election law, and with a view to
the upcoming presidential elections in 2000, demanded changes in
the election procedure and a new census to establish correct lists of
voters.

During two visits to Georgia in February and early May 2000
in my capacity as rapporteur to the European Parliament on South
Caucasus, I met with most of the VIPs in the country, including
the president and the leaders of the opposition. I must confess that
the attitude of most opposition representatives struck me as utterly
uncompromising, counter-productive and exaggerated.

I had severe difficulties in taking him seriously when Dzhumber Patiashvili, who had been deposed from his post as leader of
the Communist Party of Georgia after the April 9, 1989, massacre, shouted that the government excelled in 'disinformation',

and Vakhtang Bokhorishvili, president of a party that was loyal to Gamsakhurdia, characterized Shevardnadze as 'a Hitler'. More serious was the observation by Elene Tevdoradze, 'Georgia's grandmother' and a well-known human rights activist, that the position of ethnic minorities was deteriorating. And the leader of Labour, Shalva Natelashvili, hit a sensitive point when he asserted that Georgia was becoming a 'post-communist monarchy, just like Azerbaijan', with relatives of the president heavily over-represented in high positions in the state as well as in the private sector. However, when he claimed that 50 per cent would vote in favour of the restoration of the Soviet Union if asked, he probably fell victim to wishful thinking – although he emphasized that Georgian socialists were not pro-Russian.

Representatives of several NGOs – the Liberty Institute, the Caucasian Institute and Human Rights Watch – stated that the situation was not worse than earlier, which meant 'not very fair', but, they asserted, 'the opposition is worse'. However, they agreed that the Shevardnadze clan was spreading its tentacles into most spheres of society. Both opposition and NGO representatives made a slight distinction between the Shevardnadze clan and the 'crown prince', Zurab Zhvania. However, they underlined that he was a part of the ruling elite and as such responsible for its abuses.

Vakhtang Rchevashvili from the Socialist Party admitted that his party had the same European aspirations as the government, 'but the government has the same view of Russia as the USA has and we need more cooperation with Russia'. Nino Burjanadze, chair of the Foreign Policy Committee, and later one of the three leaders of the Rose Revolution, hoped for entry into the European Union in three or four years, and the chairperson of a subcommittee for harmonization with EU legislation reported that all Georgian parliamentary bills were checked against existing EU directives in order to avoid contradictions. The majority leader of the parliament supported these aspirations towards Europe; Zurab Zhvania proclaimed 'back to Europe', and MP Tomas Gamkrelidze praised me for using the formula 'South Caucasus' instead of the older variety 'Transcaucasia', because 'geographically Georgia is part of Europe; according to the old Greek this was part of Europe'. The attitude to NATO was less clear. Burjanadze wanted close relations with NATO, but thought that 'membership is impossible'. At the same time an official Russian newspaper speculated that Georgia might choose neutrality, on the basis of statements by the minister of foreign affairs, Irakli Menagarishvili.[15]

Georgia had voted against a proposal to exclude Russia from

the Council of Europe because of its cruel methods in Chechnya. According to Burjanadze, 'Russia's isolation is very dangerous.' She thought that relations were improving, despite Russian accusations against Georgia for supporting the Chechen rebels. The Georgians were worried that Russia would retract its agreement in the Istanbul accord of November 19, 1999, to remove two of its four military bases in Georgia. According to the *Georgian Times* the Russians feared that their retreat would be followed by a US military arrival: 'Shevardnadze has already announced that come 2005 you will see Georgia knocking loudly at NATO's door.'[16]

On February 26, 2000 the EU delegation had a meeting with an apparently tired president Shevardnadze, who chose to speak in Georgian. He praised the OSCE for having called the events in Abkhazia 'ethnic cleansing', and criticized the Russian activity in the seceded region. At the same time he supported Russia's right to defend its territorial integrity, and asserted that the Chechens 'were the cruellest among those who fought against Georgia in Abkhazia'. He also underlined that 'we are married to Russia and cannot easily separate, but we want active cooperation with NATO, member-

The author (right) with Edward Shevardnadze in 2000 (in the middle is the head of the EU delegation in Tbilisi)

ship cannot be excluded.' About the relations with the European Union he exclaimed, 'Let us into the EU immediately!' Shevardnadze admitted that 'a considerable part of the society is mixed up in corruption,' and that life in Georgia was harsh.

But the *Georgian Times* was not convinced: 'The anti-corruption threat did not mean a real anti-corruption fight at all.' The president was accused of being overoptimistic: 'The president talks about progress when citizens have not received salaries for months.'[17]

Other reports drew a similar sordid picture. The publishing company Sakartvelo ten years earlier had published 450 titles every year, but at this time it was managing only two or three. During the Soviet period a book of Georgian poems could sell 200,000 copies in the whole of the USSR. Now almost nobody could afford a book: the price of 3–4 lari (€1.50) was considered too high. 'People must choose between books and bread.'[18] The shadow economy was estimated to comprise 40 per cent of the total economy. Unemployment was at least 12 per cent. There was a permanent energy crisis, with frequent electricity cuts. The state budget had only received 25 million lari in taxes, 65 per cent of the planned amount. Foreign dept was soaring. GDP per capita was only US$600 a year, which left a large part of the population below the poverty line.

SHEVARDNADZE TURNS TO THE WEST

It is a fact that it was Shevardnadze who brought Georgia into the Russia-dominated Commonwealth of Independent States in 1993. But this was done under pressure, in order to defeat Gamsakhurdia and save the country from total chaos. After some years he was undoubtedly redirecting Georgia towards the West. One writer pinpoints the decisive turning point in 1998 – 'it was then that the Georgian government unambiguously chose a Western orientation for Georgian security and for policies'.[19] The decision to build the BTC pipeline was made, and the International Security Advisory Board (ISAB) helped Georgia to establish a strategy concept, 'Georgia and the world' (published in 2000), which proposed Georgia's inclusion in Euro-Atlantic structures. In the same year, Georgia and Israel started military cooperation. In 1999 Georgia withdrew from the CIS-affiliated security pact CSTO. In April 2000 Shevardnadze announced Georgia's ambition to join NATO within five years, and in 2002 he received the first 200 US military advisers. There were reports of plans to establish a US military base in Akhalkalaki after the Russian retreat. When the Russian base in Vaziani was closed in July 2001 it was agreed that it should not be handed over to anybody else, but with the support of Turkey it was given NATO standard, and when it was reinaugurated on June 4, 2002, a Turkish general was present. On a visit in Prague 2002 Shevardnadze formally declared that Georgia was applying for membership of NATO. On February 12, 2003, Shevardnadze declared that Vaziani could be used by US military aircraft on its way to Iraq. US military personnel were granted diplomatic status. Lots of US aid arrived during these years, at the same time as the plans for pipeline routes for oil and gas through Georgia, outside Russia (BTS, BTC, BTE), came closer to realization. And 200 Georgian soldiers were sent to the Iraq War in August 2003.

ESCALATION

According to Shevardnadze himself in his autobiography, there was nothing wrong with the strike by authorities against a television station in autumn 2001, an incident that caused the resignation of his political heir, Zurab Zhvania. Instead, he claimed that a pivotal event was the 'enforced suicide' of Nugsar Sadshaia, secretary of the State Security Council, in the spring of 2002, which led to the 'continuous loss of control over my circle of confidants'. Sadshaia's death may have contributed, as such more or less mysterious deaths usually do. But the basic causes for the deterioration in Shevardnadze's position were very different. One of many explanatory accounts was given by an economist in a French-language Georgian newspaper: 'The years of independence have been transformed into a period of unbelievable decadence, leaving but little hope for the population.'[20] A business-man in the same copy exclaimed, 'In Georgia you pay bribes under pressure. That is blackmail.'[21] Corruption and the inaction against it by the Shevardnadze regime was the main reason for the escalation of the political crisis.

I was personally drawn into the morass when at the end of May 2002 Georgians approached the European institutions with cries for help to save from massive fraud the local election of June 2, considered by most as a rehearsal for the upcoming parliamentary (2003) and presidential (2005) elections. So after some discussions in the Green Group in the European Parliament it was decided that in my capacity as Rapporteur on South Caucasus I should make a brief visit, which I did on May 30 and 31.

An experienced official of an international organization in

Georgia told me that deficiencies and flaws had increased with every election, from the local elections of 1998, via the parliamentary elections of 1999 to the presidential elections of 2000. In the debate before the local election of June 2, 2002, fears of fraud and manipulation were paramount in the Georgian media. The criticisms had led to some improvements and changes. A report by the Venice Commission of the Council of Europe, dated May 24, 2002, considered the new election law as 'an important step forward' but also noted several important 'provisions that remain highly problematic'. One possibility for fraud was the lack of trustworthy registers of voters. There had been no reliable census. As it was allowable to vote without being registered and with only doubtful identification (old Soviet IDs, pension cards without a photo and so on), voters might vote several times. The printing of ballots was also criticized. Some maintained that ballot boxes might be stuffed by additional ballots printed on top of the controlled number. A newspaper article maintained, 'Political leaders are unanimous in excluding the possibility that the elections will be conducted in an objective manner. They claim that it is highly likely that the election results will be rigged.'[22]

After the re-election of Shevardnadze as president in April 2000 Zhvania became more and more impatient with the lack of efficient measures against corruption, and with some of the president's nominations to leading positions, especially the nomination of Kakha Targamadze to the post of minister of the interior. According to Zhvania, Targamadze became the real ruler of Georgia. On August 28, 2001, Zhvania wrote an open letter to Shevardnadze in which he raised several demands, one of which was that Targamadze should be dismissed. Shevardnadze refused. At the end of October the popular and independent television station Rustavi 2, which was investigating the corruption of leading politicians, including Targamadze, was attacked by the police in order to close it down. Zhvania called a press conference, blamed Shevardnadze and promised to resign if the president dismissed Targamadze. Shevardnadze dismissed the whole government, then Zhvania resigned as speaker.

In December 2001, at the Congress of the CUG, Zhvania made a speech which criticized the government and launched the CUG as a party of 'constructive opposition'. Shevardnadze resigned as chairman of the CUG, and the congress decided to leave that post vacant and establish an Organization Committee (OC), responsible for leading the party and charged with the task of drawing up a new structure for it. Zhvania became chair of the OC. In January 2002 the Ministry of Justice registered the changes in the CUG structure.

In the same month Zhvania publicly repeated that the CUG was a 'constructive opposition'.

In March a CUG MP, Gela Kvaratskhelia, submitted a complaint to the Ministry of Justice against the decisions of the CUG Congress. This was rejected by the ministry. Kvaratskhelia then made a complaint to a district court. The court, acting according to the Administrative Code, immediately suspended the registration of Zhvania's 'new' CUG. This started a chain of actions and measures, in courts and in the Central Election Committee, which finally led to the invalidation of the list of CUG candidates delivered by the OC led by Zhvania. Instead other candidates were registered in the name of CUG by the group led by Kvaratskhelia. When I asked him, Kvaratskhelia admitted that the conflict between him and Zhvania was political. He even recognized that the decision to proclaim the CUG as an 'opposition party' was taken by a large majority, eleven to two, in the CUG's OC. But he claimed that the party members did not agree, and that several local party meetings had protested and wanted the CUG to remain a supporter of the government. Why then not let the voters decide, by not trying to block the participation of the Zhvania group in the local elections? No, said Kvaratskhelia, this was an internal party conflict that should be settled inside the party. So why not let the party members decide; why not call a new congress? Why go to the courts? Kvaratskhelia considered the approach he took the only feasible one because a 'small group' (in other words, Zhvania and his supporters) controlled the party.

The president of the Supreme Court, Lado Chanturia, told me that the court had no choice but to suspend the registration of the CUG candidates when Gela Kvaratskhelia gave in his complaint. According to the Administrative Procedure Code, First Part, Article 29, 'bringing an action in the court shall result in the suspension of the concerned administrative act'. I replied that this was absurd because it opened the door to anybody to sabotage the activity of any party, such as the registration of candidates, by making a complaint to a court. What if all parties were the victims of such complaints? Then there would be no registered candidates at all! To this Mr Chanturia replied that the Supreme Court was aware of the risk of abuse of the provision, and therefore six months earlier had tried to bring parliament's attention to the problem, but to no avail.

The chair of the Central Electoral Committee, Jumber Lominadze, a physicist by profession, told me he had tried to negotiate a solution with the conflicting factions for four hours. Outside was turmoil, the building was blocked. Finally he had no choice but to turn over the matter to the court. But his personal opinion was that the decision of the court was wrong.

Davit Kipiani, from the International Society for Fair Elections and Democracy, stated that the CUG split 'paralyzed the Central Election Committee.' The CEC had to deal with matters outside its competence, with the result that the elections were poorly prepared. The situation was so tense that there was a risk of violence; Kipiani called upon the politicians to keep calm and act according to the law.

Everybody agreed that tension had been higher before this election than earlier. Some said this was because the overwhelming dominance of the CUG had been broken. Apart from the split between the Zhvania group and Kvaratskhelia (in reality, according to most observers, working on behalf of Shevardnadze), two other groups had already seceded from the CUG, the fiercely anti-Shevardnadze National Movement and the New Right Party. The slogan of the National Movement was 'Georgia/Tbilisi without Shevardnadze'. Its leader, Mikheil Saakashvili, declared 'that it is no longer a novelty that money-making is only possible by means of having good relations with Shevardnadze'.[23]

The Zhvania group was thus in principle banned from participating in the elections. But only just before the time limit for registration, a small registered party, the Christian Conservatives, offered Zhvania its party label because, they said, they wanted to protest against the manipulations that had almost left the Zhvania group out of the election race. Thus, Zhvania and his colleagues could stand for election as 'Christian Conservatives', a label that did not exactly correspond to their politics.

The turnout of voters was higher than expected and the election was a victory for the main anti-corruption opposition parties. Seven parties overcame the 4 per cent barrier for representation. The National Movement and the Labour Party gained 25 per cent each, the New Right 12 per cent, Industry Will Save Georgia 7 per cent, Zhvania's group 9 per cent and Agordzineba (Revival, the party of the Adjara ruler, Abashidze) 6 per cent. The elections were probably fairer than expected, as these figures meant a victory for the opposition. The rump of the CUG did not manage to overcome the 4 per cent barrier.[24] Although they won the elections the opposition parties still insisted that massive fraud had been committed against them, a policy that could have been suicidal, because the government threatened to cancel the elections completely, and Shevardnadze started a movement to rebuild the defunct Citizens Union. A sign of the very high and shrill level of the debate was a report that the former minister of the interior Targamadze was preparing documents against Zhvania and Saakashvili which would prove that in the autumn of 2001 those two politicians had been planning to 'stage a coup d'état'.[25]

PREPARING FOR SHEVARDNADZE'S EXIT

The political situation in Georgia in the middle of 2002 was described in a nutshell by a newspaper report that Shevardnadze's new crown prince, the state minister, Avtandil Jorbenadze, 'did not only obtain membership of the Citizens' Union because all state officials are obliged to do so, but he saw potential in his membership to influence the party and *profit from it*' (my italics).[26] The anti-corruption opposition which won the local elections was of course not completely innocent and clean. All the leaders of the National Movement and the Zhvania group had played important roles in the ruling CUG during the 1990s. Shalva Natelashvili, leader of the Labour Party, remarked that when his party in 1999 was banned from parliament as a result of flawed election rules, the cause was legislation supported by Zhvania and Saakashvili. From the Labour Party point of view, Zhvania had been the victim of a system he had for years himself been a powerful representative of.[27]

In a chat with me on May 30, 2002, Zhvania admitted that 'now it is Misha who is the leader of the opposition'. This was probably true, despite the fact that according to an opinion poll about the popularity of Georgian politicians in the fall of 2002 both Burjanadze and Zhvania received higher positions than Saakashvili.[28] The local elections gave Saakashvili a very good platform, as mayor of Tbilisi. One commentator, however, believed that the Shevardnadze–Zhvania confrontation had actually been a diversion to smooth Zhvania's rise to power.[29]

BACK TO RUSSIA?

In 2003, before the fateful parliamentary election that provoked his demise, Shevardnadze made an agreement with Russia to reduce the role of the United Nations in Abkhazia and accepted the reopening of the Tbilisi–Sochi railway through Abkhazia. A decrease in US aid was planned, from US$100 million in 2003 to $77 million in 2004. After the regime change in Tbilisi in November 2003, the trend was reversed and the new rulers received $164 million in 2004.[30] As one commentator concludes, Shevardnadze was pro-West for pragmatic, not ideological reasons, and 'by the end of his rule he had grown ambivalent toward the US and the EU', a fact that may be part of an explanation for the Rose Revolution.[31] Another observer remarked that in 2003 the clear direction towards the West was replaced by a more ambiguous political line. While sending soldiers to Iraq, Shevardnadze also negotiated unilaterally with Russia about Abkhazia and agreed a treaty with Gazprom. He did not emphasize NATO membership and did not demand the total retreat of Russian troops from Georgian military bases as urgently as before. 'At the end of his mandate a new positioning towards Russia can be established, which is based upon the belief in the efficiency of Russia's means of influence in Abkhazia.'[32]

Thus, in 2003, there are signs both that the West, to some extent encouraged by the new opposition, which had been strengthened by the local elections of 2002, was losing patience with the inability or unwillingness of Shevardnadze to cope with corruption and other deficiencies in the Georgian society, and that Shevardnadze was trying to reach back to Russia. This was in order to resolve his problems with the breakaway regions and maybe, according to some, also to avoid pressure from the Saakashvili–Burjanadze–Zhvania group and demands that he take action against his corrupt family and clan. One illustrative example of the growing dissatisfaction with Shevardnadze in the West was the European Union's new Georgia strategy for 2003–06, which was presented in September 2003. In the introduction it is admitted that it must 'be recognised that the EU may well have underestimated the size of the challenge' (that is, to transform Georgia into a liberal, free market democracy of Western type). One of the major problems mentioned is 'evidence that influential forces in Georgia, in and outside the government, do not adequately support reform'.[33] Considering the implied and covert character of diplomatic jargon it could hardly be expressed more clearly that from a Western point of view the stage was set for a 'regime change'.

NOTES

1   Vladimer Papava, 'East European democratization, the political economy of Georgia's Rose Revolution', *Orbits*, autumn 2006.
2   *Nezavisimaya Gazeta*, August 24, 1993.
3   *Zakavkaskie voyennie vedomosti*, no, 185, October 6, 1993.
4   Eduard Schewardnadze, *Als der Eiserne Vorhang zerriss, Begegnungen und Erinnerungen* (When the Iron Curtain was torn to pieces, meetings and memories) Peter M Metzler Verlag, Duisburg 2007, p. 173.
5   Carolyn McGriffith Ekedahl and Melvin A. Goodman, *The Wars of Eduard Shevaradnadze*, 2nd edn, Brassey's, Washington D.C., 2001.

6   *New Yorker,* December 18, 2000, quoted in Silvia Serrano, *Géorgie – sortie d'empire* (Georgia – exit from the empire), CNRS Éditions, Paris, 2007, p. 228.

7   Ekedahl and Goodman *The Wars.*

8   Ronald Grigor Suny, *The Making of the Georgian Nation,* 2nd edn, Indiana University Press, Bloomington, 1994, p. 329.

9   Schewardnadze, *Als der Eiserne,* p. 365.

10 Silke Kleinhanss, *Die Aussenpolitik Georgiens – Ein failing state zwischen internem Teilversagen und externen Chancen* (The foreign policy of Georgia – a failing state between internal flaws and external possibilities), LITverlag, Münster, 2008, p. 26.

11 Peter Nasmyth, *Georgia: In the mountains of poetry,* Curzon Caucasus World, London, 2001.

12 Thomas Balivet, *Géopolitique de la Géorgie: Souverainité et controle des territoires* (The geopolitics of Georgia: sovereignty and controle of territoires), L'Harmattan, Paris, 2005.

13 Bruno Coppetier and Robert Legvold (eds), *Statehood and Security: Georgia after the Rose Revolution,* MIT Press, Cambridge, Mass., 2005, p. 115.

14 Briefing, February 23, 2000.

15 *Russkaya Gazeta,* February 19–26, 2000.

16 *Georgian Times,* February 16, 2000.

17 *Georgian Times,* February 14, 2000.

18 *Svobodnaya Gruzia,* February 25, 2000.

19 Coppetier, *Statehood,* p. 131.

20 Vladimir Sokoloff, doctor of economy and finance, in *La Vie en Georgie,* May 7, 2002.

21 Vice president of the American Chamber of Commerce in Georgia, Fady Asly, in *La Vie en Georgie,* May 7, 2002.

22 *Georgian Messenger,* May 30, 2002.

23 Ibid.

24 *Georgian Times,* June 3, 2002.

25 *Svobodnaya Gruzia,* May 29, 2002.

26 *Georgian Messenger,* July 2, 2002.

27 Per Gahrton (MEP, Greens, Sweden), rapporteur of the European Parliament on South Caucasus, 'Georgia: the struggle for power and the local elections of June 2nd', report from a brief mission to Tbilisi, May 30–31, 2002.

28 *Georgian Times,* October 13, 2002.

29 Zaal Anjaparidze, 'Preparing for post-Shevardnadze era', *Prism,* vol. 8, issue 5, May 30, 2002.

30 Balivet, *Géopolitique.*

31 Coppetier, *Statehood,* p. 144.

32 Kleinhans, *Die Aussenpolitik,* p. 91.

33 European Union. Tacis National Indicative Programme 2004–2006, *Georgia, Country Strategy Paper 2003–2006,* adopted by the European Commission on September 23, 2003.

8

KMARA – ENOUGH! THE ROSE REVOLUTION

The situation in Georgia just before the Rose Revolution of November 2003 was appalling. The economy had almost come to a standstill. The GNP was only 29 per cent of the level in 1990. Every fourth person in the urban population was without a job. An average monthly wage was about US$50, and half the population lived below the poverty line. The Council of Europe had declared that the human rights situation was not acceptable. A fifth of the population during Soviet times, about a million people, had emigrated. The central government had lost control over three provinces, Abkhazia, South Ossetia and Adjara.

To carry out fair and correct elections under such circumstances would not be easy. When in my capacity as election observer from the European Parliament, I met with representatives of the major political parties and NGOs during the week before the day of the election (November 2), the terminology was so tense that it was clear that a catastrophe was approaching. Representatives of Shevardnadze's New Georgia coalition used rude jargon and showed a complete lack of respect for the opposition parties, accusing them of wanting to give Georgia back to Russia, pursuing fascist and populist policies, and controlling most NGOs and independent media, such as the Rustavi 2 television station. Opposition representatives openly declared that the election really was about the position of Shevardnadze (although his mandate lasted until 2005) and warned that the voters' registers were not correct.

Tina Khidasheli of the Georgian Young Lawyers Association (GYLA) informed me that her organization planned to send 128 trained lawyers to Adjara, which was one of the strongholds of the regime. It was obvious that there was a special need for insight into the elections under the control of the authoritarian leader of Adjara, Aslan Abashidze, since the Adjara authorities had informed the Central Election Commission (CEC) in Tbilisi that the number of voters in the autonomous area was 290,000, compared with 216,000 at the local elections only one year earlier. However, Adjara had declared that external monitoring would not be allowed, so the chances that GYLA would be able to carry out its intention were slim.

The inflated number of presumed voters in Adjara was but one warning that inaccurate registers of voters was a likely source of falsification. Another method was the 'carousel', which means that a pre-marked ballot paper is given to a bribed voter. The voter puts this into his pocket, enters the polling station, receives an empty ballot paper, puts this in his pocket and takes out the pre-marked one, which is used for the voting. The empty ballot paper is then given to the briber outside in exchange for the agreed amount of money, marked again by the falsifiers and given to the next voter who is prepared to sell his democratic right. In some polling stations, allegedly in order to restrict the possibility of people carrying out the 'carousel', the polling booths were turned so that the voter was standing with the back towards the polling officials. In this way it was, in theory, possible for an administrator to see if a voter was fumbling with two ballot papers, the pre-marked and the empty one. A side effect was, however, that it might be possible to look over the shoulder of a voter and observe which candidate or party was marked.

Zurab Chiaberashvili of the Institute for Fair Elections expressed satisfaction with the election code but worried about the implementation. His organization was responsible for a parallel vote count, covering some 85 per cent of all polling stations. He expressed concern that the *gangabelis* (heads of the regional administrations), who had been appointed by the government, would abuse their power in favour of the regime. However, government representatives warned that abuse of power could occur in the areas where the opposition had been in charge since the local elections of 2002. Gia Nodia of the Caucasian Institute for Peace, Democracy and Development mainly worried about the minority areas, where civil society was weak and people had been told by government representatives that a vote for the opposition was tantamount to treason. Nevertheless, out of some 1,200 election rallies only a few had been violent. There had been some explosions of cars and shootings, but it was underlined that the general level of crime in Georgia was high, so a certain amount of violent trouble was nothing but normal. Also, access to mass media had been fairly equal for the government and the opposition. Several observers deplored the fact that political programmes and issues had been almost totally absent during the pre-election campaign, which instead had been dominated by tactical speculations and accusations.

According to representatives of OSCE the voters' registers had not been updated since 1991. Moreover, there were too few polling stations. It was estimated that the number would only give each voter 15 seconds to perform all the procedures of casting a vote, a fact that foreshadowed congestion, irritation and disorder in the polling stations. Nevertheless, Nana Devdariani, newly appointed director of the CEC, tried to assure everybody that any eventual faults and irregularities would be the result of technical complications and human mistakes, not of deliberate fraud. In addition, she added, 'People who have themselves manipulated elections now take it for granted that they are going to be victims of manipulations.' She had a point; all the most well-known leaders of the opposition had undeniably, as members of the Shevardnadze ruling team, been responsible for manipulating elections.

On election day, I was in charge of observing a district in a Soviet-style, grubby suburb of Georgia's third city, Rustavi, hurrying back and fro between ten polling stations on muddy and slippery unpaved streets. I did not observe any fraud or falsification with my own eyes, but I encountered thousands of protesting and swearing voters who despite valid identification cards were not allowed to vote because their names could not be found in the official, handwritten registers. I watched several quarrels and even fist fights in and outside the polling stations. Other observers saw direct manipulation. The Institute for Fair Elections proved, by parallel counting, that manipulation of figures was common at the regional level. Observers from OSCE, the Council of Europe and the European Union agreed that the election was not correct and fair. The International Election Observation Mission declared that:

the 2 November Parliamentary elections in Georgia fell short of a number of international standards. Delays and confusion over voter lists contributed to a lack of public confidence in the governmental and parliamentary authorities' capacity to manage an effective and transparent election process.

In his memoirs Shevardnadze admits, 'Both sides, the government and the opposition, manipulated limitlessly.'

DID THE OPPOSITION WIN?

The parallel count showed that Shevardnadze's New Georgia party lost, with only 19 per cent of the votes. But did the opposition win? According to the estimate by Fair Elections, the three opposition parties that had declared they were prepared to cooperate, the National Movement (NM), Burjanadze-Democrats (BD) and New Rights (NR), got 44 per cent of the votes (NM 26, BD 10 and NR 8). The Adjara ruler's Revival got 8, Labour 17, the Industry Party (IP) 7, and small parties the rest. An exit poll had very similar results. How different was this from the official result? Significantly different, but probably less so than many believe. The major difference was for the Adjara Revival party, which was given 19 per cent by CEC, while New Georgia only got slightly more than according to the parallel count, 21 per cent. This indicates that massive fraud was committed not by Shevardnadze, but by Abashidze. The inflation of Abashidze's figures hit NM and Labour the most, giving them only 18 and 12 per cent respectively, while the official results for BD, NR and IP came rather close to the parallel count: 8, 7, 6. Thus, according to the official result, the three cooperating opposition parties got 33 per cent (instead of 44 per cent). New Georgia and Revival got 40 per cent (instead of 27), which together with the 6 per cent of the Industry Party totals 46 per cent (instead of 34). Interestingly enough neither the Shevardnadze loyalists nor the cooperating opposition won a majority according to any of the counts.

The Georgian parliament in 2003 had 235 seats. Of these 10 seats from Abkhazia were not up for renewal, because of the complicated situation, and 75 seats were elected according to the majority system (based on the French model, with two rounds). Out of these 26 were won by the cooperating opposition, 23 by the government block, and 20 by independents. In the remaining districts nobody got enough votes to win in the first round. When the Supreme Court after the Rose Revolution decided to cancel the results of the proportional election, the majority seats were not touched. Thus it is possible to estimate the approximate outcome of the election in parliamentary seats according to both the official result and the parallel count. According to the official result neither the three-party opposition nor the government block would reach the required 118 seats to command a majority. If Shevardnadze had remained as president he would probably have been dependent on Labour to command a secure parliamentary majority. According to the parallel count the three-party opposition would have gained some 30 seats more than the government block, but would have needed support from Labour or from most of the independent majority MPs to reach a majority.

The Georgian Labour Party was different from most other major parties. While in 2003 it was difficult to discover programmatic political differences of importance between the other parties, which were all more or less centre-right, neoliberal, in favour of free markets and privatization, and pro-West, Labour had a clear centre-left agenda. According to Gia Nodia, 'the Labour Party of Georgia is the most successful left-wing political organization in the country'; it supported state ownership of land, opposed the privatization of electric power plants and demanded free education and health care.[1] In a directory of some 150 Georgian political parties compiled in 1999, the main priorities of the Labour Party were described as 'dynamic and balanced economics, which serves first of all people and correspondingly, state interests' and the 'realization of state protectionism, institutions in strategic spheres'. And most important, while most other parties openly displayed a strong ambition to achieve Georgian membership of NATO, the Labour Party demanded 'complete military neutrality'. It was also much more of a genuine popular movement than most other parties, reporting that it had some 90,000 members. Moreover, its leader had not been educated outside the Soviet Union; he communicated with foreigners in Russian.[2]

It is far from sure that Labour, after a fair election with an outcome as reported by the parallel count, would have supported the Saakashvili–Burjanadze–Zhvania group. While the Labour leader, Shalva Natelashvili, was very critical of Shevardnadze and had complained to the European Court in Strasbourg about the fraud in the previous parliamentary election that had barred his party from representation in the parliament, he detested the new leaders, whom he (with some logic) held responsible for most of the evils of the Shevardnadze period. Natelashvili told me two weeks after the election, but some days before the Rose Revolution, that Labour wanted to play the role of a third force. Labour was planning to join the new parliament, as it had passed the 7 per cent barrier even according to the official result. Natelashvili might have made a deal with Shevardnadze just as well as with the opposition. According to the parallel count, New Georgia, Revival, Labour and the Industry Party would have got 51 per cent of the votes.

Thus, there is no evidence to support a claim that those who carried out the Rose Revolution 'in reality' had the support of a majority of voters. On the contrary, even if the election of

Shalva Natelashvili (here on an election poster 2008), the leader of Labour, the only major party with a genuinely alternative programme, could have achieved a strategic position after the 2003 elections had there not been the Rose Revolution

November 2 had been fair, it is quite likely that it would not have given the power to the Saakashvili–Burjanadze–Zhvania group, but to a new constellation where a much more left-wing, even if somewhat populist, party, Labour, would have reached a key position. That such a development would seriously disturb the plans of some groups and interests was evident and clearly understood by most Georgian politicians. Natelashvili told me, at the same time as huge and daily demonstrations against the electoral fraud were being staged by the Saakashvili–Burjanadze–Zhvania group in front of the parliament building in Tbilisi, that he was pessimistic about the future of democracy in Georgia, because he was convinced that the demonstrators would force Shevardnadze to resign before the new parliament could legally convene. This would catapult the speaker, Nino Burjanadze, into the position of interim president, and give these people the possibility of 'staging fraudulent presidential elections'. There was no love lost between the later leaders of the Rose Revolution and Natelashvili and his Labour Party. In a meeting with European observers before the election, Zurab Zhvania stated that his party could work with the National Movement and the New Right Party but that it could not form a coalition with Labour or the Revival Party.[3] Like many other members of the Georgian establishment and foreign observers, the Saakashvili–Burjanadze–Zhvania group considered

Natelashvili to be an irresponsible populist. There is some truth in this judgement; the Labour leader is infamous for awkward statements.

Nevertheless, it is also true that his policies have been undeniably more left-wing, without being pro-Russian, and have included more about social justice, than has been common in independent Georgia, where most politicians have competed to be the most liberal, pro-market and pro-West. Was this a reason that the opposition was not satisfied with having taught Shevardnadze a lesson, and waited for his natural resignation in 2005? Was it a reason for Western powers to support a speedy regime change in Georgia? Was there a fear that despite all his earlier pro-West actions, like sending troops to Iraq, the last years of the Shevardnadze period with Labour in a key role might turn into a backlash from the point of view of Washington and Brussels?

FEAR OF ABASHIDZE

The three opposition leaders met with Shevardnadze on November 9 and had a brief talk, which produced no substantial result. The president is reported to have remarked, 'I do not intend to resign at the demand of individual politicians and a few dozen young people waving flags. If there were at least a million people, it would have been different.' However, in only a couple of days, the number of demonstrators increased considerably and about 1 million signatures demanding Shevardnadze's resignation were collected.

Then the embattled president turned to his long-time competitor, Aslan Abashidze. In his memoirs Shevardnadze recounts that after November 10, when the battle cry of the protestors was 'resign', he drew the conclusion that it was no longer possible to talk to his former collaborators Burjanadze and Saakashvili. Instead, he travelled to Batumi and convened with Abashidze. There he learned that the Adjara autocrat threatened to separate Adjara from Georgia definitively if the official election results for his region were not legalized. It is understandable that the Georgian leader did not want to risk a third secession, after South Ossetia and Abkhazia. Nevertheless, the price for avoiding such an outcome, that is, to accept a false election result in order to keep Adjara inside the Georgian state, seems very high. Moreover, this incident underlines the fact that the major manipulator was Abashidze, not Shevardnadze. If Saakashvili had not acted and the parliament that came out of the rigged election had been accepted, and Shevardnadze had been able to remain as president, it would have entailed increased power for Abashidze, not only in Batumi, but also in Tbilisi. That this prospect was frightening for many Georgians and contributed to escalating the protests into a demand for regime change is confirmed by one of the leaders of Kmara:

> The picture changed dramatically when election results from the autonomous region of Adjara propelled the regional Revival Union party into second place .... Suspicions were particularly high about the Adjara results, because the long-acrimonious relations between Adjara's pro-Russian strongman, Aslan Abashidze, and Shevardnadze had thawed in the months before the elections. This led some to speculate that the two had reached a deal to trade support for votes.[4]

When I met with Zurab Zhvania and Nino Burjanadze in Tbilisi on November 14, permanent demonstrations were going on in the centre of the city, along Rustaveli Avenue. They expressed worry that the irascible Saakashvili would go too far and create a snowball effect which nobody would be able to control. They admitted that they did not actually agree with the demand by the demonstrators for Shevardnadze's resignation, and that they disowned any kind of threat to the personal security of the president. They expressed a wish of finding a compromise solution through outside mediation. At the same time they refused to enter a parliament set up according to the falsified result. Nevertheless, they wanted to de-escalate the conflict, stop the daily demonstrations and instead start serious negotiations. Saakashvili opted for the opposite approach, and as very often, those who take the initiative and switch from words to deeds get the upper hand and determine the development. On November 22 Zhvania had moved to the position of Saakashvili and told a European Parliament delegation, only hours before the actual takeover, that the only solution was the resignation of the president. One of his main arguments was that Shevardnadze was bringing in Abashidze loyalists from Adjara. It is obvious that even if the opposition might have been prepared to live another two years with Shevardnadze as president, they were not willing to accept a position of real power over the whole of Georgia for Aslan Abashidze.

PEACEFUL TAKEOVER

Of course it is not known in every detail what happened during the almost three weeks that lapsed from the elections to November 22, when Mikheil Saakashvili, with his followers, carrying roses in their hands, erupted into the inauguration ceremony of the new parliament (composed according to the official, falsified result), interrupted Shevardnadze's speech and scared him, or his bodyguards, into leaving through a back door. Saakashvili immediately took over the empty rostrum, sipped from Shevardnadze's still tepid tea and also took over the country, both symbolically and practically. Shevardnadze, however, declared a state of emergency, and for some hours it was not clear whether Georgia was going to be thrown once more into civil war.

The next day Zhvania and Saakashvili visited Shevardnadze in his residence in Krzanisi just outside Tbilisi. Russian and Western diplomats were active and finally the president promised to resign, obviously after having received far-reaching promises not only concerning his and his family's personal security, but also concerning his property and financial situation. The whole world congratulated him on his wisdom. He received a letter from US President George W. Bush on December 1, of which he proudly publishes a facsimile in his memoirs, with thanks for 'guiding Georgia from the darkness of civil war toward democracy and market economy and establishing close friendship with the USA. I am grateful for your support on Iraq and your leadership on counterterrorism in the Pankisi Gorge.' Shevardnadze even offered to give good advice to his followers, but 'unfortunately the developments after the Revolution became something else, liberal values were ignored, massive televised arrests and dismissals followed and a pressure upon judges and enterprises without precedence was registered', he complains in his memoirs.

One of the newly elected parliamentarians who watched the nonviolent coup d'état from a ringside seat was Gia Gachechiladze, leader of the Green Party. From a peak in influence with 11 MPs in 1992, the Green Party had had a shadowy existence since Zhvania and most of his collaborators had switched their loyalties to Shevardnadze, something that quite a few of those who remained considered to be treason. While Gia and his followers had for many years criticized the Zhvania group because of its cooperation with Shevardnadze, after the split between Zhvania and Shevardnadze they decided, somewhat paradoxically, to stand for the election of 2003 on the list of Shevardnadze's New Georgia coalition. 'I was MP for 28 minutes', Gia snorted bitterly about a year after the Rose Revolution. He told me that Georgia had become a 'mixture of Hoxha's Albania and Hitler's Germany'. He was of course still influenced by bitterness when he made this bizarre comparison. But I must admit that a lot of the observations that Gia made directly after

the Rose Revolution have later been made by a growing number of
Georgian and foreign journalists, disappointed supporters of Saakashvili and Co., and international organizations for human rights and
democracy (see the following chapters).

WAS IT A CIA-LED COUP?

A left-wing evaluation of the Rose Revolution was formulated as
soon as early December on the World Socialist Web Site: 'It was a
US-led coup!'[5] A similar conclusion was made by a German website:
'A revolution in Georgia? Hardly.'[6] It was alleged that some of the
observers who had reported that the November 2 election had been
falsified were funded by US-sponsored institutions. The US ambassador, Richard Miles, had been deeply involved. As Goltz remarks,
Miles had been US Ambassador to Azerbaijan, Serbia and Georgia,
and 'there had been a coup in each of the countries he had been
posted to'.[7] US-supported members of the anti-Milosevic Serb Otpor
had trained Georgian youngsters in modern non-violent methods to
achieve a 'regime change'.

I asked Zhvania shortly after the takeover about the Otpor connection. He replied, 'What is wrong with one peaceful revolutionary
movement getting support from another?' In this he was right, of
course. The Georgian equivalent of Otpor, Kmara (Enough), had
been created by students some years earlier, and had close relations
to the US-sponsored Liberty Institute. Kmara, like many similar
youthful protest groups all over the world, was explicitly peaceful
and introduced new ways of acting politically. One of the most visible and efficient methods was simple political graffiti. Small teams
of Kmara activists spent nights painting 'Kmara' on walls all over
Tbilisi and other cities. Also, after the elections, when demonstrations were supervised by security forces, Kmara girls gave flowers
and sandwiches to the soldiers and policemen.[8]

Critics remarked that Saakashvili had studied in the United States,
as had several of his ministers. Other leading personalities in the new
regime had worked with the Soros Foundation, which spent tens
of millions of dollars in supporting the opposition against Shevardnadze. Several new ministers were former collaborators of Soros.[9]
The minister of defence had studied at Harvard's Kennedy School,
the minister of energy came from the US-financed PA Consulting, and
as his first minister of foreign affairs Saakashvili appointed Georgia's
ambassador to Washington. Does this prove that the Rose Revolution

was merely a US-planned coup? Probably not. An article on the World Socialist Web Site indirectly admitted that it was more complicated, when it quoted the first speech to the nation by Interim President Burjanadze, where she promised 'not to deviate from the strongly pro-Western policy which has been pursued by Shevardnadze'.[10] Lincoln A. Mitchell, who was a representative of the National Democratic Institute in Tbilisi before, during and after the Rose Revolution, and later has become overtly critical of the Saakashvili regime, goes to great length to prove that the US involvement in democracy building in Georgia in the 1990s and early twenty-first century did not aim at toppling the Shevardnadze regime. He has an argument that sounds rather plausible: 'Given how difficult it was for the Bush administration to recruit countries to join the "coalition of willing" (in Iraq) we can be reasonably certain the administration would not have done anything to remove a pro-war government from power'.[11]

According to Kmara activist Tina Kandelaki, the Rose Revolution was not planned at all, nor even intended to take place. Kmara was 'a revolt against corruption and kleptocratic government', but the perpetrators did not anticipate regime change as a result of the election in 2003, 'they hoped only to influence the presidential elections of 2005'.[12] Zhvania, in an interview in early January 2004, stated that 'I can tell you that even two days before President Shevardnadze's resignation he still had the chance to avoid the most dramatic scenario. People were not looking for a revolution.'[13] The theory of a US-planned coup was also discarded at a seminar at the Institute of Political Science at the Georgian Academy of Science at the end of April 2004.[14] A dozen participants saw a straight line from the election in 1990 of the nationalist Gamsakhurdia up to the Saakashvili regime. The main ambition had all the time been to establish a functioning state. According to this hypothesis Shevardnadze did not fall because he was not sufficiently pro-West, but because he achieved nothing but a corrupt house of poverty.

However, other observers take a somewhat different position. While admitting that the main foreign policy strategy paper of the Shevardnadze regime, 'Georgia and the world' (2000) was indeed written by Western consultants, it is estimated that the paper was just a number of 'loose statements'. This has changed with the Saakashvili regime, which has given 'military reform a new impulse'.[15] Another writer emphasizes that 'the spontaneous background of the Rose Revolution must be doubted'.[16] Nevertheless, it was not obvious even to the Big Brother, and later infamous enemy of Georgia, Russia, how to classify the Rose Revolution. One poll revealed that the initial reaction among Russians was clearly positive. However during the following year a reversal became visible.[17]

Russian attitudes towards Georgia (in percentages)

Month/year	Negative	Positive
August 2002	39	22
January 2004	10	41
July 2004	22	29

Among all theories about the character of the Rose Revolution, one of the most awkward is probably one suggested by a couple of Russian authors, who hint that there could have been a pro-Russian coup, had the Rose Revolution not taken place.[18] It is, of course, not uncommon in the history of revolutions and coups that a takeover of power in a state is made by one group primarily in order to thwart a similar action by quite another group. The possibility of a 'pro-Russian' take-over in Georgia in 2003, however, seems remote.

At the same time there is nothing to substantiate the idea that it was a kind of liberation from dictatorship. Shevardnadze was no Stalin; his regime was just a corrupt mixture of clan and mafia mismanagement. In 2003 the Georgians did not lack 'freedom'; they had had it, more or less, for a decade. Freedom of expression had been considerable, civil society was relatively strong. The main problem was the material standard of living, which had deteriorated to a great extent. Those who supported the ousting of Shevardnadze did it less for ideological reasons and more because they hoped for a higher standard of living. Thus it was logical that one of the most noticed promises by the new regime was to double the pensions for close to a million pensioners – from the equivalent of US$6 to $12 a month. That was not much. Nevertheless, it was probably more than the state could afford. The previous regime had emptied the wallet of the state. One reason everybody was aware of was, of course, corruption. However, among many Georgians there was also much disappointment with the liberal economy which, at least in theory, had replaced the Soviet centrally planned system. What if somebody suggested remedying the ills and combating poverty, but not by more of the liberal reforms which, in the eyes of many, had so far failed?

The alternative to the Rose Revolution was neither a pro-Russian coup, nor some kind of Shevardnadze dictatorship, but rather a mixture of Labour's economic and social policies, Abash-idze's authoritarian style and good relations with Moscow, and

Shevardnadze's lenience towards dissident opinions and the 'informal' economy. The Rose Revolutionaries obviously feared such an option, and so did quite a few centres of power in the West. The fundamental problems of Georgia, such as corruption, would of course not have been resolved by a Shevardnadze regime dependent on Labour and Abashidze. The conflicts with Russia might have been assuaged, without the country becoming a satellite. Political freedom would not have been improved, but nor would it have been abolished. According to this hypothesis a continued Shevardnadze regime in 2003 would have been different from the Shevardnadze regime previously. It might very well have been less prepared to follow directives from Washington, less keen to join NATO and support the US imperial ambitions in the area. The showdown with the opposition would have been postponed until the presidential election of 2005. Maybe Abashidze would have tried to succeed Shevardnadze, but it is extremely unlikely that he would have had any chance of winning enough support outside Adjara, even if the elections were just as unfair as in 2003. Maybe the leader of Labour would have gained strength from the key role of his party and felt strong enough to be a serious candidate for presidency. Nevertheless, I find it difficult to believe that Shalva Natelashvili could have won an election against a trustworthy opponent.

If the perpetrators of the Rose Revolution had abstained from removing Shevardnadze in 2003 they would have had very good chances of winning the presidential election of 2005. Who would have been their candidate? That is far from clear. Without the drama of November 22, 2003, Saakashvili would not have been such an obvious candidate for the opposition. Both Zhvania and Burjanadze would have had the chance to be number one. Maybe such thoughts were behind an article in a Georgian newspaper in October 2008 about the 'February 2003 conspiracy', where it is claimed that a plan to topple Shevardnadze was investigated by the authorities as much as nine months before it happened, but that the replacement was intended to be not Saakashvili, but 'somebody else'. In the same article it is alleged that Shevardnadze 'regrets that Zurab Zhvania did not become president'.[19]

If this analysis is credible, and if others had similar thoughts during the fall of 2003, it is clear that several persons and groups and players in the Great Game considered the prolongation of the Shevardnadze regime, with support from Abashidze and with Labour in a key role, as very hazardous. At the same time there was a relatively broad popular dissatisfaction that was skilfully exploited and organized by the leaders of the Rose Revolution, with support from Western, mainly US-sponsored, institutions and persons.

NOTES

1 Ghia Nodia and Alvaro Pinto Scholtbach, *The Political Landscape of Georgia*, Eburan Academic, Delft, 2006. Nodia expressed the same evaluation of the Labour Party in a personal interview with the author in July 2009.
2 International Centre for Civic Culture, *Political Parties of Georgia, Directory 1999*, Tbilisi, 1999.
3 Report on the elections 2003 by the European Parliament observers, DV/5360EN.doc.
4 Georgi Kandelaki, *Georgia's Rose Revolution: A participant's perspective*, Special Report 167, July 2006, US Institute of Peace <www.usip.org>.
5 Barry Grey and Vladimir Volkov, 'Georgia's 'rose revolution' – a made-in-America coup', *World Socialist Web* December 5, 2003.
6 *Grazwurzelrevolution,* January 2004.
7 Thomas Goltz, *Georgia Diary: A chronicle of war and political chaos in the post-Soviet Caucasus*, M. E. Sharpe, Armonk, N.Y., 2006, p. 231.
8 Kandelaki, *Georgia's Rose Revolution.*
9 For example Minister of Justice Papuashvili, Minister of Education Lomaia and Minister of Economy Rekhviashvili.
10 World Socialist Web Site, December 29, 2003.
11 Lincoln A. Mitchell, *Uncertain Democracy: U.S. foreign policy and Georgia's Rose Revolution*, University of Pennsylvania Press, Philadelphia, 2009.
12 Kandelaki, *Georgia's Rose Revolution.*
13 Zurab Karumidze and James V. Wertsch (eds) *'Enough': The Rose Revolution in the Republic of Georgia 2003*, Nova Science, New York, 2005, p. 35.
14 *Svobodnaya Gruzia*, April 17, 2004.
15 Bruno Coppetier and Robert Legvold (eds), *Statehood and Security: Georgia after the Rose Revolution,* MIT Press, Cambridge, Mass., 2005, p. 75 and p. 4.
16 Gaidz Minassian, *Caucase du Sud, la nouvelle guerrre froide* (South Caucasus, the new cold war), L'Harmattan, Paris, 2007, p. 162.
17 Coppetier, *Statehood*, p. 257.
18 Mikhail Leontiev and Dmitrij Zhukov, *'Nezavisimaya' Gruzia – bandit v tigrovoj shkure* ('Independent' Georgia – a bandit in a tiger's hide), Yauza Press, Moscow, 2008, p. 286.
19 *Asaval-Dasavali,* October 27, 2008.

9

THE REVOLUTIONARY HONEYMOON

After taking power, the revolutionary triumvirate, Saakashvili, Burjanadze and Zhvania, had a dramatic flying start. A typical action was a lightning visit by Saakashvili to Tskhinvali, followed by his remark afterwards that he regretted not having been arrested by the authorities of the breakaway region! The shock therapy was appreciated by many, but also irritated several groups and probably made some into outright enemies. One analysis stated that the three leaders 'moved swiftly to reinvigorate the state, strengthen executive power, pare back corruption in government, disrupt criminalized networks, restore central authority in the often quarrelsome province of Adjara, create a trustworthy domestic police force, and collect taxes to sustain a revenue-starved government'.[1]

One of the most visible actions was a deep-seated reform of the traffic police. During one of my visits some years before the Rose Revolution I noticed that all cars, except ours, which was marked as belonging to the government, were stopped by police. 'Do you fear an attack?' I asked, bearing in mind the civil wars of the early 1990s. 'No', replied the president of the Parliamentary Committee for Judicial Affairs, who was accompanying us, 'the police officers are just collecting their salary.' After the regime change the new government sacked thousands of underpaid police officers who had created a tradition of corruption, and employed new and fresh people who immediately received a decent salary from the state. A similar move was made to eradicate the old and bad tradition of buying university exams. This was achieved by moving the responsibility for examinations from individual universities to a central state authority, which robbed the corrupt teachers and professors of the 'commodity' they had used to sell to the students.

While both these reforms could be understood as consumer-friendly improvements of everyday life, they may also be defined as measures to increase the authority of the state. According to many assessments, the Georgia of Shevardnadze was on the verge of becoming a failed state. While Shevardnadze has maintained that the reason he did not defend his position in November 2003 by resorting to the security services was a wish to avoid bloodshed, others have recalled that large parts of the security service did not obey his orders simply because they had not even been paid the low salary they were entitled to. From this point of view, strong measures to increase the authority of the state were of course both legitimate and necessary. A strong state was also considered necessary to recover the lost territories. Thus, it was no coincidence that the defence budget in 2005 reached 300 million lari, which was ten times as much as in the last Shevardnadze budget. The entire state budget increased rapidly, from 7.1 per cent of GNP in 1995, to double that in 2005. At the same time GNP grew, although it was still far below that of the Soviet period. While GNP in 1994 was only 23 per cent of the GNP of 1989, that figure had grown to 50 per cent by 2005.

SUCCESSES AND FAILURES

One commentator lists five major successes of the Rose Revolution:

- The state was made to function.
- The restructuring of the armed forces.
- Respect for popular wishes.
- The solution of the Adjara issue.
- The normalization of Armenian–Georgian relations.[2]

Most observers agree with the first, second and fourth of these, while the third and last can be disputed. However, more and more analyses have pointed at the negative aspects of the frenetic ambition to construct a strong state. Many commentators have criticized the constitutional amendments made rapidly after the presidential election of January 2004, when the power of the president was increased at the expense of parliament. Shortly after the Rose Revolution several television stations and newspapers were closed, which according to Papava was 'a major setback for democratic development, but a setback largely unnoticed by Saakashvili's Western friends'.[3]

    Gia Nodia has carried out an evaluation of several aspects of political and social development, such as the electoral process, civil society, independent media, independence of the judiciary and the degree of corruption. The sum of the indicators (where 1 is best and 7 worst) for these aspects for the years 1999 and 2006 respectively reveal a slight deterioration (from a total score of 20.5 to 22.75). Only one aspect, civil society, improved a little.[4] In another overview it was reported that out of 24 indicators on security, rule of law and welfare, 14 – a small majority – did not change after the Rose Revolution. Six improved: the control of territories and borders, security, elections, corruption and collection of taxes. Four deteriorated: the independence of the judiciary, civil liberties, the abuse of power of state authorities and external debt.[5] Despite dramatic actions and some admitted successes, in 2005 Georgia was still one of the most corrupt countries of the world, on a level with Cambodia, at number 130 out of 157. Interestingly, a German researcher concluded that 'Georgia can even in 2006 be classified as a failing state.'[6] As early as December 2004, readers of the *International Herald Tribune* learned from one of the most keen advocates of political and democratic reforms, Tina Khidasheli, president of Georgian Young Lawyers, that the 'Rose revolution has wilted'.[7]

The growing criticism against the new Georgian regime was taken note of in Moscow. In January 2005, *Izvestia* carried an article that claimed, 'The honeymoon between Georgia and the Council of Europe is over'.[8]

THE PRESIDENTIAL ELECTION OF 2004

After the resignation of Shevardnadze, the new leaders were keen to act according to the constitution. The speaker of the parliament, Nino Burjanadze, became interim president. One observer, Lincoln A. Mitchell, elaborately describes a tough, but covert, power struggle between Saakashvili, Burjanadze and Zhvania.[9] Theoretically this might be true to some extent, although not even Mitchell is able to refer to any overt signs. If Burjanadze and Zhvania had ambitions for the number one position, they kept them to themselves. Actually, Zhvania told me in connection with the local election of 2002 that he accepted that Saakashvili had grown into the leader of the anti-Shevardnadze camp. While this does not necessarily imply that Zhvania had already given up all plans to succeed Shevardnadze in 2005, it is clear that by his interruption of Shevardnadze's inauguration speech on November 22, 2003, Saakashvili created an accomplished fact, which determined the issue in his own favour.

As it turned out there was no real competitor for Saakashvili. Labour and Revival boycotted the election. There was virtually no election campaign, and 99 per cent of paid advertising was in favour of Saakashvili.[10] Saakashvili's wife has admitted that campaigning was 'superfluous', and described her own contribution as a 'triumphal procession' during which she felt like Julia Roberts.[11] Only 1.7 million voters were registered, compared with 3.2 million for the elections of November 2, 2003. Zurab Chiaberashvili, who had now switched position from the NGO Fair Elections, which was responsible for the important parallel count in 2003, to the position as head of the Central Election Committee, claimed that this was because of the large number of 'dead souls' in the 2003 registers.

Nevertheless, if official figures indicating a total population of more than 4.5 million were true, there should have been at least 3 million adults entitled to vote. Not surprisingly quarrels about voter registration did not end in November 2003, but were to haunt Georgian elections for years. The somewhat ironical outcome of what was supposed to be the first completely fair and democratic election in the history of Georgia was that Saakashvili won with figures that recalled Soviet 'elections'. In an election with high participation, 86 per cent of registered voters (albeit a significantly lower percentage of the population of voting age), Saakashvili received 96.27 per cent of the votes; second came a certain Temur Shashiashvili with 1.85 per cent.

I followed the presidential election in the eastern province of Kakheti. When Mikheil Saakashvili early in the evening of January 4, 2004, celebrated his victory with a press conference in Tbilisi where he spoke in Georgian, Russian, English and French, I was still observing the counting of votes in the little snowy village of Gombori. While sipping local wine and chewing *gozinaki* (cakes of nuts and honey) and *churchkhelas* ('sausages' made of nuts, wrapped up in grape skin), I was listening to a tedious speech by a self-appointed *tameda* (toastmaster). There was a cosy atmosphere in the polling station, light years from the squabbling and quarrelsomeness and disunity during the election of November 2, 2003. Then nothing had been offered to me by the Georgian functionaries.

In Gombori, beside their native Georgian, people spoke only Russian. Everybody knew that electricity and oil came from Russia. Despite this, almost everybody voted for the US-educated candidate who was known to be keen on Georgian membership of NATO. Out of 408 votes Saakashvili received 369. Maybe the inhabitants of Gombori had read an interview with him two days before the election in the Russian-language Georgian newspaper *Svobodnaya Gruzia* (Free Georgia), where he asserted that the Russians were the closest cousins of the Georgians and that there was no hurry to join NATO. The five competitors to Saakashvili received 14 votes together. There were 25 ballot papers initially classed as spoiled, but most of them were probably later added to the votes in favour of Saakashvili. On one of these a voter who was not satisfied to stick to the rules and simply circle Saakashvili's name had also written 'I am in favour of him.' The female chairperson of the election committee asked me for advice. I replied that this ballot would probably be accepted in Sweden because there was no doubt about the voter's intention. The same applied to all the ballot papers where voters had emphasized their wish to support Saakashvili by crossing out the other five names. The chairperson wanted to approve them, but a young man intervened. 'No, it is impossible,' he insisted. 'Our victory must be totally clean.' He introduced himself as a member of the ruling National Movement. Now he was in charge! He could afford to be steadfast on principles of justice and fairness in front of a foreign observer. He did not want to tell me how long he had been a member of the National Movement. A week, a month, a year? Saakashvili himself had been minister of justice under Shevardnadze only 27 months earlier. Everywhere the same old people had been given new roles. The revolution had not always meant a change of personnel, only a change of labels.

I encountered enormous hope in the polling station in Gombori. What took place there was of course no real election, although there was no fraud. It was a hugely popular party, a festival for the hope of change. 'I earn 30 lari [€9]', said the toastmaster. 'That is too little to make a living.' Yes it was, just as it was not enough for the million pensioners to live on about €5 a month. Saakashvili had promised double, but the state coffers were empty. I could not help making a little speech in honour of the Georgians. 'I have been in Georgia many times. You have a secret that I still do not understand. You earn 10, 20, 30 lari. That is not enough to survive on. Nevertheless, you do survive and even thrive and offer a foreigner wine and *gozinaki*! Please, teach me how to live without money.' Everybody roared with laughter. The loudest laughter came from the young women who were in charge of administrating the election and did look not at all like peasant women, but were dressed in the same way as the women in Tbilisi. Life in Georgia went on. 'If he does not keep his promises he will share the fate of Shevardnadze,' shouted the toastmaster menacingly. 'Then we will replace him!' But nobody would have guessed that only a few years later demands to replace Saakashvili would be heard from growing street choruses all over Georgia.

THE BRAIN OF THE REVOLUTION

The day after the presidential election I met with 'the brain' of the Revolution, as some observers had started to call Zurab Zhvania, the de facto prime minister, in his office in the government building in central Tbilisi. Zurab was relaxed, but seemed worn out and tired, although he admitted that he had allowed himself to sleep enough for the first time in a very long period. However, he smoked a lot and probably did not exercise at all. He smiled mildly when I reminded him that some people, including some of his old collaborators in the Green Party, wondered how his democratic credibility could be trusted since he had collaborated closely with Shevardnadze for almost a decade and been his unofficial crown prince for quite some time. He replied that he was not ashamed of that period. Georgia had been torn to pieces by civil war when Shevardnadze was brought back home in 1992. Then there was no better alternative. He added:

> However, I am probably the only politician in the former USSR, who voluntarily has left such a high position of power as I did in the autumn of 2001, since Shevardnadze had refused to act with strength against corruption and, furthermore, sent his security forces to harass the free television station Rustavi 2.

It is true that Zurab Zhvania then took a step into the unknown. He was very close to ending up in the dustbin of history. However, he managed to make a comeback. He interrupted our chat because of a telephone call from Nino Burjanadze, who would remain as interim president until the inauguration of Saakashvili on January 25. 'We are preparing a rapid change of the constitution in order to create a position of prime minister, a real head of government,' he told me. I recalled having heard from an EU official that Saakashvili would probably prefer to stick with the existing situation, since in this construction the president was head of government, not the 'state minister', who was nothing but a coordinator under the president. I asked, 'But will Saakashvili accept such a position now when he has been elected by more than 96 per cent of the votes? Why would he refrain from being almost as powerful as an American president?' Zurab smiled again, and asserted that 'Misha' would keep all agreements about the distribution of power within the triumvirate of leaders. I believed him. It would of course be stupid of Saakashvili to transform Zhvania from a loyal supporter and collaborator to a bitter adversary. 'We will not split up,' Zurab emphasized:

> We must not deceive people, not run away from the responsibility. Now we have a unique opportunity when the Georgians are united and we are free to do almost whatever we like. We receive a large number of proposals. The worst swindlers will be put on trial. However, not Shevardnadze personally. He still lives in the presidential palace and has 25 bodyguards. We want him to remain in Georgia. It proves that Georgia is a democracy, that a former president is neither dead, nor refugee in exile, nor prisoner, but is able to be a normal, free citizen.

An interesting detail, maybe symptomatic of the nonviolent character of the Rose Revolution and the fact that the principal adversaries had been close collaborators only a short time earlier, was that Saakashvili was also living in the presidential complex, for the sake of security. This caused a flood of jokes about how 'Misha' and 'Shevy' met in the corridors in the middle of the night for sentimental chats about old times. Nevertheless, it was no joke but probably true that Shevardnadze, when asked if he had voted for Saakashvili as president, replied, 'That is close to the truth.'

Zurab told me he was worried because of the absence of what he considered any real political opposition. He took neither Labour nor his own old friends in the Greens seriously. My impression was that there was some honest uneasiness in Zurab's worry that the new regime might appear to be a one-party regime. At the same time he was not prepared to lower the barrier at the upcoming parliamentary election from 7 to 5 per cent, as representatives of European institutions had proposed. He was not free of 'revolutionary' zeal and the temptation to exploit a situation of almost total power to get things moving fast, without having to cope with an irresponsible opposition.

I could not help asking Zurab about claims that he and his colleagues were nothing but puppets in the US struggle for global dominance. 'Don't you have to cooperate with Russia, which is your neighbour and controls your access to energy and your breakaway provinces?' Zurab protested with indignation. 'We are aware of the importance of Russia. Nevertheless, we want to approach Europe, even become members of the European Union. However, NATO is not urgent, I have just talked to Misha and agreed that we should keep a low profile on that.' Was he serious? Was there a difference between Zhvania and Saakashvili concerning NATO? Not in principle, but perhaps in intensity.

On another point he confirmed a piece of information I had had difficulty believing, that the salaries of the new government were being paid by the multibillionaire George Soros. He emphasized that formally it was a fund including contributions from other sources, such as the UNDP. Nevertheless, it was correct that the West paid the salaries of the Georgian ministers! The argument he gave was that earlier a salary for a minister had been 200 lari (about €80). That was too little, and it forced ministers to make some additional income on the side, or even take bribes. Now, the West paid them some 2,000 lari plus US$1,000, which was quite enough to live on a 'ministerial level' in a country where the monthly salary of a university professor was no more than 100 lari. According to Zurab this system had given Georgia its first non-corrupt government in ages. Sometimes a good end is allowed to justify extremely untraditional means.

TOWARDS ONE-PARTY DEMOCRACY?

On March 26, 2004, two days before the partial rerun of the annulled parliamentary election of November 2, 2003, Prime Minister Zhvania told EU observers that he wanted the opposition to be represented in parliament, but that a reduction of the 7 per cent barrier would need a constitutional change. He regretted that the issue had only been raised recently, which was not correct. I had myself brought up the matter with him that January, and European representatives had long since warned that the 7 per cent barrier might produce a one-party parliament. This almost came true. According to preliminary results only the ruling National Movement, with which the United Democrats of Zhvania and Burjanadze had merged to form one united ruling party, seemed to have received enough votes to obtain representation.

This outcome caused considerable consternation. Matyas Eosi of the Council of Europe stated that even if a one-party parliament reflected the will of the voters, it 'cannot reflect the wide diversity of views indispensable for meaningful debates on Georgia's future'.

Nino Burjanadze, who had resumed her position as speaker of parliament, blamed the opposition for having 'equivocated' and 'failed to unite'.

When the official result was published on April 18, it emerged that Georgia would not after all go down in history as the first one-party democracy. The New Rights/Industrialists received 7.96 per cent of the votes, and got representation, while the Labour Party only received 6.01 per cent and was left outside the Parliament. In addition it was emphasized that the opposition would be strengthened by some of the MPs who had been elected on November 2 according to the majority system, a result that had not been annulled. The day before the election Gela Danelia, the representative of the Labour Party, had predicted in front of the European observers that his party would not be allowed representation in the new parliament. He blamed this on 'massive fraud' and threatened 'a further revolution if this did take place'. When his forecast came true Labour representatives promised to file complaints to every possible international institution, but nobody in the West was prepared to take Labour's accusations seriously. Only several years later would some Western observers begin to understand that the takeover from Shevardnadze by some of his closest collaborators did not change Georgian society as deeply and rapidly as had been taken for granted.

RECONCILIATION WITH RUSSIA?

In fact, while the new regime continued and escalated the rapprochement with the West, some friendly gestures were also made towards Russia. Saakashvili symbolically made his first visit abroad as president to Moscow, and Zhvania was one of very few state leaders apart from Russia's closest allies who welcomed the outcome of the Duma elections in December 2003.[12] In the spring of 2004 President Saakashvili proposed an oil pipeline from Russia via Georgia to the Mediterranean. He also offered Russia joint border supervision between Georgia and Chechnya. The Russians replied by alluding to the possibility of easing the visa requirements for Georgians.[13] Putin praised the Georgian leadership and promised to respect the territorial integrity of Georgia.[14] Russia was helpful in deposing the autocrat of Adjara in the spring of 2004, and it also, in an agreement on May 30, 2005, agreed to withdraw from the remaining military bases by 2008.

An almost immediate economic effect of the regime change was an increase in money transfers from Georgians abroad, which grew by US$37 million. A considerable part of these transfers came from representatives of the old regime who had emigrated and sent money back to their relatives. Many sought refuge in Russia, which caused money transfers from Russia to increase by 40 per cent, making up a total of 38 per cent of all money transfers into the country. Thus, paradoxically, Georgia's economic dependence on Russia increased.[15]

In other ways too Russian involvement in the Georgian economy grew considerably after the regime change. According to Vladimer Papava, 'the new Georgian government fully supported the entry of Russian capital into the Georgian economy during the broad-scale privatization of government-owned enterprises following the Rose Revolution'. One example was the takeover of the United Georgian Bank by the Russian state-owned Vneshtorgbank.[16]

DETERIORATING RELATIONS WITH RUSSIA

If Georgia's political relations with Russia could be described as somewhat ambiguous during the first part of 2004, they started to deteriorate after the summer. On September 1, a school in Beslan, North Ossetia, was attacked and seized by a group of Chechen fighters who took the schoolchildren as hostages. When the drama was over two days later, not only had all the aggressors but one been killed, 334 civilians, 186 of them children, were also dead. Although it was obvious that (apart from the hostage-takers) those who were responsible for the catastrophic outcome and the slaughter of all the children were the hard-line and incompetent Russian authorities, some Russian military and political groups tried to blame Georgia, hinting that Georgia had intended to take revenge for the loss of its own South Ossetia by supporting an attack in North Ossetia.

When I met Zurab Zhvania in the autumn of 2004 he was unimpressed and calm, and asserted that he did not believe there would be Russian military action against Georgia. He regretted, though, that Russia found it so difficult to refrain from acting like an imperialist superpower, and wondered why Russia did not see the link between separatism in Georgia and the same phenomenon in Russia. He recalled that Shamil Basayev, who claimed responsibility for the Beslan outrage, had been fighting against Georgia in Abkhazia in 1993, which according to Zurab was practically tantamount to fighting on the side of Russia. That meant that Russia had fed a snake at its breast. He compared this to the fact that the United States had sponsored Usama bin Laden to wage war against Soviet troops in Afghanistan. 'Why don't superpowers learn from their mistakes?' he sighed.

The minister of defence, Georgi Baramidze, who was like Zurab a former Green activist, was also calm when I met him in the Ministry, which still had as its neighbour the Russian military headquarters for South Caucasus. However, he told me about several planned measures which indicated military rearmament, partly with US support. So was Georgia aligning itself with the West after all? On the same day as I met with Zurab, an English-language newspaper in Tbilisi published an editorial on the recently terminated CIS summit meeting in Astana, which claimed that it was time for Georgia to make a choice – either to deepen the cooperation with Russia and scrap all plans for membership of the European Union and NATO, or to leave the CIS.[17] 'That is the most stupid thing I have heard,' commented Zurab when I related this proposal to him. 'Russia is a very troublesome neighbour, but it is our neighbour. We have no choice but peaceful cooperation – with all sides.'

THE END OF THE HONEYMOON

Around the time of the first anniversary of the Rose Revolution more and more worrying reports and critical statements indicated that the honeymoon was approaching its end. The Caucasus Reporting Service reported that 'growing numbers of NGOs and parliamentarians, including some previous close to Saakashvili and his revolutionary team, have accused the government of back-pedalling on democratic values and of bending the law in pursuit of alleged corruption suspects'.[18] A businessperson, who had not paid taxes for years would be dramatically arrested in the middle of the night by masked Special Forces, the whole drama being transmitted live on major television channels. They would be locked up for a few weeks or months, then released in exchange for a suitable amount of dollars paid to the state cashier. The whole procedure was totally lacking in normal legal process.

According to Papava these procedures were not only illegal, they also created possibilities for a new type of corruption, through the extra-budgetary accounts, outside public scrutiny, which were replenished through 'voluntary contributions' by businesses under the threat of otherwise being punished for tax evasion. 'If pre-revolution functionaries had pockets open for bribes, their successors – who may have closed pockets – certainly have open bank accounts.'[19]

A report from the Human Rights Information Centre (HRIC), called 'Human Rights in Georgia after the Rose Revolution', admitted that the untraditional methods of the government had resulted in increased tax revenues, regular payment of salaries and pensions, and improvement in public services.[20] Nevertheless, the continuous contravention of human rights had created a situation that could best be described as 'an atmosphere of fear'. The report also criticized the constitutional changes which had increased the power of the president, giving him the authority to dissolve parliament and to appoint judges. One specific accusation was that during a television transmission after a riot among prisoners, the president had urged the police to 'shoot in order to kill and to destroy every criminal who is making trouble'. Freedom of assembly had been restricted, the report asserted, and it mentioned as proof a new rule against street vending in Tbilisi, which had caused an animated debate. Even the freedom of the press had been restrained: Reporters Sans Frontières had (according to the HRIC report) reduced Georgia's rating for the freedom of its mass media from 74th to 94th place (out of 167 countries).

A kind of acknowledgement of these problems could be found in a report by the Embassy of Georgia in Brussels to the European Parliament delegation for South Caucasus, where the existence of 'serious difficulties' concerning human rights was admitted.[21] The Embassy recalled that the president of Georgia in 2002 (Shevardnadze) had proclaimed Georgia to be a 'zone free of torture'. 'Now it is time to implement that statement.' Nevertheless, the Embassy was proud of the anti-corruption campaign. Over 20 officials of the old regime had been apprehended and forced to pay back what they owed the state, in all 45 million lari (some €20 million).

The economic stagnation was still serious. It was true that the GNP growth was around 10 per cent, but industrial production remained very low. In that respect in 2004 Georgia was only number nine among former Soviet republics (excluding the Baltic countries), behind Belarus, Tajikistan and Moldova, which were not usually regarded as forerunners in this respect.[22] Half the population was estimated to be living below the poverty line (which was fixed at 110 lari – about €45 – a month).

Great hopes were attached to the BTC pipeline, the construction of which had started in the spring of 2003. Employment during the construction phase and fees from users of the completed transport route were expected to boost the economy. However, some possibly negative aspects and hazards were observed by ecological movements. One problem that caused concern was its route through the National Park of Borjomi, which contained the sources of the famous Borjomi mineral water, appreciated all over the former Soviet Union. The presence of an oil pipeline in the vicinity of the wells was not considered to be very good publicity. A London-based campaigning organization claimed that the pipes, which were to be buried in the soil, would rust and dissolve, which might lead to hazardous subterranean emissions. The campaign maintained that the BTC might lead to 'serious crimes against humanity, eruption of regional conflicts, and poor people's loss of income and life environment'.[23]

Just before the end of 2004 the government was reshuffled. Most attention was paid to the transfer of the minister of internal affairs, Irakli Okruashvili, to the post of minister of defence, and the creation of a new post for the former minister of the economy, Kakha Bendukidze, who became minister for coordination of economic and administrative reforms. Restoration of territorial integrity, reinforcement of the military forces and cutting down heavy bureaucracy were proclaimed as major goals of the new government..

Both the United States and Turkey were presumed to be assisting in Georgian rearmament. According to the outgoing minister of defence, Gia Baramidze, military support from the United States would reach US$60 million. Georgia also announced an increase in its presence in Iraq, which would make the Georgian contingent number 8, compared with number 28 out of 34 in 2004. It was declared that the military build-up was intended to strengthen the Georgian power of resistance against Russian pressure, and to prepare Georgia for an entry into NATO.

Around and immediately after the first anniversary of the Rose Revolution it was obvious that the regime was growing impatient with the stagnation in several fields of action, especially the restoration of territorial integrity. Many signs indicated that the hawkish trend in the regime had been reinforced, and that the choice was being made to seek a closer alliance with the United States in order to reach a strength that would allow some kind of forceful activity, in order to get back Abkhazia and South Ossetia. It was a risky game at a time when the real, material dependence on Russia for energy, export and investments was still huge. At the same time disapproval of the situation was growing, and reports such as the one cited above, with critical observations and remarks, were starting to appear from all kinds of international watchdogs. One year after the Rose

Revolution a Georgian political scientist working in France summarized the mood in Georgia: 'Almost one third of the electorate is not satisfied with Saakashvili, but does not see any other alternative.'[24]

NOTES

1 Bruno Coppetier and Robert Legvold (eds), *Statehood and Security: Georgia after the Rose Revolution*, MIT Press, London, 2005, p. 3.

2 Gaidz Minassian, *Caucase du Sud, la nouvelle guerrre froide* (South Caucasus, the new cold war), Éditions Autrement, Paris, 2007.

3 Vladimer Papava, 'Georgia's hollow revolution: does Georgia's pro-Western and Anti-Russian policy amount to democracy?' *Harvard International Review*, 2008.

4 Ghia Nodia, *Nations in Transit 2005: Georgia*, Freedom House, 2005, p. 1.

5 Pamela Jawad, *Diversity, Conflict, and State Failure: Chances and challenges for democratic consolidation in Georgia after the 'Rose Revolution'*, Cornell University Peace Studies Program, Occasional Paper no. 30-3, December 2006.

6 Silke Kleinhanss, *Die Aussenpolitik Georgiens – Ein failing state zwischen internem Teilversagen und externen Chancen* (The foreign policy of Georgia – a failing state between internal part failure and external possibilities), LIT Verlag, Münster, 2008.

7 *International Herald Tribune*, December 8, 2004.

8 *Izvestia*, January 26, 2005.

9 Lincoln A. Mitchell, *Uncertain Democracy*, University of Pennsylvania Press, Pittsburgh, 2009.

10 European Parliament report on the 2004 presidential election, DV/5360EN.doc.

11 Sandra Elizabeth Roelofs, *Die first lady of Georgië, het verhal van een idealiste* (The first lady of Georgia, the story of an idealist), Archipel, Amsterdam, 2005, p. 264.

12 *Svobodnaya Gruzia*, December 8, 2003.

13 Russia's consul in Tbilisi, *Svobodnaya Gruzia*, March 30, 2004.

14 *Svobodnaya Gruzia*, March 31, 2004.

15 Vladimer Papava, 'The Baku–Tbilisi–Ceyhan pipeline: implications for Georgia', in S. Frederick Starr and Svante E. Cornell (eds), *The Baku–Tbilisi–Ceyhan Pipeline*, Central Asia-Caucasus Institute and Silk Road Studies Program, Johns Hopkins University, Baltimore, Md., 2005 <www.silkroadstudies.org>.

16 Vladimer Papava, 'The essence of economic reforms in post-revolutionary Georgia: What about the European choice?' *Georgian International Journal of Science and Technology*, vol, 1, issue 1, pp. 1–9, 2008.

17 *Georgian Messenger*, September 17, 2004.

18 By Sebastian Smith in Tbilisi, *Caucasus Reporting Service*, no. 263, November 25, 2004.

19 Papava, 'Georgia's hollow revolution'.

20 December 14, 2004, <www.ecoi.net>.
21 Report by the Embassy of Georgia to the European Parliament, October 6, 2004.
22 *Svobodnaya Gruzia*, December 29, 2004.
23 <www.bakuceyhan.org.uk>.
24 Thornike Gordadze, interview with Célia Chauffour, *Caucaz Europenews*, November 22, 2004, <www.caucas.com>.

10

THE DEATH OF ZHVANIA – THE REVOLUTION LOSES ITS BRAIN

In the morning of February 3, 2005 I received an SMS from my friend Nato Kirvalidze, with the short and blunt message: 'Z dead'. My immediate thought was that Zurab had been assassinated. I called back, and Nato confirmed that Zurab Zhvania, the prime minister and our friend, was dead. However, the information she could give was far from unambiguous. She said that the government had already declared that Zurab and a political collaborator, the vice governor of Kvemo Kartli province, Raul Usupov, had been poisoned by carbon monoxide from a defective Iranian-made heater, while they were having a late supper together.

Nevertheless, unanswered questions began to pile up during the first hours after the prime minister's bodyguards found the two corpses. Today that situation has not changed, despite the publication of several Georgian and international reports. Almost all the Georgians I have asked, including Zurab's wife, mother and brother, are convinced that he was assassinated. However, there is no clear, unanimous or credible explanation of who could be responsible or how the killings were perpetrated. There are considerably more questions than answers.

A GREEN REALIST

Zurab Zhvania was born on December 9, 1963, in Tbilisi. His mother had a Jewish mother and an Armenian father, so he had a considerable portion of the multi-ethnicity of Georgia in his genes and social background, something that ought to be a major asset in any modern multi-ethnic society. However, during his two years outside the power elite, from late 2001 until the Rose Revolution, he was repeatedly attacked in public for this reason. His Armenian ancestry was especially exploited in more or less racist terms by the last minister of the interior of the Shevardnadze era, Kakha Targama-dze. Zhvania took his academic exam at the Faculty of Biology in Tbilisi in 1985, and worked there as a teacher until he was elected a member of parliament in 1992. In the 1980s he became active in the growing ecological movement, which developed all over the Soviet Union under the relatively liberal conditions of the Gorbachev period.

A crucial role in this process was played by the struggle against the Caucasian Railway project. The only railway connections between Russia and the South Caucasus were (and still are) one line along the coast of the Black Sea and another along the coast of the Caspian Sea. For a long time there had been vague plans to construct a railway somewhere in the middle of the Caucasus mountain range, directly from Tbilisi to Russia. In 1974 Kavgiprotrans, a subsidiary of the Soviet Ministry of Transport Construction, was ordered to explore the idea, and made a pilot plan, which was approved by the Soviet government in 1984. The project was for a double-track railway, 188 kilometres in length, to be constructed from Tbilisi, along the Aragvi river northwards, through 15 tunnels and 85 bridges, into North Ossetia. The government presented the project as important to the economic development of Georgia and the other South Caucasus republics, but growing numbers of opponents doubted the benefits

Zurab Zhvania founded the Green Party, then became Shevardnadze's designated successor, but he changed parties in 2001 and was one of the leaders of the Rose Revolution in 2003. Here (second left) with the author (right) and other Green MEPs in 2000.

and began to list all the possible hazards and perils. They presented environmental, demographic and economic objections, and referred to the lack of transparency during the decision process. They highlighted threats to fauna and flora, increased erosion, disturbance of the local microclimate and pollution of the water supply. There was also concern that dozens of historical monuments and archaeological sites might be damaged. In 1987 the debate escalated, and in June some 800 well-known writers and intellectuals signed a petition, complaining about the lack of *glasnost* during the decision-making process. On August 29 a consultative committee recommended further investigations before a final decision. A moratorium on the project was immediately imposed. Since then the project has been dead.[1] According to later accounts by Zhvania, experience from the struggle against the Caucasian Railway project was a vital factor that brought him to launch a Green Party in Georgia.

The first time I met Zurab Zhvania was at a conference for Green Parliamentarians in Stockholm in January 1990. He came from a distant and unknown country, and told us that he had established a Green Party – in the Soviet Union. We thought that was impossible, but Zurab had made it! He was member of the Secretariat of the Coordination of European Greens from 1989 to 1993. The Georgian Greens contested the first multi-party election in Georgia on October 28, 1990, but did not manage to win any seats.

Later, in the beginning of 1992, when Gamsakhurdia had been toppled and Georgia was ruled by a military junta, Zhvania was active in luring Shevardnadze back to Georgia. He once told me that he 'brought Shevardnadze back as the only solution to save the country from either chaos or dictatorship'. However, Shevardnadze does not mention Zhvania in this respect in his memoirs. According to Shevardnadze he was approached in Moscow by three other personalities: Otar Litanishvili, a painter who was the mayor of Tbilisi in 1992–93; Ramaz Chkhikvadze, a famous actor from the Rustaveli Theatre; and Irakli Batiashvili, who was the head of the Georgian Secret Service in 1992–93, and later a member of parliament. One reason that Shevardnadze did not mention Zhvania might of course be the disappointment he felt when Zhvania, despite having become regarded as his chosen successor, defected to the opposition in 2001. Or did Zhvania exaggerate his importance in bringing Shevardnadze back? I turned to Nato Kirvalidze, one of Zhvania's closest collaborators of that time, and received the following reply:

In early 1992, when Zurab and David Berdzenishvili (and I) had visited the European Parliament in Strasbourg, on our way back home we stopped in Moscow for some days. Zurab went several times to see Shevardnadze. After some time, during an argument between Zurab and David, which I witnessed, David was saying that now he knew why Zurab was visiting Shevardnadze, accusing him of trying to convince Shevardnadze to return to Georgia. Thus, I can confirm that Zurab visited Shevardnadze in Moscow in 1992, though of course I do not know for sure what they talked about, except David's guess later.

My conclusion is that Zhvania did in fact play a major role in bringing Shevardnadze back to Georgia. This fits very well with his pragmatic approach to politics, which did not mean that he was not sincere in his basic convictions. In fact he always remained identified as Green, although he left the Georgian Greens in 1993 to head Shevardnadze's new ruling party, the Citizens Union of Georgia (CUG). A decade later, he wrote in a booklet about the first 20 years of the European Greens:

> Having served as Chairman of the Parliament for six years and now as the leader of the opposition, I came to know and be acquainted with many different political families, organizations and leaders. However, I cannot but say that my most sincere and trusted friends remain those very people of the Green Group in the European Parliament and the Green Federation.[2]

It was typical that when he was invited to make one of the keynote speeches at the Congress of the European Greens in Rome in the spring of 2004, he chose to make what most listeners qualified as a genuinely green outline of priorities, compared with the possibly better known participant, the German minister of foreign affairs, Joschka Fischer, who delivered a more conventional speech without clear green highlights. I heard many rank and file Greens comment that it was 'paradoxical' that a formally no-more-green prime minister of a small former Soviet republic touched deep green feelings more convincingly than the leader of the most powerful Green Party in the world.

In the elections in October 1992, the Georgian Greens won eleven seats and formed a Green Group, which was joined by one independent MP. The election of October 1992 was technically unique because it was based on the preference principle (after the Irish model). This system was advocated by Zhvania, who even invited an Irish expert on consensus and preference voting systems to Georgia. The success of the Greens in 1992 was partly due to this election system, as they got most of the second and third-choice votes. Maybe the Green success was one reason that the system was later abolished.

The next time I saw Zurab was in 1993 in Georgia. The country was on the verge of collapse. He took me from Tbilisi to Kutaisi, which I have described in Chapter 7. Here I only want to make a brief addition, relevant for what it shows of Zurab's personality. At one point during the stay in Kutaisi I was introduced to 17 generals from the government troops that were supposed to mobilize against Gamsakhurdia's forces. 'And how many soldiers do you have?' I asked. The answer was: 'Maybe 50.' Zurab liked to tell this story over and over again. He saw the absurd numerical relation between generals and soldiers as symbolic of Georgia at that time.

After the parliamentary election of 1995 Zhvania became the speaker of the parliament, a position he retained until his resignation in November 2001. After I became the European Parliament rapporteur for South Caucasus in 1999 I met with him once or twice a year. In June 2002 Zhvania officially announced his departure from the ruling CUG, and on June 6 he established a new parliamentary group, the Democrats. On June 17 he became the leader of a new political party, United Democrats, which stood for the parliamentary elections of November 2, 2003 under the label 'Burjanadze Democrats'. After the Rose Revolution he first became state minister, then after an amendment to the constitution, on February 17, 2004 he was appointed prime minister.

ZURAB AS POLITICAL PSYCHOTHERAPIST

Of all the meetings and encounters I had with Zurab Zhvania, a visit to Adjara in his company in March 2004 stands out as the most thrilling but also the most instructive. Zurab emerged as a fully fledged political psychotherapist. Had the way he handled the autocratic leader of the province, Aslan Abashidze, been elevated to a general rule for Tbilisi in handling its recalcitrant provinces, the situation in the country might have been very different.

Adjara, in the far southwest of Georgia, bordering on Turkey, was for a long time a part of the Ottoman empire, until it was conquered by Russia in 1878. Since the treaty of Kars in 1921 between Turkey and the USSR the region has been an autonomous republic of

Georgia. Most of the 420,000 inhabitants are ethnic Georgians, and Muslims. Adjara never tried to formally secede from Georgia, but its ruler at this time, Aslan Abashidze, behaved like a sovereign feudal prince, refusing to pay taxes to the central government and keeping his own militia. Adjara was for most practical purposes outside the control of Tbilisi. However, Abashidze always participated in the Georgian power struggle, through a political party and a television station. These instruments were most often used to support Shevardnadze, in exchange for Abashidze being left free to act in his own fief. After his re-election as president in 2000, with the support of Abashidze, Shevardnadze visited Batumi, the capital of Adjara, together with Zhvania, and granted Adjara status as an economic free zone. In connection with the Kodori crisis in the autumn 2001 Shevardnadze again visited Batumi, which caused a rumour that Abashidze would be appointed prime minister. However, instead he was made negotiator between Georgia and Abkhazia, a task which he did not succeed in bringing to a successful conclusion. This may have been the first step towards his political demise.[3] Nevertheless, the major blow to his position was of course the Rose Revolution. When the new president, Mikheil Saakashvili, wanted to visit Adjara on March 15, 2004, but was denied entry, the Georgian government imposed an economic blockade.

Only two weeks later I was in Georgia as an EU observer of the parliamentary elections. In the early morning of the election day, March 28, I was preparing to go to Gori to observe some polling stations, when I received a call from Zurab Zhvania, who asked me to accompany him instead to Adjara. An hour later I was in a small airplane together with Zhvania and six of his closest colleagues.[4] After an hour's flight we landed in Poti and continued by cars towards Adjara, at the border of which we passed a checkpoint at full speed without any reaction by the heavily armed guards. Some distance into the region we were met by an elderly representative of the regional government, Vakhtang Abashidze, a relative of the ruler. During the whole day our cars moved around in Adjara and stopped outside polling stations. People gathered, at first dumbfounded to see Zhvania, but later obviously having been informed that he was there by the radio and television. They asked questions, mostly about practical matters such as agriculture, prices and taxes. After initial hesitation, the reactions grew more openly approving, even cheerful. There was clearly an appreciation of the interest shown by the central government. In my capacity as official election observer I was able to make brief visits to polling stations, where I was assured by representatives of parties and NGOs that the procedures were correct and smooth.

Nevertheless, Zhvania was not convinced. 'The difficulty will come when the polling stations are closing and exit polls show that Abashidze is losing. Then he might send his thugs to crush the ballot boxes and set fire to the polling stations,' he warned. To anticipate such events he made an appointment with Abashidze in the afternoon. We arrived at his palace, where I stayed in a huge hall while Zhvania and Abashidze disappeared. Giorgi Abashidze, the 30-year-old son of the feudal ruler, who had been made mayor of Batumi by his father, strolled by in jogging shoes, loosely fluttering trousers, a black T-shirt, a silly smile on his lips and a general appearance which brought to mind rumours about his drug addiction. He complained that he had not been allowed to vote when he had arrived at a polling station because he had had no ID card that indicated his domicile. I was left waiting together with Vakhtang Abashidze for hours for Aslan and Zurab. Vakhtang was big and heavy, and was sweating floods. He murmured, 'Allegations that we would threaten anybody is just rubbish, we would only do damage to ourselves.'

Finally Abashidze and Zhvania appeared and I said *dozvidanye* (farewell). But it was too early: we were invited for dinner. It was rather chaotic. Zurab was talking on his mobile all the time. Aslan discovered that I could communicate in Russian and started a long lament, accusing the Tbilisi regime of having sent *spetsnaz* (commando) troops to kill him. He was absolutely no mafia leader, despite his son-in-law being an Italian! The Tbilisi government had sent disguised policemen who were attacking his television station Iberia! His *gangabeli* (local administrators) were calling and complained about provocations by members of the National Movement! The Tbilisi government wanted to eradicate all opposition! Adjara had always defended itself, even against the Persians! 'Why should I invite all these NGO people and observers if I wanted to provoke?'

Suddenly a piece of paper was delivered to the dinner table. It quoted an assertion by the director of the Central Election Committee that the election in Adjara was characterized by fraud. Aslan flew up. Zurab was irritated too. He had not been given any such information by his representatives in Adjara. He denied the CEC allegation to the media. At 8 pm both Aslan and Zurab left the palace and held an improvised press conference in the street. The polling stations had closed, and no great trouble had erupted. We left and headed for the home of a member of the National Movement.

However, we had almost no time to take our seats at dinner before Aslan called and claimed that Georgian *spetsnaz* troops, disguised as election observers, were approaching in order to assassinate him. Zurab denied this. Nevertheless we immediately got up and drove at high speed to Abashidze's palace. Now the situation had changed: the palace was surrounded by heavily armed and masked warriors, loyal to the Adjara ruler. Aslan was agitated. We accompanied him into a large room. Aslan sat down for some minutes, then left the room and returned. Suddenly he started to show a video film. For an hour we had to watch a film about motorboats, made by his company. 'The best armed motorboats in the world,' he assured us. I asked Zurab what was the point of this. Zurab just shook his head. It was past midnight. Then Aslan showed us another video, of a children's opera in Batumi that he had financed. What did this mean? What was he trying to tell us: that he was a good guy and loved children? It was 3 am. Nothing special happened.

Aslan started to make sketches of the positions of his troops a couple of weeks earlier when there had been a crisis with Saakashvili. Suddenly he rose with a jump and pointed at the ceiling. 'Do you hear? Georgian airplanes, they are landing troops to kill me!' Zurab denied this and assured him, 'Georgia does not have any airplanes capable of night flight.' Aslan did not believe him. Zurab called the minister of defence, who confirmed this to Aslan. It was now 4 am. I began to understand that I was watching a kind of therapy. The aim was to keep Aslan calm until the votes were counted. At 5 am Aslan and Zurab went outdoors to meet the media once more. I asked some journalists who had been in the street during the night if they had heard any airplanes. The reply was, absolutely not. There had been no sound in the sky during the whole night.

We left Batumi at 6 am and drove the 400 kilometres to Tbilisi in seven hours. Later I noticed from the election results that Abashidze's Revival party had not reached the 7 per cent barrier. Nevertheless, in Adjara Revival had been the largest party, with 51 per cent against 43 per cent for the ruling National Movement. However, Abashidze usually got 99 per cent in Adjara. Some kind of change was in the pipeline. The Tbilisi government issued an ultimatum demanding that Abashidze disarm his private militia and submit to the central administration. Abashidze replied by announcing a regional state of emergency on May 2, and blew up the three main bridges linking Adjara to the rest of Georgia. Russia, however, did not support Abashidze, but mediated a solution which entailed the emigration of Abashidze and his clan to Moscow, and the reintegration of Adjara into Georgia, albeit with the continued status of autonomy. The regional election after the departure of the Abashidze clan was a landslide victory for the National Movement, which won 28 of the 30 seats. Revival ceased to exist.

WAS ZHVANIA ASSASSINATED?

In principle the official theory of the cause of Zhvania's death is far from unlikely. The permanent energy crisis had contributed to the creation of a large market for all kinds of temporary heating devices, more often than not of doubtful technical quality. During the year preceding the death of Zhvania several dozen lethal accidents with gas heaters were reported from all over Georgia. At the same time, however, murder was not an uncommon cause of death among Caucasian politicians. In October 1999 the prime minister of Armenia was killed together with seven other high-ranking politicians during a shoot-out in the Armenian parliament. Edward Shevardnadze was the subject of three major assassination attempts during his period as the president of Georgia. Zhvania had made numerous enemies during his twelve years at the top level of Georgian politics, especially since the Rose Revolution. Among possible perpetrators the grapevine mentioned supporters of the deposed Adjara autocrat Abashidze, businessmen who had been ruined by the tough anti-corruption measures, and former state officials who had lost their jobs during the purges against bribe taking and red-tape bureaucracy. Some mentioned people who had belonged to the power elite during the Shevardnadze period and had now been reduced to unpersons or even been forced to emigrate. Others speculated about the involvement of foreign intelligence services: most often Russian, Abkhazian or South Ossetian, but Western agencies were also mentioned. Sometimes even his competitors among the leaders of the Rose Revolution, most often Mikheil Saakashvili, were indicated as possible organizers of the killing.

Pictures from the flat on Saburtalo Street where Zhvania and Usupov were found showed a bottle of cognac and a backgammon board. This indicated that the two friends had had a late-night supper together, which triggered gossip about the nature of their relationship. This has been vehemently refuted by everybody who knew Zurab personally.[5] Several critics, among them Zurab's brother, claim that the scene was a set-up: the bodies were brought to the flat from elsewhere, maybe with the deliberate purpose of tarnishing the

A poster used by the opposition during the election campaign of May 2008, saying, 'Zvhania is dead, everything is possible'. Most Georgians believe that the premature and mysterious death of Zhvania has had negative repercussions for their country.

memory of the victims. Usupov's father claimed that his son did not rent that flat. One piece of information to support the argument that the dead men had not spent the night in the apartment was that none of their fingerprints was detected there.

The prime minister's bodyguards made contradictory and ambiguous statements. Some of the claims about mobile telephone calls do not fit with cellphone company logs. Other alleged discrepancies include the official claim that when the bodyguards arrived to check why Zhvania was not answering calls on his mobile, they pushed opened a window – but it was later found to be bolted, and could not be opened with a simple push. On the other hand, had the window been open from the beginning, there would not have been a lethal build-up of carbon monoxide in the flat. According to a journalist from Mze TV, only a few hours after Zhvania's death the minister of internal affairs, Vano Merabishvili, claimed that it was thought to be gas poisoning because those arriving at the flat had smelled gas. When he was reminded that carbon monoxide has neither smell nor colour, and can only be detected using technical devices, the interview was cancelled and the tape confiscated. The way the autopsy was carried out also led to critical questions; and information from the gas company that the gas supply to the flat had been cut off at the time makes the death appear even more mysterious.

A technical report by a team from the FBI led to much argument in Georgia.[6] While I have written on my copy 'as far as I understand this implies that it was monoxide poisoning,' it is true that no such conclusion was explicitly drawn in the report. It was presented in the Georgian media as corroborating the claim that the heater could produce lethal emissions of monoxide, which stirred a lot of criticism. Officials did not gain credibility by explaining that this was an error of translation.[7]

Zhvania had used to fill ashtrays with his cigarette butts, and some were left in the flat, but they did not have the shape that was typical of Zhvania's butts. This was also mentioned as a suspicious fact. Furthermore, some slips of the tongue by prominent people also helped to enhance suspicions. President Saakashvili himself at an international scientific conference mentioned the 'assassination' of Zhvania, before he corrected himself to 'the death' of Zhvania. And when launching a Ukrainian version of her autobiography, the first lady, Sandra Roelofs, claimed that the publication had been delayed by the 'assassination' of Zhvania.[8]

Some sceptics mention the occurrence of other violent events around the time of Zhvania's death as further proof of the untrustworthiness of the official version. A French observer notes that there was an armed attack just before Zhvania's death, and several people were killed immediately afterwards, and cites rumours that Russian intelligence was involved.[9] One of Zhvania's collaborators, Georgi Shelashvili, was found to have shot himself on February 4, 2005. A short time later the medical expert who was finalizing the report on the death of Zhvania and Usupov was killed by a former classmate, who is reported to have committed suicide.

Several of these rumours and sceptical opinions and statements have been published in the Georgian media. On May 17, 2006, the weekly *Georgian Times* published a claim that Zhvania was shot by a very highly placed government official close to the president because he refused to give a group around Saakashvili part of the revenue from the sale of Poti harbour and airport. In October 2007 the opposition television channel Imedi showed a film, *Without bullets*, made by a well-known film producer, Vakhtang Komakhidze, about several of the most mysterious aspects of Zhvania's death. Imedi was owned by the finance tycoon Badri Patarkatsishvili, who stood as candidate for the presidency in January 2008 and died shortly afterwards. In

November 2007 the regime made an attack on Imedi and closed it down.[10]

Based on these and other rumours, discrepancies and mysterious details, it is not only ordinary people and close relatives of Zhvania and Usupov who have expressed suspicions about the official version of events; so have politicians and celebrities. One is the leader of the Labour Party, Shalva Natelashvili, who has repeatedly accused the regime of having killed Zhvania, even suggesting that the actual killing occurred in the presence of President Saakashvili, who according to Natelashvili has a 'smile of Satan' on his face.[11] On September 25, 2007, the former minister of defence, Irakli Okruashvili, asserted that he did not know whether Zhvania was assassinated, but he did know for sure that the corpses had been moved from another place to the infamous flat in Saburtalo Street. According to Irina Sarishvili-Chanturia, leader of a small opposition party, Zhvania was choked to death in one of the cars of President Saakashvili's escort.[12]

In March 2006 Edward Shevardnadze told the *Washington Post* that he did not believe the official version of the death of Zhvania, because 'he was murdered'.[13] And a couple of years later in an interview in a Georgian newspaper, Shevardnadze said, 'Zhvania should not have run into the confrontation with Targamadze.' (Targamadze was minister of internal affairs when Zhvania cut his links with the Shevardnadze regime in 2001.) Shevardnadze's account was very cryptic. There were hints that Zhvania had invited Russian businessmen who according to Targamadze were spies, and the US intelligence had got involved; and it was also implied that Zhvania believed Targamadze had tried to ensnare him in order to be able to arrest him as a spy. It is a fact that Zhvania and Targamadze had fierce public rows during the years between Zhvania's defection and the Rose Revolution. The interviewer asked, 'So if he hadn't resigned, could he have become President?' Shevardnadze replied: 'Well, might be ... at least he would have stayed alive.'[14]

In reality no serious investigation into the death of Zhvania is going on. This may be compared with the amazing news that the Georgian Parliament in November 2009 decided to establish a special commission to investigate the death in 1993 of the first president of Georgia, Zviad Gamsakhurdia – and to appoint one of his sons as its chairperson – despite the fact that almost nobody doubts that Gamsakhurdia took his own life in desperation when he understood that his case was lost (see Chapter 6).[15] In this perspective the reports that special measures will be undertaken by the administration of Tbilisi to prevent the kind of monoxide poisoning that

Zhvania is supposed to have died of about five years ago, appear as either a bad joke or the height of cynicism.[16]

REPERCUSSIONS OF THE DEATH OF ZHVANIA

In retrospect, Zhvania's death in early February 2005 seems to constitute a turning point in the modern history of Georgia. Most observers admit that with Zhvania gone, the balancing 'brain' of the Rose Revolution was gone too, and what was left was mostly the 'heart' (Saakashvili) and to a certain extent the 'face' (Nino Burjanadze, speaker of the parliament). Since Burjanadze's shift to the opposition in 2008 only the 'heart' is left at the top of the Rose Revolution regime.

Immediately after the death of Zhvania, observers warned that without his 'more conciliatory approach to the conflicts with separatists in Abkhazia and South Ossetia', the risk of violent eruptions had increased. Several commentators claimed that Zhvania had had a moderating influence on Saakashvili. 'Zhvania was very even-tempered,' said Alexander Rondeli, president of the Georgian Centre for Strategic and International Studies. 'He had the ability to find a rational solution to any problem.'[17]

During a visit to Georgia in October and November 2006 I asked everybody about their opinion of Zhvania. Salome Zurabishvili admitted that she had been against him as a former *politruk* of Shevardnadze, but now was convinced that he was also a 'genuine democrat'. Myraz Alashvili at *Svobodnaya Gruzia* said the Zhvania was the only person who could have created balance, 'alive he would have been in the opposition'. Giorgi Sapashvili of Civil Georgia considered Zhvania to be 'a soft person who solved problems softly'. Gia Gachechiladze, general secretary of the Green Party, asserted that Zhvania had been in favour of building an oil pipeline from Iran, via Armenia and Georgia to Russia, a project which was later stopped by the Americans (see Chapter 12). Gia Khukhashvili of Resonansi characterized the death of Zhvania as 'a catastrophe for the country'. Even if Zhvania was 'not an angel and did dirty things, he was a statesman and a democrat'. Khukhashvili compared the death of Zhvania with the famous *Murder on the Orient Express* by Agatha Christie: 'everybody wants to get rid of him and everybody participates'. In July 2009 former minister of economy Vladimer Papava told me that 'Zhvania was clever and he was killed.'

Another image was given by a left-wing critic, who claimed that

Zhvania 'was involved in all the privatizations' during which dubious deals typically 'took place between the hours of 2 and 3 am', a habit that had left 'potential foreign investors embittered'. Despite such ominous hints, it was admitted that 'Zhvania is regarded as a dove'.[18]

Zhvania as philosopher

During his brief period out of office from 2001 to 2003 Zhvania delivered a series of lectures to students of the Georgian Institute of Public Affairs, which were published, on the basis of his notes and taped recordings, after his death – in Georgian in 2005, and in English in 2009, with support of the Greens in the European Parliament.[19] It is a remarkable book, which gives substance to Zhvania's label as the 'brain' of the Rose Revolution. Few European politicians would be able to match the extensive and deep erudition shown in this book about European political history. He mentioned the theories and writings of philosophers like Hobbes, Locke and Montesquieu, to underpin his analysis of the prerequisites for good democracy in general, and especially in Georgia. Of special interest is his lengthy denouncement of the ethno-religious brand of Georgian nationalism which has had such devastating consequences. Over and over again he emphasizes that the minorities are not only citizens with equal rights, they constitute an integral 'part of this nation'. He praises King David the Builder for having demonstratively visited mosques and synagogues and paved the way for tolerance, and scourges contemporary Georgia for being the only 'nation that can openly burn thousands of copies of the Bible (only because they were produced not by the Georgian Church but by Baptists) and remain unpunished'. He even states that he thinks 'Georgia is an artificial concept', a statement that would make Gamsakhurdia turn in his grave.

This does not mean that he hesitates about Georgia's right to independence from Russia, but he blames the classical national movement for not having brought the minorities on board. He mentions that when Ossetians wanted to join the Georgian national movement in the 1980s they were not welcomed but treated as secret agents of the KGB. The solution to the conflicts with the breakaway regions he sees in 'regionalism', and he states that 'Abkhazia should have political autonomy, just like the Tskhinvali region.' He even recalls having proposed to the Abkhazian leader Ardzinba 'to have a two-chamber parliament and always appoint an Abkhaz the chairman of the Senate,' and to give the Abkhaz the right of veto on certain issues.

He is of course highly critical of Russian policy, as I have shown earlier in this book, and he blames the Kremlin for a lot of Georgia's problems. At the same time the United States and NATO are rarely mentioned. His grand idea is not to move Georgia from being a satellite of USSR or Russia to being the same of the United States, but to make Georgia really independent, not only politically but also economically. A major way of securing the independence in his thinking is to make Georgia important to the world, and because of the lack of oil, gas, gold or similar resources the only way to international importance he can find is to become a 'transit country'. Thus he praises Shevardnadze for having launched the concept of the Silk Road, and supports all projects for pipelines and communication routes through Georgia. However, his goal is not to punish Russia. On the contrary, he suggests that when Russia has understood that the BTS, BTC and so on are inevitable, 'we should tell Russia: You see it doesn't make sense to oppose each other. What could be your interest?' Why not propose to Russia, he says, a pipeline through Abkhazia to Novorossiysk and further? Such a project, he assumes, might console both Russians and Abkhazians. Thus, it is obvious that the thinking of Zurab Zhvania just before the Rose Revolution was rather different from the policy of Mikheil Saakashvili. Was he aware of such a difference of approach when he made his lectures? Perhaps.

A student asks why Zhvania and Saakashvili are not united. Zhvania assures that they are in fact working together. However, he also adds, 'There are tactical issues that I don't agree with him on. In general I am very cautious about the possibility of a revolutionary development, because I deeply believe that any revolution in the end yields very bad results.' Even if he hurries to deny that he is accusing Saakashvili of being a revolutionary, he cannot help admitting that his political partner 'often has such impulses'. To my mind it is obvious that Zurab was worried about what an unchecked Saakashvili could undertake. That is probably the explanation for his lengthy discussion about the need for checks and balances in any democracy. Maybe he also looked into the future when he regretted that in the Georgian constitution 'presidential power is quite inadequately balanced by the parliament'. With this background it is worth noting that less than three months before the Rose Revolution, Saakashvili at a press conference accused Zhvania of being a 'weathercock', who might very well rejoin the ranks of Shevardnadze if he received an appropriate offer.[20]

THE DEATH OF ZHVANIA 149

A GREAT LOSS

The difference in approach between Zhvania and Saakashvili was noticed in Moscow. In October 2007 the Russian Duma adopted a statement on 'Antidemocratic policy by the Georgian authorities and breach of human rights in Georgia', where it was stated that the death of Zhvania 'made it impossible to implement a constructive program for resolving the Georgian–Ossetian conflict'. The Duma also demanded a more careful and independent investigation into the causes of Zhvania's death.[21]

Thus, there was broad consensus that the death of Zhvania was a great loss not only for Georgia, but for the whole region. Despite the fact that Zhvania's first replacement was one of his old colleagues, Zurab Nogaideli, it soon became apparent that a new era had begun. Of course, any hypotheses about what would have happened in Georgia had Zurab Zhvania not died in February 2005 are mere guesswork.

In Sweden we have had a similar situation since the assassination of prime minister Olof Palme in February 1986. Like the death of Zhvania, Palme's death is shrouded in mystery. Although it is clear that he was assassinated, his murderer has not been caught. A great number of theories have been presented, many of them claiming that without Palme's assassination Sweden would today have been a different country. In fact nobody knows whether Palme's premature disappearance from the political scene had any impact at all. The same is of course true for Zhvania. However, I am convinced that even if personalities do not determine history, they have a real, and sometimes considerable, importance. That was the case with Olof Palme. That is undoubtedly also the case with Zurab Zhvania.

I am sure that the development of the Rose Revolution would have been different with Zurab Zhvania as prime minister. Alternatively, a political clash might have forced him to leave the political company of Saakashvili, as so many others of the original team behind the Rose Revolution have found it necessary to do. In both cases, with Zhvania either as acting prime minister or as active member of the opposition, Georgia today would have been different.

The crucial question is, did somebody realize that Georgia without Zurab Zhvania would be different from Georgia with Zurab Zhvania? And did somebody consider Georgia without Zhvania preferable? And did that somebody go from words to deeds?

NOTES

1　Stephen F. Jones, 'The Caucasian Mountain Railway Project: a victory for glasnost?', *Central Asian Survey*, vol. 8. no. 2, pp. 47–59, 1989.

2　Arnold Cassola and Per Gahrton (eds), *Twenty Years of European Greens 1984–2004*, European Federation of Green Parties, Brussels, 2003.

3　*Georgian Times*, October 13, 2002.

4　Mikhail Machavariani, leader of the parliamentary group of the ruling party, Georgi Tsetereli, minister of social affairs and labour, David Treshlashvili, director of the Prime Minister's Office, Alexander Lomaia, minister of education and science, Zurab Nagasheli, minister of finance and Giorgi Garashvili, minister of culture.

5　Goltz mentions the 'obscure death of Prime Minister Zurab Zhvania in a secret sex flat with his male lover' (Thomas Goltz, *Georgia Diary: A chronicle of war and political chaos in the post-Soviet Caucasus*, M. E. Sharpe, Armonk. N.Y.. 2006, p. 247). Minassian alleges that Zhvania is 'connu pour son homesexualité' (known for his homosexuality) (Gaïdz Minassian, *Caucase du Sud, la nouvelle guerrre froide* (South Caucasus, the new cold war), Éditions Autrement, Paris, 2007, p. 58.

6　'Report on FBI testing in Tbilisi, Republic of Georgia', file no 163A-TI-3, March 14, 2005.

7　Vakhtang Komashidze, 'Special Report Georgia: questions linger about Zhvania death', *Caucasus Reporting Service*, no. 327, February 16, 2006.

8　Russian Wikipedia.

9　Minassian, *Caucase du Sud*, p. 164.

10　*Izvestia*, October 8, 2007.

11　*Izvestia*, December 17, 2007.

12　Russian Wikipedia.

13　Paul Quinn-Judge, 'Shevardnadze the survivor', *Washington Post,* March 19, 2006.

14　Makvala Berianidze in *Asaval-Dasavali,* October 17, 2008.

15　*Civil Georgia,* 6 November 2009.

16　*Georgian Times/Rustavi 2*, 6 November 2009.

17　*Caucasus Reporting Service*, no. 327, February 16, 2006.

18　Patrick Richter, 'Two mysterious deaths in Georgia's 'Rose Revolution' regime', World Socialist Web, February 2005.

19　Zurab Zhvania, *The Privilege of our Generation,* GIPA, Tbilisi, 2009.

20　BBC Monitoring, *Georgian Parliamentary Election Guide*, November 2, 2003.

21　*Izvestia*, October 2, 2007.

11

SAAKASHVILI, THE FAILED LIBERATOR

When Mikheil Saakashvili was inaugurated on January 25, 2004, as the youngest president in Europe, symbolically at the grave of King David IV, he promised to give priority to the fight against corruption and the restoration of Georgia's territorial integrity. However, one commentator concluded, there were clear hints that it was the latter goal that made the 'heart' of the Rose Revolution beat with extra strength, as he was also quoted as having emphasized that 'Georgia's territorial integrity is the goal of my life'.[1] The same day he was presented by the BBC as 'a crusader against corruption and an enemy of poverty'. Fourteen months later, on May 10, 2005, US president George W. Bush, on a visit in Tbilisi, praised him and exclaimed, 'Because you acted, Georgia is today both sovereign and free and a beacon of liberty for this region and the world.' In nationalist Russian eyes he was instead a 'typical Georgian tsar'.[2] Common to most observers, irrespective of their general appreciation of Saakashvili, is an emphasis on his emotional and disquieting unpredictability and inclination to authoritarian behaviour.

Ilan Greenberg of the *New York Times* recorded how, during an interview in 2004, the Georgian president was interrupted by an urgent telephone call, during which he suddenly shouted 'To jail!' and put down the receiver.[3] In his second inaugural speech, on January 20, 2008, Saakashvili made a promise which most observers would consider very typical of his style: 'Today I make a commitment to you that our efforts to build a Georgia without poverty will take concrete form within the next 50 working days.'[4] In fact, when his second term started Georgia was still corrupt and poor, still divided, with two regions seceded.

MINISTER, MAYOR, PRESIDENT

Mikheil Saakashvili was born in Tbilisi in 1967 to an academic couple. He graduated from the School of International Law in Kiev and studied in the United States. In 1995 he was approached by Zurab Zhvania, who convinced him to join the Citizens Union and stand for the elections. In parliament he was in charge of reforming the judiciary and the police, and in October 2000 he was appointed minister of justice. However, after less than a year he resigned, after having been involved in open controversy with several other members of the government, accusing them of corruption. He founded the National Movement and was elected mayor of Tbilisi in 2002.

Saakashvili's reputation for hasty and emotional actions was confirmed during his first year as president. His swift intervention in Adjara in May 2004 surprised even Zhvania, as did the failed attempt to repeat the Adjara success in Ossetia. In August 2004 Saakashvili threatened to open fire on Russian ships bringing tourists from Sochi to Sukhumi.[5] When in December 2004 he replaced the Zhvania loyalist Georgi Baramidze with Irakli Okruashvili as minister of defence, the nomination took place in the middle of night in front of the entire Kodori Brigade, which had been put on alert with short notice; and, of course, in front of television cameras. The president gave Okruashvili the order to give the highest priority to the reintegration of separatist regions.

When he was new in office President Saakashvili asserted that he just needed an ordinary apartment to live in with his family. When a British writer in 2005 tried to take a photo of what in reality was a new palace-like domicile for the presidential family, he was detained: 'For the first time since Romanian police destroyed my photographs of Ceausescu's new Palace of the People seventeen years earlier, in July 1988, I saw my amateur photography deleted from the record – in democratic Georgia.'[6]

As a matter of fact, in the summer of 2009 an enormous presidential palace, overlooking the river Mtkvara and visible from most parts of the city, was inaugurated. It is designed after the model of the White House in Washington by the Italian architect Michele Delucci, who in addition to normal pay was rewarded with Georgian citizenship. When proud President Saakashvili showed the building to a group of schoolchildren he underlined that it had cost only 12 million lari, 0.18 per cent of the state budget. And he explained that 'this is the first huge governmental construction in Georgia for two

The new presidential palace overlooking Tbilisi, constructed on the model of the White House in Washington DC. The Italian architect was granted Georgian citizenship as a reward for his work.

thousand years', the purpose of which is to show that Georgia is 'eternal and immortal'.[7]

The visit by President Bush to Tbilisi in May 2005 was regarded as a major political achievement for Saakashvili. It was followed by an official visit by the Georgian president to Washington the following year, which lead to a commitment by Bush to support Georgia's aspiration to become a member of NATO. After Bush's visit the campaign against the Russian military bases in Georgia was escalated. On May 30, 2005, it was agreed that they would all be dismantled by 2008, which they were. In October Saakashvili dismissed his minister of foreign affairs, Salome Zurabishvili, initially a French citizen of Georgian descent who was the ambassador of France in Tbilisi when she was appointed (and promptly given Georgian citizenship). She immediately formed a new political party, Georgia's Way, and was to be only the first of a growing number of close colleagues of the president to join the opposition.

A briefing note from the European Parliament in 2006 reported, 'Georgia is now the second poorest country in Europe, after Moldova.' While the GNP growth was relatively high, 7 per cent in 2005, the economic improvement did not reach the population. There were also difficulties in attracting foreign investment. Despite the conflict with Russia, the main source of investment was Russian capital. While some Georgians were uneasy about this, Ms Zurabishvili told representatives of the European Parliament in January 2006 that 'a bigger Russian stake in the Georgian economy could mean a clear Russian interest in its developing well'.[8]

During the first half of 2006 critical remarks about developments in Georgia became common in the West. Charles A. Kupchan, professor of international affairs at Georgetown University, asked whether Georgia was 'reverting to tyranny', and maintained that 'the bloom is off the Rose Revolution. Saakashvili's accomplishments have been undercut by the excessive concentration of power in his own hands – what the intelligentsia calls the "Putinization" of Georgia.'[9]

During a meeting of the EU–Georgia Parliamentary Cooperation Committee in September 2006, the debate about the worrying reports on democracy and human rights in Georgia became heated. The head of the Commission Delegation to Georgia, Torben Holtze, drew attention to the fact that 'free media are not flourishing, as could have been expected'. Neither was investment taking off. Holtze also asked how increased defence expenditure could be justified when education, health care and other needs were so great, and noted that inflammatory rhetoric was driving public opinion in the wrong direction.[10]

In 2006 several reports gave a troubling picture of the development of human rights and democracy. GYLA asserted that 'according to international ratings there is ample evidence that freedom of expression has decreased since the Rose Revolution'.[11] Human Rights Watch wrote, 'Human rights abuses continue unchecked in many spheres following patterns established under former governments.'[12] Human Rights in Georgia went further: 'Step by step, Georgia is acquiring all the signs of a police state.'[13]

While a report from a British human rights group alleged that even at the first presidential inauguration on January 25, 2004, 'people could have been forgiven for suspecting fascist leanings on the part of the new president,'[14] the Georgian Republican party put the title on one of its critical pamphlets, 'From Rose Revolution to Neobolshevism (President Saakashvili's political choice)'.[15]

The local election in October 2006 became a huge victory for the ruling United National Movement (UNM), which won 88.8 per cent of the 1,733 seats in local assemblies. Second came a coalition of Conservatives and Republicans with 3.2 per cent, third Labour with 2.3, fourth the Industrial Party with 1.6 and fifth Georgia's Way with

0.2 per cent. However, only 47.4 per cent of registered voters took part in the election (in Tbilisi it was only 34.7 per cent). Numerous voters considered the election to be, if not manipulated, at least dominated by the ruling party. The ODIHR report noted that public debates were organized, but 'regrettably, the UNM did not engage in these debates'.[16]

Nevertheless, other observers were quite happy with the situation in Georgia. At a press conference in Tbilisi on September 13, 2007, the co-rapporteurs of the Council of Europe declared, 'In a remarkably short time, Georgia has made stunning progress in carrying out substantial economic, judicial and state reforms.'[17] The UN Human Rights Committee in October 2007 welcomed 'the significant legislative and institutional changes that have been introduced with a view to consolidating the rule of law' in Georgia.[18]

THE NOVEMBER CRISIS, 2007

A dramatic hint of serious troubles came on September 25, 2007, when the former minister of defence, Irakli Okruashvili, appeared on the Imedi television channel and accused his former boss of being an oppressor, and having harmed the Georgian church, covered up the truth about the death of Zhvania and ordered the assassination of the business tycoon Badri Patarkatsishvili.[19] However, possibly even more devastating for the reputation of the president was Okruashvili's allegation that the Saakashvili family had a business empire worth 'billions' and that the president's fight against corruption was only 'window dressing'. Okruashvili did not present any tangible evidence for his allegations, which were vehemently denied by the President's Office.

Nevertheless, some observers believed that Okruashvili might become a serious challenger to Saakashvili. He was arrested on September 27 and released on bail on October 8, when he publicly recanted. A couple of weeks later he left for Germany, where he applied for asylum and claimed that the recantation had been made under pressure. The Okruashvili incident was in a way typical of the absurd situation. There were some demonstrations protesting about his arrest, but he had no support among the other opposition parties.

Thus, when ten opposition parties joined in a National Council, there was no formal connection to the Okruashvili incident. The next step was mass protests in several regions and outside the parliament in Tbilisi on November 2, where 50,000 people gathered on Rustaveli Avenue to support the United Opposition. The regime answered by announcing higher pensions and salaries, and some amendments to the electoral law. Nevertheless, the opposition was not satisfied. One of my friends in Tbilisi explained, 'The problem is that Misha has lost the trust of the public; a lot of people who went out on the streets to protest were not supporters of Okruashvili, but they protested against the current regime.'

The explosion came on November 7, 2007, when 'Tbilisi sank into chaos and violence, with hundreds of people reported injured after police used force to break up mass protests,' as reported by the Caucasus Reporting Service.[20] The government declared a state of emergency. The Imedi television station was closed down by police forces bursting into its building in the middle of ongoing transmissions. Imedi was at least partly owned and controlled by the business tycoon Badri Patarkatsishvili, who for a mixture of reasons, some honourable, some less so, had ended up as a main opponent of Saakashvili. The regime lost its temper in the face of these mass protests. Georgia's human rights ombudsman Sozar Subari, who was assaulted by police during the violence, stated, 'Today Georgia turned off the path of being a "beacon of democracy" down the road of being a country where human rights count for nothing.'[21]

In a televised address on the evening of November 7, Mikheil Saakashvili blamed Russia's FSB intelligence service for the unrest, and claimed that his measures, including the state of emergency, were in harmony with Western democratic practice. A paradox, typical of much Georgian politics, is that those who were accused of being steered by Russia presented a demand for Georgia's rapid membership of NATO! The Green Party expressed fear that 'the current government of Georgia will attempt to establish a totalitarian dictatorship,' which might sound like a gross exaggeration. But similar worries were expressed by all sorts of groups and observers. The International Crisis Group asked whether Georgia was 'sliding towards authoritarianism'.[22] GYLA in a letter to foreign ambassadors claimed that 'although all legislative requirements were properly pursued, state authorities have nevertheless dispersed peaceful protesters who were on hunger strike'. Human Rights Watch stated that 'the fragility of Georgia's commitment to human rights and the rule of law was revealed on November 7, 2007'.[23]

While the overwhelming majority of comments, both Georgian and international, disregarded the accusation that the protesters were Russian agents and put the major blame for the violence on the

Saakashvili regime, there were some diverging views. One example was the Swedish–American Silk Road Program, which maintained that the brutal crackdown by the Georgian authorities could be explained by the 'genuine belief that the situation risked developing into considerable domestic turmoil. These fears should be viewed against the background of Russia's relentless challenge to Georgian statehood.'[24]

Nevertheless, when in the spring of 2008 the *Harvard International Review* published three articles on the November crisis, the expert authors unanimously placed the blame on the Saakashvili regime. Former minister for the economy Vladimer Papava declared that 'Georgia's experience calls to light the folly of equating a pro-Western and anti-Russian orientation with democracy'.[25] Stephen Jones stated, 'Rather, what the debacle on Tbilisi's streets showed, yet again, was the West's ability to be shocked by the actions of its own illusory creations.'[26] Even the enthusiastic supporter of the Rose Revolution, Lincoln Mitchell, was worried: 'Georgia seems to be moving towards consolidating a strong, but not particularly democratic, regime.'[27]

On November 8, President Saakashvili announced early presidential elections on January 5, 2008. This was not, as might have been believed, a victory for the opposition, but a cunning move in order to regain lost political territory. According to the constitution, parliamentary elections were supposed to be held several months before presidential elections. However, the huge parliamentary majority of the ruling National Movement in December 2006 decided to hold presidential elections first and parliamentary elections after that, during the autumn of 2008. One of the main demands of the opposition during the November demonstrations was that parliamentary, not presidential, elections should be arranged in the spring of 2008. With his clever manoeuvre Saakashvili, while creating an impression of democratically giving in to the demands of the opposition for early elections, in fact maximized the chances of his own political survival. While it was considered highly possible that the National Movement would risk losing its majority in a parliamentary election, it was supposed that Saakashvili, despite all, would be able to exploit his charismatic capabilities in a presidential election.

After some weeks the state of emergency was lifted and the Polish former dissident Adam Michnik, editor in chief of *Wyborcza Gazeta* in Warsaw, was brought in to broker a deal with Imedi, which, according to Saakashvili, was intended to guarantee that the television station could no more be used as 'a weapon in the hands of Patarkatsishvili'. The station was back on the air in the middle of December, but suspended its broadcasts again two weeks later because of alleged external pressure.[28]

Half a year after the events took place, the EU–Georgia Parliamentary Cooperation Committee made a statement that deplored 'the use of force to disperse peaceful demonstrators on 7 November 2007, the subsequent temporary silencing of two opposition-controlled television stations and the declaration of a state of emergency'.[29]

An example of the agitated mood among the Georgian opposition was a newspaper interview with a member of the so-called Georgian Academy, Gela Dolidze, who predicted that 'Saakashvili will falsify the presidential election which will cause the people to fill the streets in protest; Saakashvili will strike back, there will be a bloodbath and Saakashvili will end like Ceausescu.'[30] Several of Georgia's major human rights organizations, GYLA, Transparency International/ Georgia and International Society for Fair Elections and Democracy, immediately formulated 'Ten preconditions for free and fair elections in Georgia'. Was there a serious fear among NGOs and opposition parties that the Saakashvili regime might resort to what it had characterized as the major evil of its predecessor, falsifying elections? It was hard to believe. Nevertheless, the existence of such a fear was undeniable.

THE PRESIDENTIAL ELECTION OF 2008

The early presidential election of January 5, 2008, for the first time in the history of Georgia, was a contested political struggle. At all previous presidential elections there had been only one serious candidate – successively Gamsakhurdia, Shevardnadze and Saakashvili, all of whom had won with an overwhelming majority. Now a considerable part of the opposition had united behind a single candidate, Levan Gachechiladze, a successful wine producer, member of the New Right Party and activist during the November 2007 protests. He was considered to have a fair chance by several observers. However, there were several other opposition candidates, so it was clear that votes critical of the regime would be split and Saakashvili would be number one in the first round. But would he get more than 50 per cent or would he have to face a united opposition in a second round? The political scientist Ramaz Sakvarelidze was of the opinion that 'a second round is unavoidable, because none of the candidates will get more than 25 percent of the votes'.[31]

Most of his colleagues agreed, and several of them assumed that Saakashvili would have difficulties in winning if forced to face only one opposition candidate in a second round. Even the incumbent himself admitted to the *Financial Times* that 'it will be much more difficult for us in the second round'.[32]

One of my guides in Georgian politics was Tiko, a young woman who had returned to Georgia after studies in the United States and Germany, and had been an active supporter of the Rose Revolution. Now she was disappointed and feared that the regime would abuse its power to guarantee the incumbent a comfortable victory in the first round. There had been some improvement concerning the crucial problem of voters' lists, she admitted, but still there were many problems, especially that supplementary lists would be allowed. This meant that people who did not find their names in the voters' list would nevertheless be allowed to vote and be registered on a handwritten list. The opposition feared that this possibility could be abused for multiple voting. If exit polls and the first result indicated that Saakashvili would get just about 50 per cent, only a fairly small portion of the total vote would have to be falsified in order to guarantee a victory in the first round. And, Tiko asserted, 'there is more intimidation of voters than ever, more than during Shevardnadze. Employees are fired because of their opinions and there is intimidation against people who want to rent halls for meetings of the opposition.' Tiko quoted Saakashvili as having said in a television transmission that the 'opposition could be flushed down the toilet'. 'They ridicule us,' she complained, and was worried by the fact that all politicians mixed religion with politics. 'Christianity is not used less in Georgian politics than Islam is in some of our neighbouring countries!'

In one of several pre-election reports OSCE/ODIHR noted that health care vouchers for pensioners prominently showed the number 5, Mikheil Saakashvili's number on the ballot paper. Although the authorities asserted that the vouchers had been planned before the election was called, the report maintained that 'there is evidence to suggest that the distribution has been used for campaign purposes, blurring the separation between state activities and candidate's election campaign'.[33] A few days before the election, Freedom House published a report under the title 'Freedom in Georgia takes a step backward in 2007'. Some reasons given were the lack of alternative voices, the fragile media landscape and the violent crackdown of November.[34]

The day before the election I went to a press conference held by

the United Opposition. I was the only foreigner; the other 50 journalists were all Georgian. The international (Western) media apparently
were not interested. The opposition accused the regime of all kinds
of abuse of power, but it did not present anything like an alternative
political programme. The representatives of the opposition were as
least as pro-Western as the regime, and the repeated accusations by
the regime that the opposition was pro-Russian, even teleguided by
Russian intelligence, seemed utterly absurd.

Mikheil Saakashvili was of course much more impressive and
charismatic, and the world media did show up when later the same
day he met the press, after having addressed a huge mass meeting.
While, as usual, giving a very energetic impression, Saakashvili
also looked pressed and exhausted. Was he worried that his use of
violence against a political demonstration two months earlier would
now backfire? He did his best to prove that he was still the master of
the game, sometimes by telling the truth, sometimes by exaggerating,

Saakashvili addressing an election rally. He was elected in the first round, which
according to the opposition was a result of fraud. This started a campaign which
is still ongoing demanding the resignation of the president.

sometimes by stretching the truth a very long way. 'We fired 50,000 policemen, some of them are of course critical. Shouldn't we have done it? Yes!' he exclaimed, and nobody could contradict him. 'We attack the opposition best by explaining our programme; they have no programme, they just attack us,' he asserted and only exaggerated a little. 'Georgia is a wonderful success concerning corruption, we are even less corrupt than some Scandinavian countries,' he said, which was blatantly untrue.

A group 'Misha' would not get any votes from were some women in their 40s, whom I met at a lunch at the home of the former minister of the environment, Nino Chkhobadze, one of the Green veterans who had followed Zurab Zhvania to the Shevardnadze camp. However, she had not followed him in his last political move and remained sceptical of the Rose Revolution. Among Nino's guests was a teacher of Georgian literature who complained about the abolition of the study of old Georgian poetry in some school classes. Another one was a pianist who had had a guaranteed contract in the Soviet Union and during the Shevardnadze period. But now, under the rule of US-trained management experts, her job had been removed from the state budget as an unproductive expenditure. They all agreed that culture and education had been impoverished because of the newly imported neoliberal and materialistic ideology, alien to the most basic aspects of Georgian identity.

The night before the election, one of the Georgian television channels tried a new approach: a debate between the possible first ladies. Not all of them had agreed to participate, but Mrs Gamkrelidze, wife of the leader of the right-wing Industry Party, Mrs Natelashvili, wife of the Labour leader, and Mrs Saakashvili were present. If the debate was looked upon from the perspective of the dramaturgic rules of a television show, there is no doubt that Sandra Roelofs, alias Mrs Saakashvili, was the winner. The young Dutchwoman, who had met her husband during studies in Strasbourg, impressed by her openness and by speaking the Georgian language, according to my Georgian friends, with almost perfection. But did this young, modern, Western woman convince her likes among the Georgians? Tiko was not the only young, modern, Western-educated woman in Georgia who by the end of Mikheil Saakashvili's first period as president was fed up and disappointed with the 'revolutionary' regime. Another one was Anna Dolidze, former director of GYLA, who the day before the election summarized the situation in an article on the web in the following blunt way:

After years of darkness and cold it is no longer an exception that gas and electricity is available. The traffic police don't require bribes to afford a beer with their lunch and it is no longer easy to buy a speedy way through the bureaucracy for five dollars. Roads are being built and the banking sector of Georgia is gaining confidence. But such things did not cause the Georgians to move into the streets in November 2007, but the transformation of democracy to a myth with increased abuse of power, breach in the communications with the people and intolerance of dissidents.[35]

I spent the election day visiting polling stations in Tbilisi and Marneuli, south of the capital, where a high proportion of the population is Azeri. All public signposts were bilingual, though with not Azerbaijani as the second language, but Russian. This was a reminder that Russian has survived as the lingua franca that allows for communication between people of all nationalities. 'In Marneuli everybody votes for the ruling party,' I had been told by a member of the opposition. 'There is a set phrase that claims that if a chair is made candidate for the presidency, the Azeris will vote for the chair.' The explanation given for this by Georgians is that memories from the Soviet system, and knowledge about the authoritarian regime in Baku, have convinced the Azeris that they are better off if they keep good relations with those who are in power. However, an alternative explanation could be that the local authorities, who are most often ethnic Georgians, have found methods to create an imposed loyalty to any regime in Tbilisi.

Such assumptions were confirmed when I visited some polling stations in Marneuli and the offices of the two major candidates. In the polling stations some information in Azerbaijani could be found. The general impression, however, was that there was a mess. At the office of the United Opposition I was immediately surrounded by angry party workers who complained about all kinds of fraud, manipulation and falsification. The mood was tense and irritated. In the office of the ruling party some blocks away it was completely calm and I was welcomed by a functionary who beamed with self-confidence: 'At least 90 per cent of the Azeris will vote for Saakash-vili. About the Georgian voters I am less sure, but we will win in the first round!' While talking with me he received a telephone call warning that the opposition might carry out violent actions of sabotage. I felt unsure whether the threat was real or just something staged for my benefit in order to prove how irresponsible the opposition was.

In Tbilisi I followed a friend to a congested polling station in the Saburtalo district. She did not reveal to me which candidate she intended to vote for, but her argument had a leaning towards Saakashvili:

> I think the opposition is exaggerating and lacks tangible alternatives. They just complain and accuse the government for abusing its power. And when they promise something, it cannot be taken seriously. Gachechiladze has promised to release all prisoners! And Patarkatsishvili has promised to give one billion dollars from his own wallet to the poor! Such promises are not serious.

I could only agree. My friend also related one of many rumours about Patarkatsishvili:

> He became one of the super-rich oligarchs in Russia by stealing cars on an industrial scale. And when his construction firm was repairing inside the Kremlin they stole the original gold panels and covered it over with cheap gold paint. Maybe such things cannot happen in normal countries, but in the 1990s Russia wasn't normal.

Before even a fraction of the votes had been counted, at 1 pm on January 6, the BBC announced to the world that Saakashvili had won a 'landslide victory'. The same day the Swedish minister of foreign affairs, Carl Bildt, congratulated Georgia for having carried out 'the most democratic election' that had ever been held in the country. He rejected accusations by the opposition about fraud as an attempt to 'sabotage an election they could not win'.[36] It was to be another five days before that bubble exploded. On January 10, under the headline 'Georgian election massively falsified', the German newspaper *Frankfurter Rundschau* published an interview in which the president of the election observation group of the OSCE, Dieter Boden, claimed that chaotic conditions had characterized the situation in many polling stations, and that he had received reports from his observers about 'widespread and serious breaches of the rules at the count of votes, among other things through gross, careless and premeditated fraud'. Similar statements had been made by the opposition on the election day, but they were rejected by Bildt and other Western commentators as lies by bad losers. Nevertheless, the opposition did not lack arguments.

The first official result, which after a long delay was published by the Central Election Committee (CEC) on the morning after the election, gave Saakashvili 57.58 per cent of the votes. This figure, however, was founded only upon a small fraction of the total number of electoral districts, 229 out of 3,512. Before this, during the election night, a final result was pre-announced several times, but the director of the CEC emerged in front of several hundred impatient journalists once every hour and regretted that an unexpected snowfall, a technical problem, or disputes in the local election committees had delayed the count. Early results came in from Zugdidi, a district close to Abkhazia where many refugees from the seceded province had voted, and Saakashvili was still popular because of his militant promises to reconquer Abkhazia and South Ossetia. In Zugdidi the incumbent was reported to have received more than 70 per cent of the votes.

The official forecast was pretty well corroborated by an exit poll, commissioned by television stations loyal to the regime, published at 4 pm on election day, which gave Saakashvili 52.5 per cent, Levan Gachechiladze 28.5, Arkadij Patarkatsishvili 6.0, Shalva Natelashvili 5.5, David Gamkrelidze 3.6, and two marginal candidates Georgi Maisashvili 0.8 and Irina Sarishvili-Chanturia (the only woman in the race) 0.4 per cent. This was the exit poll that stayed put on television screens during the following four hours of continued voting. Another exit poll was taken by some Ukrainian organizations, and gave a rather different picture: Gachechiladze 31.0, Saakashvili 24.4, Patarkatsishvili 20.3, Natelashvili 12.4, Gamkrelidze 7.3, Maisashvili 0.6 and Sarashvili 0.1. These figures, however, were never shown by the major television stations.

I was present among a bunch of lingering journalists at 3.30 am in the night after the election, when the exhausted director of the CEC informed us that we had waited in vain. Ninety percent of the foreign journalists were Russian or Russian speaking. The interest by Western media was limited. In the West it was supposed to be already settled that the candidate of the West had made it through with a 'landslide victory'. I happened to stand just beside the director of GYLA, Georgi Chkheidze, when the chief of the CEC gave up. Chkheidze groaned, 'This doesn't look good!' It was obvious that he suspected foul play, without saying so explicitly. Some Georgian journalists, though, expressed loudly what many thought: 'The result is not so good for the regime, so they are spinning it out and playing for time.'

Two days later I was present when CEC had a public meeting about all kinds of complaints of irregularities. Most of them were shelved. Here I quote only one example from a long list: 'At 11.20 am Gela

Mtvishvili from the Human Rights Centre reports that there is chaos in polling station number 19 in Kabala. Members of the election committee tell the voters to designate number 5 (Saakashvili), and people vote several times without showing their identity cards.'

The attack by Carl Bildt on the Georgian opposition, which was unique among EU politicians, was the main news item on the pro-regime television station Rustavi 2 for the evening news of January 6. I happened to be in the company of one of the closest advisors of the opposition's would-be prime minister, Salome Zurabishvili. He was completely taken aback and urged me to tell the Swedish public that his chief was no less pro-West, and especially pro-European, than Saakashvili. That was of course true, which made the one-man crusade of the Swedish minister of foreign affairs against the Georgian opposition even more awkward. As a matter of fact, when his statement was made, it was still not clear who was going to win. When about one-third of the districts were counted at 11 pm on January 6, the percentage for Saakashvili had sunk to only a few tenths of a per cent above the crucial 50 per cent level, which made it seem probable that a second round would take place.

At the same time as the presidential election took place, a referendum was held about Georgian membership of NATO. At his press conference the day before the election, Mikheil Saakashvili admitted that this time he might not get 96 per cent of the votes, as in 2004, 'but NATO will get it', he promised. As most of the opposition candidates, including Gachechiladze, were just as keen on NATO membership as the government, that did not sound very far-fetched. The first exit poll, then, probably was a shock for many, indicating only 61.1 per cent yes votes. The official result, given some days later, was a little better for the friends of NATO: 77 per cent in favour, 23 against. Nevertheless, 77 per cent is rather different from 96 per cent. And after all, the fundamental question remained: could the official result be trusted?

When the official outcome of the presidential election was finally published on January 13 nobody was surprised that it returned the presidency to Mikheil Saakashvili after only one round, with 53.41 per cent of the votes. According to the official figures Gachechiladze came second with 25.67 per cent, followed by Patarkatsishvili 7.1, Natelashvili 6.55, Gamkrelidze 4.05, Maisashvili 0.78 and Sarishvili-Chanturia 0.19. The *Economist* exclaimed: 'Misha bounces back – Mikheil Saakashvili duly re-elected as Georgia's president, but he is a somewhat chastened man.'[37] The immediate reaction by

GYLA was to call to attention hundreds of complaints about fraud which had not been dealt with properly. On January 14 the three main Georgian election observer organizations, GYLA, ISFED and Transparency International, in a joint press release announced that they did not agree with a statement made by the chief of the CEC on Rustavi 2, that the presidential election had been 'maximally democratic, maximally transparent and maximally fair'. The OSCE/ODIHR in its final report concluded that:

> the distinction between State activities and the campaign of the ruling United National Movement (UNM) party candidate, Mr. Mikheil Saakashvili, was blurred. In addition other aspects of the election process, notably vote count and tabulation procedures, as well as the post-election complaints and appeals process, further presented serious challenges to the fulfilment of some OSCE commitments.[38]

Other reports from different groups of foreign observers expressed different degrees of criticism.[39] The opposition staged large demonstrations and demanded that a second round be held.

One result that probably worried the regime and showed that the opposition was serious and stronger than expected was that Saakashvili lost Tbilisi. He got only 32.56 per cent, while Gachechiladze won by 40.43 per cent – and this was according to the official result.

A couple of weeks after the election the government was reshuffled to contain a wider circle than the narrow group of veterans of the Rose Revolution. However, in the night of February 12–13 Georgian politics was hit by one more of those sudden and mysterious deaths that have been poisoning the atmosphere for so long. This time the victim was Badri Patarkatsishvili, aged 52, who allegedly was felled by a heart attack. This did not prevent the respected Caucasus Reporting Service from carrying the news under the headline 'British police say death of Georgia's richest man is "suspicious"'.[40] Some rather typical remarks were uttered, exemplifying the tension in Georgian political life. A supporter of Patarkatsishvili, David Shukakidze, stated that 'the Georgian authorities handed out a death sentence to Patarkatsishvili when they began their dirty campaign against him'. Another opposition politician, Georgi Khaindrava, claimed, that 'this government drove Patarkatsishvili to his death with their dirty insinuations'. Georgi Bokeria of the ruling National Movement party replied stoically, 'On the day a person dies, it is usual practice to say something good about him or say nothing at all. So I won't say anything.' Patarkatsishvili, who lived in London, was considered by the Saakashvili regime to be a criminal and a traitor. The authorities published a tape recording which was alleged to reveal how Patarkatsishvili offered a police officer US$100 million to assassinate Interior Minister Merabishvili. This incident, together with Patarkatsishvili's style and his tarnished reputation as an oligarch, created apprehension among other opposition groups, and even made the brother of Zurab Zhvania leave Patarkatsishvili's campaign team only days before the presidential election.

The Russian newspaper *Izvestia* asked after the presidential election, 'Does Georgia await a new revolution?'[41] This was probably more a sign of wishful thinking than the result of deep analysis. Nevertheless, the opposition continued to demand a second round at the same time as it prepared for the approaching parliamentary election.

THE PARLIAMENTARY ELECTION OF 2008

One slogan of the opposition was directed against 'thieves of votes', that is, the president and the government. Regime representatives accused the opposition of being a bunch of 'criminals' and 'traitors', supported by Russia, while the opposition retorted by labelling government people as 'terrorists' and 'fascists'. One research institute, in an understatement, observed that 'Georgia's political debate has failed to focus on the contents of policies, as the main forces have focused their campaigns on discrediting each other, leaving very little room for constructive political debate.'[42]

On January 29, 2008, most major opposition parties and blocks agreed on a joint memorandum outlining 17 demands, and setting February 15 as a deadline for the government to agree, otherwise the protests would be resumed. Compared with the earlier demands for the outright resignation of Saakashvili, these proposals were more modest and realistic. They dealt with issues such as a recount of disputed votes during the presidential election, release of all political prisoners and investigation of the excessive use of force on November 7. The opposition also insisted that the majoritarian system should be abolished. There were some talks between the government and opposition representatives, and according to some sources even progress. But on March 12, the huge regime majority in the parliament suddenly decided to increase the number of seats to be elected by the majority system from 50 to 75 (out of 150), which

caused the opposition to start a hunger strike.[43] An event that added
to the tense situation, but also to the hopes among opposition parties
for a tangible success at the polls, was the surprising decision at
the end of April by Nino Burjanadze to resign from the ballot of
the ruling National Movement. Allegedly she was just angry with
the composition of the electoral list and presented no political arguments, but many observers believed that she felt that the regime was
in for escalating unpopularity and that she did not want to be part
of such a development.

The situation in Georgia after the presidential election created an
expectation that the opposition might win a majority in the parliament provided the election was not 'stolen' through manipulations
by the regime. Thus, the dismay was great when the official results
showed a landslide victory for the United National Movement. Out
of the 75 proportionally elected seats the government got 60. Only
three out of eleven opposition parties passed the 5 per cent barrier,
down from 7 per cent after internal as well as external pressure.
Out of 75 majority seats, the ruling party received 70, the opposition only five (including two for a party that did not pass the 5 per
cent barrier). This meant that the regime could generate the two-
thirds majority required for constitutional amendments by a good
margin. The opposition rapidly gave its verdict: massive fraud. The
preliminary report by the international observers contained quite a
lot of criticism, but was phrased so that it could be presented by the
government, as well as most international media, as approval.

When I met with Salome Zurabishvili shortly after the election,
she was disappointed with the Europeans: 'The too hasty approval
by the OSCE and the EU will make lots of pro-European Georgians
furious and disappointed.' Zurabishvili even compared the Georgian president to Vladimir Putin. A similar opinion was expressed
by the opposition newspaper *Resonansi*, which appeared after the
election with the headline: 'The ghost of Putinization'. And in an
interview in the same newspaper the political scientist Soso Tsikarishvili fully supported the accusations by the opposition against the
regime, and declared that 'unfortunately fraud and manipulations
have increased'. When I met with him personally and asked how
that judgment corresponded with the fact that a parallel vote count
by independent groups had shown almost the same result as the
official one, Tsikarishvili explained that the methodology of fraud
had developed. One example, even mentioned in the OSCE report,
was 'problems with inking'. All voters are supposed to be marked
on one finger with indelible ink after having voted. Tsikarishvili

explained to me that if this had not been done, it was not just an example of regrettable negligence, but a part of a very sophisticated fraud method where large groups of voters, extended families or clans, were bribed to abstain from voting and hand over their ID cards to agents of the ruling party who voted in their place.

The Georgian Green Party in a report to the European Greens in Brussels claimed that 'such an outcome was possible only after fraud and falsification, which was done in a more professional manner than at any election before'.[44]

Many Western Europeans probably consider allegations about election fraud by the venerated Saakashvili regime to be wild conspiracy theories by 'bad losers'. One OSCE observer, at the press conference in Tbilisi the day after the elections, publicly accused the opposition of not having understood an important element of democratic states, that the losers in elections should congratulate the winners! But to everybody who has observed several Georgian elections, it its clear that the ploy Tsikarishvili described is only one of several very imaginative fraud tricks which cannot be discovered by parallel counting of votes.

There were probably other contributing causes than fraud for the landslide victory of the government. The opposition was divided, populist and had no alternative political programme. There was virtually no debate about political programmes, only about who was the most despicable liar, oppressor, abuser of power and manipulator, which made many voters rather exhausted and depressed. The paradox was that the very pro-West opposition was feeling deceived by the West. Or as it was put by Tsikarishvili, 'More and more Georgians who are basically pro-West get the feeling that the West, primarily the USA but also the EU, don't care about democracy in Georgia but only has an interest in having Georgia as a strategic ally against Russia. They want us to be satisfied with third-class democracy, but we aren't!'

Some commentators believed that the huge victory of the ruling party could have been caused by some dramatic developments in Georgia's external relations. The flaring conflict with Russia was so beneficial for the regime that Salome Zurabishvili even dared hint that it was just a planned illusion: 'What has been happening recently between Georgia and Russia suggests to me certain coordinated actions between the two countries,' she told a news agency the day after the election.[45]

At a large demonstration with thousands of participants on the

Georgian National Day, May 26, 2008, the opposition parties escalated their accusations against the Saakashvili regime of ruling the
country on the basis of electoral fraud and suppression of alternative
opinions. Levan Gachechiladze, who came second at the presidential election in January, threatened that the opposition would refuse
to take the few seats they won according to the official result and
prevent the new parliament from convening 'if necessary by force'.

After three and a half months (during which time a war had
erupted in South Ossetia), on September 9, 2008, the International
Election Observation Mission (IEOM)[46] published its final report,
which stated that while the new Georgian electoral code was 'gener-
ally conducive to conducting democratic elections, it contains new
provisions which created an unequal playing field in favour of the
ruling party'. Furthermore, the report underlined that the vote count
and the tabulation of results 'were assessed more negatively' by
IEOM observers, who also reported signs of 'ballot stuffing'.[47]

After the elections the protests by the opposition continued. When
the new parliament convened on June 7 it was almost exclusively a
regime event, most opposition MPs having chosen to refuse to take
their seats.

GOOD FOR BUSINESS, NOT FOR THE POOR

The Rose Revolution regime has been praised for its struggle against
corruption, despite the extremely unorthodox methods that have
been used. However, it is an undeniable fact that Georgia's 79th
position on the ranking list of corruption, according to Transparency International, is on the same level as countries such as Serbia
and Saudi Arabia, and lower than China, India and Mexico.[48]

One awkward effect of the campaign against corruption has been
the weakening or abolition of rules for the protection of consumers.
When some rules about food quality were relaxed in 2007 the motive
given by the responsible authority was that a source of corruption
had been removed.[49] However, an expert from the IMF told me that
'they prefer to abolish rules which can be abused for corruption
instead of abolishing corruption'.

The main achievement of the new regime has been to strengthen
state institutions, which has allowed a considerable increase in the
collection of state revenues, the regular payment of pensions and salaries to state employees, and the efficient functioning of basic services,
such as distribution of electricity and maintenance and construc-

tion of roads. GNP growth has been comparatively high during the period, usually around 10 per cent annually. The economic dependence on Russia is still high, but a slight change in the trade pattern has become visible. In 2006 Turkey took over as Georgia's main trading partner, while Russia was still the number one country from which Georgia imported goods.[50] An 'aggressive privatization' has been carried out. The rating of Georgia by international investors and financial institutions has improved. One remarkable example is that Georgia's ranking on the list of the best countries to do business in soared from 112 in 2005 to 37 in 2006. In the 2009 *Doing Business Report* the country continued to climb, and reached position 15 out of 181 economies.

Nevertheless it is obvious that the regime has not fully understood the relation between Western economic liberalism and the rule of law. Privatization has often been carried out through extremely arbitrary methods, alienating considerable parts of the population. At one stage restaurant owners were asked to give their property as 'gifts' to the state, after having been reminded that they had acquired it in the first place by corrupt measures. At another stage, small shops, booths and stalls close to metro stations in Tbilisi were targeted and destroyed in order to make room for major buildings, such as the Kempinski hotel. Often no prior notice and no opportunity to appeal was given; owners and inhabitants were sometimes forced to leave overnight. According to a German analysis, 'the confiscation issue in Georgia shows that international organizations and the Georgian government differ in their understanding of the rule of law'. Nevertheless, despite this basic contradiction in the perception of liberal economy, the World Bank and the IMF 'are satisfied with the Georgian government's policies, which favour radical liberal reforms'.[51]

Other international organizations have also been delighted. The UNDP has lauded Georgia for its deregulation of the labour market, its trade liberalization, and especially for its introduction in 2005 of a low (12 per cent) flat income tax, after the model of a similar reform in Russia in 2001. The European Bank for Reconstruction and Development (EBRD) has expressed contentment with Georgian privatization policies, according to its homepage, which mentions as a good example that 'significant progress has been made in power sector reform' through the sale of two major regional power distributors and six power stations to a Czech company in February 2007. EBRD also with obvious pleasure notes that 'the privatization of municipal water companies and the commercialization of municipal public transport services has started'.[52] One of the most approving reports was published by a Swedish business-sponsored neoliberal think tank in August 2008, just after the Ossetia War, under the title 'Georgia – the shining star in the reform sky'. There are, according to the report, virtually no clouds at all in the Georgian heaven; the future is radiantly bright, provided the policy of the Saakashvili regime is continued.[53]

So why have people not been satisfied with the situation? Do most Georgians agree with the evaluation by GYLA's Anna Dolidze from November 2007 (quoted above) that the flaws in the democratic life of the country are more important than the undeniable improvement of some aspects of the economy? This may be true. However, another fact may also be of considerable importance -- the remaining poverty, the lack of social security and the growing socioeconomic gaps. The favourite theory of unbridled economic liberalism, that unrestricted growth in the wealth of an upper class automatically 'trickles' down to everybody, including the poor, has not come true. While, according to a study commissioned by the UNDP, the perception by Tbilisi residents of the socioeconomic situation four years after the Rose Revolution was 'substantially better' than of the period prior to November 2003, they were 'nevertheless overwhelmingly negative still'. Seventy-one per cent gave a negative, and only 1 per cent a positive assessment. Asked about their view of the direction of the ongoing socioeconomic development, those interviewed showed a slightly decreasing pessimism, but still 37 per cent thought that things were getting worse.[54]

Even the prime minister admitted in 2007 that 25 per cent of the population still remained below the poverty line and that 300,000 were unemployed. The International Crisis Group noted in a report on the November clashes that 'a significant segment of the population has not benefited from the reforms, and social disenfranchisement threatens cohesion'. One of Mikheil Saakashvili's slogans during his re-election campaign was 'Georgia without poverty', which may have been an indication that the regime had begun to understand the limits of the 'trickle-down' theory.[55]

In April 2008 a European Commission report observed that 'as regards labour law and rights at work, no progress can be reported as regards unrestricted strike rights'. It was underlined that 'the labour code contradicts both EU standards and the European Social Charter'. It was further observed that 'on the social situation, no progress can be reported as regards poverty reduction and social welfare'.[56]

In order to help Georgia pay for reconstruction of infrastructure and buildings damaged by the war, a donors' conference in

October 2008 granted the country US$4.55 billion, a sum that was even larger than the World Bank and the IMF had estimated was needed. Nevertheless, the double shocks of the Ossetia War and the global recession have seriously hampered the development of Georgia's economy. There has been a decline in foreign investments and a slowdown in the economic growth to 2.1 per cent in 2008, with a contraction of 3.2 per cent during the second half of the year.[57]

If the Saakashvili regime has been able to cope with the internal political crisis thanks to the positive aspects of the neoliberal economic policy, despite the fact that large parts of the population have been left behind and socioeconomic inequality has deepened, what about the prospects if the effects of the war and the global recession are obstructing further strengthening of the state finances and thereby the possibilities of improving infrastructure and services? What if Georgia's enormous dependence on imported goods for maintaining a reasonable standard of living – imports are four times the value of exports, and 80 per cent of consumer goods are imported – causes considerably higher prices without concomitant higher revenues for large parts of the population?

For many reasons the usually Georgia-friendly Russian newspaper *Novaya Gazeta* reported at the beginning of 2009 that nobody in Georgia believes that Saakashvili will be the first president in the history of the country to remain in office for his full legal term, which in his case ends in January 2013. However he is a shrewd politician, and nobody knows whether the overt and often furious opposition that he is the subject of in Tbilisi is supported by the majority of the population, which lives outside the capital.[58]

NOTES

1   Pamela Jawad, 'Diversity, conflict, and state failure: chances and challenges for democratic consolidation in Georgia after the 'Rose Revolution', Cornell University Peace Studies Program, Occasional Paper no. 30-3, December 2006.

2   Mikhail Leontiev and Dmitrij Zhukov, *'Nezavisimaya' Gruzia – bandit v tigrovoj shkure* ('Independent' Georgia – a bandit in a tiger's hide), Yuaza Press, Moscow, 2008.

3   Ilan Greenberg, 'The not-so-Velvet Revolution', *New York Times Magazine*, May 30, 2004.

4   Website of the Georgian president <www.president.gov.ge>.

5   Antonenko, p. 248 in Bruno Coppetier and Robert Legvold (eds), *Statehood and Security: Georgia after the Rose Revolution*, MIT Press, Cambridge, Mass., 2005.

6   Mark Almond, 'Black Roses: Georgia's reformers fall out – Georgia's transition from "people power" to Caucasian cockpit', <http://markalmondoxford.blogspot.com/2007>, November 3, 2007.

7   *Golovinskij Prospekt*, no. 29, July 20–26, 2009, <www.golovin-ave.fortuna-7.com>.

8   European Union, 'Note on Georgia: Political and economic situation, EU relations', DGEXPO/B/PolDep/Note/2006/124.

9   Charles A. Kupchan, 'Wilted rose', *New Republic*, February 2006.

10   EU–Georgia Parliamentary Cooperation Committee, September 12, 2006, Tbilisi.

11   GYLA, *Freedom of Expression in Georgia*, 2006.

12   <http://hrw.org/english/docs/2006/01/18/georgi12229_txt.htm>.

13   <www.humanrights.ge>.

14   'Georgia 2005: Rose Revolution justice', <www.bhhrg.org>.

15   Republican Party, Tbilisi, February 2006.

16   OSCE/ODIHR Limited Election Observation Mission, *Municipal Elections, October 5, 2006, Final Report.*

17   Parliamentary Assembly of the Council of Europe (PACE), 'Stunning progress achieved in Georgia is an example for the whole region and beyond', September 19, 2007 <http://assembly.coe.int/ASP/Press/StopPressView.asp?ID=1958>.

18   <http://www.ohchr.org/english/bodies/hrc/docs/CCPR.C.GEO.CO.3.CRP.1.pdf>.

19   <www.km.ru, September 26, 2007.

20   Giorgi Kupadze, 'Street battles rock Georgian capital', *Caucasus Reporting Service*, no. 418, November 7, 2007.

21   Ibid.

22   International Crisis Group, *Georgia: Sliding towards authoritarianism?* Europe Report no. 189, December 19, 2007.

23   Human Rights Watch, 'Crossing the line – Georgia's violent dispersal of protestors and raid on Imedi Television', December 2007.

24   Svante E. Cornell, Johanna Popjanevski and Niklas Nilsson, 'Learning from Georgia's crisis: implications and recommendations', Central Asia-Caucasus and Silk Road Studies Program, Johns Hopkins University, Baltimore, Md., December 2007 <www.silkroadstudies.org>.

25   Vladimer Papava, 'Georgia's hollow revolution: Does Georgia's pro-Western and anti-Russian policy amount to democracy?' *Harvard International Review*, 2008.

26   Stephen Jones, 'A tale of two rallies', *Harvard International Review*, 2008.

27   Lincoln Mitchell, 'What was the Rose Revolution for? Understanding the Georgian revolution', *Harvard International Review*, 2008.

28   *Caucasus Reporting Service*, no. 420, November 22, 2007.

29   Statement by EU-Georgia Parliamentary Cooperation Committee, April 29–30, 2008.

30   Alia, November 22, 2007 <www.regnum.ru>.

31   *Interpress News*, January 8, 2003.

32 *Financial Times*, January 4, 2008.
33 *Civil Georgia*, December 29, 2007.
34 *Rustavi2* website, January 8, 2003.
35 Anna Dolidze and Irakli Jibladze, 'Anatomy of Georgia's anti-revolution', <www.theglobalist.com>, January 3 and 4, 2008.
36 Carl Bildt, Utrikesminister (minister of foreign affairs), Uttalande, Utrikesdepartementet (Statement, Ministry of Foreign Affairs, Sweden), January 6, 2008.
37 *Economist*, January 10, 2008.
38 OSCE/ODIHR Election Observation Mission, 'Georgia extraordinary presidential election, 5 January 2008', Final Report, March 4, 2008.
39 <www.newsgeorgia.ru> February 8, 2008.
40 *Caucasus Reporting Service*, no. 431, February 13, 2008.
41 *Izvestia*, January 8, 2009.
42 Niklas Nilsson and Svante E. Cornell, 'Georgia's May 2008, parliamentary elections: setting sail in a storm', Central Asia-Caucasus Institute and Silk Road Studies Program, May 2008.
43 *Caucasus Reporting Service*, no. 440, April 17, 2008.
44 Georgian Greens' report to the European Greens, May 15, 2008.
45 *Caucasus Reporting Service*, no. 445, May 22, 2008.
46 A joint undertaking by OSCE/ODIHR, OSCE Parliamentary Assembly, PACE, the EU Parliament and the NATO Parliamentary Assembly.
47 *Civil Georgia*, September 11, 2008.
48 Transparency International, London/Berlin, 26 September 2007.
49 *Golovinskij Prospekt*, no. 16, May, 2007, <www.golovin-ave.fortuna-7.com>.
50 Economist Intelligence Unit, 'Georgia country report, March 2007', <www.eiu.com>, 2007.
51 Lili Di Puppo, 'International and national approaches to the fight against corruption in Georgia: different methods, different objectives?' Forschungsstelle Osteuropa an der Universität Bremen, contribution presented at a Conference on Crises and Conflicts in Eastern European States and Societies: Stumbling Blocks or Stepping Stones for Democratization? Warsaw, September 2–8, 2007, <www.changing-europe.org>.
52 *GeorgiaCountry factsheet*, <www.ebrd.com/projects>.
53 Johnny Munkhammar and Jon Millarp, *Georgien – den lysande stjärnan på reformhimlen* (Georgia – the shining star on the reform sky), Timbro, Stockholm, August 28, 2008.
54 UNDP Georgia, 'Report on the non-observed economy in Georgia', Summary of new statistical estimates, Economic analysis and policy recommendations, June 30, 2007.
55 International Crisis Group, *Georgia: sliding towards authoritarianism?*
56 Commission of the European Communities, *Progress Report Georgia*, Brussels, April 3, 2008, SEC(2008) 393.
57 World Bank, *Georgia Profile*, 2009.
58 *Novaya Gazeta*, March 23, 2009.

12

THE OSSETIA WAR 2008 – A CONSPIRACY, BUT BY WHOM?

Immediately after the start of the 'five days war' between Georgia and the Russian Federation in August 2008, the Institute for War and Peace Reporting[1] dared state that 'everyone agrees that the Georgian army launched an attack at 11.30 pm that night (August 7)'.[2] Since then a great number of reports have agreed with this conclusion about the direct beginning of the war. The overall impression given by all these accounts is that both sides were well prepared and had in fact been mobilizing for quite some time, both politically and militarily, including carrying out major military exercises, while lying in wait for each other in order not to bear the blame for having started a war. Just after the beginning of the assault, the programme on the television station Rustavi 2 was interrupted for an announcement that Georgia had decided to 'restore the constitutional order' in the Tskhinvali Region (South Ossetia). Twenty-four hours later President Saakashvili called for international assistance and support against 'the Russian aggression', while at the same time claiming that Georgian troops controlled all of South Ossetia with the exception of a small mountain village.[3] As a matter of fact Russian military forces did not need much more than a day to push back the US-trained and Israel-armed Georgian army. On August 11 the former Soviet Communist Party mouthpiece *Pravda* boasted that 'the Americans admit that in South Ossetia it was not a Georgian but an American Army that was defeated'.

The truth was of course more complicated. Two weeks after the war the International Crisis Group gave the following summary:

> Moscow's initial moves into South Ossetia as large-scale violence broke out there on 7–8 August were in part a response to a disastrous miscalculation by a Georgian leadership that was impatient with gradual confidence building and a Russian-dominated

negotiations process. But Russia's disproportionate counter-attack … constitutes a dramatic shift in Russian–Western relations.[4]

One possible starting point for the escalation might have been the announcement on March 4 by the newly appointed Georgian minister of reintegration, Temuri Yakobishvili, that Georgia was withdrawing from the four party Joint Control Commission which had been monitoring the ceasefire in South Ossetia since 1992. Another possible starting point might be the formal cancellation by Russia two days later of its adherence to the international trade sanctions against Abkhazia, which Georgia publicly interpreted as an 'attack upon the sovereignty and territorial integrity of Georgia'.[5] This was followed a month later by an order by President Vladimir Putin to Russian authorities to establish 'special relations' with Abkhazia and South Ossetia.[6] In July Russian forces held a military exercise, 'Caucasus 2008', in the Russian North Caucasus region, which some observers described as a 'dress rehearsal' for what later happened, at the same time as other observers gave the same label to a joint US–Georgia military exercise, 'Immediate response'.

THE FINAL ESCALATION

On August 1 several Georgian policemen were wounded by Ossetian gunfire. The next day South Ossetia announced that it was evacuating children to North Ossetia, which Georgia interpreted as a preparation for violence. South Ossetia said that three militiamen and three civilians had been killed by Georgian bullets. On the following days reports about killings and attacks, as well as mutual warnings and accusations, escalated from Georgia, South Ossetia and Russia. A Russian journalist reported that the town of Tskhinvali was the goal of Georgian artillery shelling on August 6.[7] However the next day President Saakashvili, in a televised address, offered an immediate ceasefire, ordered Georgian forces to stop shooting and proposed 'full autonomy' to South Ossetia. This superficially peace-friendly move was interpreted as a trap, not only by South Ossetians and Russians, but also by independent commentators, one of whom observed that the same night 'Saakashvili went for the military option.'[8]

Georgia has afterwards maintained that its attack was a reply to the movement of Russian troops into South Ossetia through the Roki tunnel from North Ossetia. This argument has been refuted by

Russians and South Ossetians as well as by independent observers and Western media. During the night between August 7 and 8 Georgian spokespersons made no reference to any Russian attack, but explained the Georgian assault only by referring to the 'restoration of the constitutional order' in South Ossetia. Several eyewitnesses claim to have seen no Russian troops move southwards until after the Georgian onslaught upon South Ossetia. Three months after the war the *New York Times* concluded that 'no conclusive evidence has been as yet presented by Georgia or its Western allies that Russia was invading the country before the Georgian attack'.[9]

'OPERATION CLEAR FIELD'

The Georgian attack was codenamed 'Operation Clear Field', which South Ossetia has interpreted as a covert acknowledgement that the real aim was ethnic cleansing of Ossetians. Initially Georgian troops advanced and killed many Ossetians and several Russian members of the peacekeeping forces. Ossetians and Russians accused Georgia of committing genocide, which was obviously a gross exaggeration. However both the BBC and Human Rights Watch reported that Georgian soldiers committed war crimes during their attack and occupation of Tskhinvali.[10] The situation changed rapidly, however, and by the afternoon of August 9 Russian troops had forced the Georgians out of Tskhinvali. The whole of South Ossetia was abandoned by the Georgians, including the Georgian-populated villages.

Georgians who had not had time to escape were often badly treated or even killed by South Ossetian militias. Russian troops continued into Georgia proper and killed several civilians. Gori was especially hard hit, but so were other towns and villages in Georgia proper, such as the harbour town of Poti, where a part of the Georgian fleet was sunk. The Abkhazians exploited the chaos to evict Georgians from the Kodori valley, the only part of Abkhazia that had been under Georgian control. Tens of thousands of refugees were moving in different directions.

The rapid defeat and retreat of the Georgian troops has been explained by the intervention of a military superpower, Russia. The Russian journalist Arkadij Babtjenko, who covered the war for *Novaya Gazeta*, has another explanation. In fact, the high-tech equipment of the Georgian forces was superior to the relatively low technological level of the Russian and Ossetian military hardware.

But something else was obviously inferior among the Georgians, according to Babtjenko – their fighting spirit! 'Maybe they hadn't understood the point of the war, they were not prepared to die for a united Georgia.'[11]

CEASEFIRE

On August 12 President Medvedev ordered Russian troops to end all military operations in Georgia, and the next day all the belligerent parties – Russia, Georgia, South Ossetia and Abkhazia – accepted a peace plan proposed by the acting president of the European Union, French President Nicolas Sarkozy. At the last moment Mikheil Saakashvili managed to delete a paragraph in the proposed agreement that called for continued discussions on the future status of the secessionist regions. His aim was to prevent any impression that Georgia might accept a change in the formal status of South Ossetia and Abkhazia, but as the world got to know, Russia came to quite an opposite interpretation. With no agreed prospect for further discussions about the status of the seceded territories, which had not been under Georgian authority since the early 1990s, on August 26 Russia recognized their sovereignty, using the recognition of Kosovo by many Western governments as a precedent. If President Medvedev had signed an agreement promising further talks about the status of South Ossetia and Abkhazia it might have been difficult for him to recognize their statehood.

There had been quite a number of warnings that this was what might happen as a result of the unilateral recognition of Kosovo by the West. One example was a joint statement by the Greens in Georgia and Azerbaijan in February, which stated that 'the independence of Kosovo must not become a precedent for other conflicts, such as in South Caucasus'.[12]

The Russian recognition of Abkhazia and South Ossetia was condemned by the European Union, the Council of Europe and most Western states. The right-wing Swedish minister of foreign affairs, Carl Bildt, said that 'the independence of South Ossetia is a joke'.[13] He obviously did not take into consideration that at least ten recognized UN members have less than 50,000 inhabitants. What about Liechtenstein, with half the number of inhabitants of South Ossetia and 25 times less territory, which is a full member of the United Nations, the Council of Europe and EFTA? Several Swedish experts of international law retorted that there was nothing illegal in the Russian recognition.[14] However, the EU Tagliavini report takes an opposite view, and states that 'recognition of breakaway entities such as Abkhazia and South Ossetia by a third country is ... contrary to international law'.[15]

Only hours after the Russian recognition of Abkhazia and South Ossetia on August 26, President Saakashvili in a televised speech compared the Russian action with annexations and conquests by Hitler and Stalin, and made an effort to internationalize the issue, by claiming that 'Georgia's economic success, further development of our democracy is no longer a matter between us and Russia; this is a matter between Russia's current illegal authorities and the rest of the civilized world.'

THE AFTERMATH

On August 13 I received an email from a friend in Tbilisi who complained about the lack of reliable information. 'The Georgian authorities talk about 200 dead, despite rumours mentioning 2,000, some say 4,000, we even hear 7,000.' Other rumours said that Russian troops were starting to invade Tbilisi in order to topple the Saakashvili regime. Some nationalistic politicians in Moscow were calling for just that. In such a situation a strong urge for national unity was natural. One Georgian newspaper reported that 'the opposition expresses its solidarity with the government'.[16] On August 21 more than 50 NGOs called upon 'the entire society to unite to achieve a single objective – to force Russian occupational forces out of Georgia'.

At the same time there were critical newspaper voices against the United States: 'Despite the fact that we have soldiers in Iraq, the Americans haven't helped us with weapons or soldiers!' As a matter of fact the United States organized an airlift that brought back 2,000 Georgian soldiers from Iraq. The European Union earmarked 1 million for humanitarian aid. Nevertheless, a Georgian soldier told the *International Herald Tribune,* 'North America and the European Union spit on us.'[17]

Less than a week after the ceasefire, I received an email which well expressed the desperate feelings among Georgians who normally rejected military chauvinism:

> I and my friends helped a peaceful demonstration yesterday. 'Join us for peace!' was my message to the world. Aleko didn't join the demonstration, he was standing aside gloomy. He was in

Tskhinvali and Gori last week. He said he saw too many dead bodies to walk around with a stupid banner which is just a voice to nowhere. Join us for peace? Sure, but peace costs and also democracy costs. So what is the price of peace? Did the European diplomacy lose against Russia, or did they sell Georgia for a few barrels of oil?

The direct results of the war in human casualties and material damage are not easy to estimate. The EU Tagliavini report estimates that Georgia suffered 170 military servicemen, 14 policemen and 228 civilians killed and 1,747 wounded. There were 67 Russian military servicemen killed and 283 wounded. The South Ossetians had 365 casualties, including both military servicemen and civilians.[18] According to reports by Human Rights Watch and Amnesty, both sides violated international law during the war.[19] The president of the South Caucasus Delegation of the European Parliament, Marie Anne Isler-Beguin, reported on August 19 from a rapid visit to the war zone about 'looting, killing, burning, and the destroying of houses, kidnapping etc. …vandalizing and destroying of everything "Georgian"', carried out by unidentifiable military personnel behind the advancing Russian forces.[20] The Bank of Georgia estimated the material damage at US$1 billion. Media reports put the cost for Russia at US$2.5 billion. All parties, Georgia, Russia and the South Ossetians, have started judicial proceedings in international courts, accusing the other sides of atrocities, war crimes and attempted genocide.

After the war Abkhazia demanded that the international community should prevent Georgia from having its own military forces, alleging that during its periods of independence Georgia has started seven wars.[21] On September 9 Russia officially announced that it would keep some 3,700 troops in South Ossetia and Abkhazia under bilateral agreements. International observers arrived at the border areas on October 1, and Russia completed its withdrawal from Georgia proper on October 8. NATO has decided to increase its presence in the Black Sea region.

The European Parliament on September 3 could not avoid admitting that the war was started by Georgia, when 'during the night of 7/8 August 2008 the Georgian army launched a surprise artillery attack on Tskhinvali followed by a ground operation using both tanks and soldiers aimed at regaining control over South Ossetia'. Nevertheless the only explicit 'condemnation' by the European Parliament was directed against Russia.[22] The Parliamentary Assembly of the

Council of Europe, one month later, was more even-handed; it criticized both Georgia and Russia and made concrete demands to all involved parties.[23]

The closest allies of Russia were conspicuously silent. As observed by the independent Russian newspaper *Nezavisimaya Gazeta,* at a meeting by the members of the CSTO on August 22, nothing was said in support of the Russian intervention in Georgia.[24]

CONTRADICTORY CONSPIRACY THEORIES

Was the Georgian–Russian war the result of a Georgian–American–Israeli conspiracy in order to lure Russia into a trap and thereby create a basis for a new cold war, for the benefit of the arms industry, not least in Israel, which has been rearming Georgia for several years?[25] This hypothesis was presented by the left-wing researcher Michel Chossoudovsky.[26] Several others have presented similar ideas. According to Russian media reports, as far back as 2006 Georgia finalized a plan codenamed 'Tiger jump', the aim of which was, with US support, to force Russia to withdraw its peace forces from Abkhazia and South Ossetia.[27] The Russian writers Mikhail Leontiev and Dimitri Zhukov claim that 'the Americans set their dog against us'.[28] Even a US lawmaker, Representative Dana Rohrbacher, put the blame upon Georgia.[29] So did quite a few Georgians. In September 2008, the former minister of defence, Irakli Okruashvili, said to Reuters that he and Saakashvili together 'drew up military plans in 2005 for taking both Abkhazia and South Ossetia'.[30] On November 25 Erosi Kitsmarishvili, Georgia's last ambassador in Moscow, maintained that President Saakashvili had been on the verge of a military operation against Abkhazia in the spring of 2008. In December another former minister of defence, Georgi Karkarashvili, told the BBC that it was obviously untrue that the Georgian troops in South Ossetia had only undertaken defensive action.[31] On Christmas Eve the former Georgian ambassador to the United Nations, Irakli Alasania, claimed that 'the President of Georgia is responsible for engaging Georgia in this provocative war'.[32]

On September 4 an open letter by 80 Georgian intellectuals, authors and journalists, was published in *Resonansi,* demanding an open and honest debate, instead of the 'extensive propaganda currently underway blaming everyone, aggressive Russia, the ignorant West, the opposition, Russian spies etc., everyone, except for the authorities themselves'.[33]

Quite an opposite conspiracy theory has been proposed by Georgian officials, Western think tanks and Russian opposition media. Just after the end of the war Pavel Felgengauer of *Novaya Gazeta* published extensive arguments that the war was a provocation by the Kremlin to lure Saakashvili into a trap in order to clear the way for a comeback for Russia as the superior watchman in Caucasus and as a superpower on the world stage.[34] One of Putin's former advisors, Andrei Illarionov, also expressed his conviction that Russia had prepared and started the war.[35]

Both these opposing theories, in varying forms, have since gathered supporters. Even the pro-western Central Asia-Caucasus Institute acknowledged that 'hawks in the Georgian government had been drafting plans to re-take at least parts of the conflict zones by force, despite strong warnings by Georgia's Western allies'. However it maintained that 'while Tbilisi may well have used disproportionate force against Ossetians, Russia's aggression against Georgia appears well prepared and pre-meditated'.[36]

Maybe the German weekly magazine *Der Spiegel* was closest to the truth when it concluded that both sides mobilized during the summer in a kind of 'chicken race'.[37] Perhaps both the Kremlin and Mikheil Saakashvili set traps for each other. And perhaps both, from their own point of view, gained something. At least for some time the militant opposition against Saakashvili closed ranks with him and stopped their open criticism. Although this political truce did not last very long, it contributed to enhancing his prestige in the West, which paved the way for stronger promises than before, at least initially, from several capitals that Georgia's entry into NATO is just a matter of time. At the same time the Kremlin, while losing sympathy and even prestige in the West, won support at home and respect in those parts of the world that are keen to see the reestablishment of some counterbalancing power to the global hegemony of the United States.

According to one hypothesis the South Ossetia issue is, at least partly, an offshoot of the Middle East conflict. Chossoudovsky's observation that there is a strong Israeli support for the Saakashvili regime has been confirmed by other sources, for example by the veteran Israeli peacenik, Uri Avnery, who has reported that several Georgian government ministers at the time of the August war had grown up in Israel, and that at least two are Israeli citizens.[38] And one of the few state leaders who openly supported Russia was the president of the only remaining (moderately) militant Arab state, Bashar al-Assad of Syria. Despite this, it seems very far-fetched

184 GEORGIA

to regard the South Ossetia issue as an extension of the Palestine issue.

A STRUGGLE ABOUT DEMOCRACY?

Another popular hypothesis is that the Georgian–Russian confrontation is about democracy – the Democrats of the Rose Revolution versus the authoritarian Russian bear under Putin and Medvedev. But despite the indisputable fact that Russia is becoming worryingly more and more authoritarian, as shown not only by foreign observers but primarily by courageous Russian human rights activists, protesting intellectuals and honest mass media, such as *Novaya Gazeta*, Russia today is very far from a Stalinist dictatorship. As the Austrian diplomat and former official in the European Commission, Albrecht Rotbacher, underlines in an otherwise rather anti-Russian book, the authoritarian Putin–Medvedev system is not a dictatorship but constitutes a 'huge humanitarian and civilizational step forward', compared with most of its predecessors.[39] A group of Swedish experts on Russia, while admitting that the Yeltsin period may have been politically more democratic, underline that 'the Russians have never been so economically free as today'.[40]

That Georgia still has a long way to go before it qualifies as a fully fledged democracy, has been shown in this book. Thus, to describe the Russian–Georgian conflict, and especially the South Ossetia War of 2008, as a clash between dictatorship and democracy is missing the point and a distortion of facts.

An astounding paradox has been detected by the former minister of economy of Georgia, Vladimer Papava, who in spring 2008 made the observation, 'After the Rose Revolution Georgia opened its doors to Russian capital which has continued to flow despite the embargo on Georgian exports that Russia initiated in spring 2006.'[41] According to the Russian Embassy in Tbilisi, the Russian investments in Georgia trebled in 2007, to US$92.6 billion from $34.4 billion the previous year.

This phenomenon has been noticed in the Georgian public debate by some members of the opposition, who maintain that the whole Georgian–Russian confrontation is a smokescreen to conceal Russian economic imperialism in collusion with the corrupt power elite of Georgia. To support such assertions some mention the fact that only a couple of months after having acceded to power, President Saakashvili made a Russian financial oligarch, Kakha Bendukidze, minister of the economy. Although he is of Georgian decent, Bendukidze was a

Russian citizen, settled in Russia. His nomination was interpreted by the mouthpiece of the Russian government, *Rossijskaya Gazeta*, as a sign that Georgia was going to replace the Soros people with persons who were more Russia-oriented. Bendukidze later became minister for economic reform, and until January 2008 headed a privatization campaign under the slogan 'We sell everything except our honour'.[42]

Just after the August War the Green Party of Georgia published a long list of key Russian purchases of Georgian companies in the banking, transport and industry sectors, under the headline 'Expansion of Russian capital in Georgia. What foreign policy direction does the Georgia government have in reality?' And a Georgian website, two weeks after the eruption of the war, reported, 'The Georgian Government remains loyal to the Russian investors even during the recent Russian–Georgian conflict. Russian capital, including the banking sector, energy, oil, mobile communications, plants, air companies, have all felt comfortable in Georgia up till now.'[43]

Another example of the difficulty in cutting all links to Russia even during a war was the repercussions of Georgia's decision on September 2, 2008, to cut off diplomatic relations and to introduce restrictions to the opportunities for Russians to be granted visas to Georgia from September 8. Russia immediately stopped issuing entry visas for Georgians. On September 4 Georgia retreated and announced that Russians would be issued visas as before, at border stations.[44]

The manifest Russian presence in Georgian economy, despite the war, and the unwillingness of the Tbilisi rulers to intervene against the economic tentacles of the Big Bear, is of course no proof of a covert conspiracy. Nevertheless such a rational observer as Vladimer Papava told me in September 2009 that there are two Georgias, a rhetorical one which is anti-Russia and pro-democracy and a real one, which is controlling the media and judiciary and thrives on Russian money. His blunt explanation for the strong position of Russian capital in Georgia was either bribes or some other means of covert control of Saakashvili, who he alleged worked in a KGB department during the Soviet period. In any case it is obvious that money plays an enormous, albeit often hidden, role for all players, from local Ossetian and Abkhazian smugglers and Russian and Georgian soldiers who sell arms to 'freedom fighters', via international arms dealers and the power elite of the region, who may increase their meagre state salaries through privatizations and special accounts, to the very big actors, Russia, the United States and the European Union, which compete for control over fossil fuels.

When Russian bombs started to fall over Gori, one American commentator, close to the Pentagon, hysterically warned that Russia, as the result of the war, 'can then monopolize Caspian energy flows to Europe and use that power and those revenues to corrupt and subvert European political institutions peacefully'.[45] Therefore it was probably with of a sigh of relief the American diplomat Matthew Bryza on August 23 publicly exclaimed, 'Russia has not tried to damage the oil pipeline Baku–Tbilisi–Ceyhan.'[46] The flow of oil in the pipeline, which was estimated to transport 1.2 million barrels every day, was then interrupted by an explosion in Turkey for which Kurdish rebels took the responsibility, which is an interesting reminder that a threat against the energy supply to the West may originate from other causes than power-greedy monopolists in the Kremlin.

COUNTERMOVES AGAINST RUSSIAN RE-EMERGENCE?

One trend, which was not taken much notice of in the West, was reported by the Central Asia-Caucasus Institute at the end of July 2008: Russia was trying to break up the Baku–Tbilisi–Ankara alliance through high-level visits to Azerbaijan and Turkey. In Baku President Medvedev and his colleague Aliyev signed a treaty of friendship and strategic partnership, and in Ankara the Russian foreign minister Lavrov discussed the possibilities of opening the border between Turkey and Armenia. The CACI analysis of these developments comments that a precondition for improved Armenian–Turkish relations is a solution to the conflict about Nagorno-Karabakh between Armenia and Azerbaijan, which Russia obviously has been trying to bring about.[47] Because Russia is a trustworthy ally of Armenia, such a solution must be some kind of compromise from the Azeri demands for a total return to the situation before the secession. But a compromise solution sponsored by Moscow is hardly in the interest of the Saakashvili regime. That may be a reason why it was considered urgent to take action before a precedent for the seceded territories in South Caucasus, inspired by the Kremlin, was set by a solution to the Nagorno-Karabakh conflict. If such considerations contributed to Saakashvili's decision to act, it was a failure, because on November 2, 2008, the presidents of Russia, Azerbaijan and Armenia signed a common declaration on Nagorno-Karabakh for the first time since 1992, pledging to find a 'political settlement' to the conflict.[48]

If the Georgian attack could thus be seen as more directed to stop Russia's re-emergence as a power broker in the region, than to reconquer South Ossetia, the violent Russian counterattack might be seen as directed not against Georgia, but against the other side in the Great Game, or as it is expressed by the American Colonel Jon E. Chick, a member of the military faculty at the National War College's Department of Strategy and Policy, 'The Russian military action cannot be regarded as a simple punishment of Georgia aimed at rendering the country militarily impotent. It is rather to be seen as a message to the U.S. that Russia can act at will against Georgia or any other U.S.-interests in Eurasia.'[49]

However, in the eyes of many Russians the conflict with Georgia is but a minor part of a much greater play, where the West is planning the same end for the Russian Federation as for the Soviet Union. One of many such signs was a small news item from the Russian news agency Regnum in April 2008 with the headline 'The orange predict the breakdown of Russia in 2010'. The origin of the item was a statement by Ukrainian, not Georgian, anti-Russian nationalists, but taking into account the close relations between Yushchenko in Kiev and Saakashvili in Tbilisi, it is hardly surprising that some Russians consider Ukraine and Georgia as allies in a conspiracy to bring down the Russian Federation.

As Russia, through the Shanghai Group, seems to be establishing a new power bloc together with China and the Central Asian oil states that have common frontiers with the problem child of the United States and NATO, Afghanistan, there is no need to be a conspiracy theorist in order to believe that in fact there do exist dreams in some Western power circles that the Russian Federation should end up in the same dustbin as the Soviet Union. Maybe some Western politicians want the clock to be turned back to the time before Peter the Great when Russia was a backward marginal country which Europeans did not have to care about. Maybe some Russians believe that the West intends to make come true what the American historian Marshall T. Poe claims actually happened in 1991, that the 'Russian time came to an end'.[50]

DISSIDENT VOICES

There was no lack of dissident Russian voices during the August war, from best-seller writer Boris Akunin, born in Tbilisi as Grigory Shalvovich Chkhartishvili, to writers in oppositional newspapers such as *Novaya Gazeta*, *Nezavisimaya Gazeta* and *Kommersant*. The liberal party SPS, a union of right-wing forces, openly supported the Georgian side, and some liberal politicians handed out badges announcing 'I am a Georgian', which provoked the newspaper *Izvestia* to accuse them of being 'against the Russian people'.[51] Some peaceniks had time to set up their banners in Red Square before being arrested. In *Novaya Gazeta* the author Gleb Shulpjakov wrote, 'The conflict gave the power elite a chance to show a new non-Soviet, non-barbarian policy. But it happened as has happened to Moscow, which could have been a world metropolis, but has become an Asian backyard.'[52]

In Georgia, because of the enormous pressure for national unity, most dissident voices waited some time. Nevertheless Nino Burjanadze declared while Russian troops were still deployed in Georgia proper that 'it would be a major mistake to seek a way out by NATO, USA or EU,' and that there is a need for a new policy 'where relations to Russia are put on a rational track'.[53] She also accused her own government of having jumped into a trap set by the Russians.[54]

THE EUROPEAN UNION BLAMES GEORGIA MOST, WHICH EMBARRASSES THE EU PRESIDENCY

On September 30, 2009, an EU-sponsored committee led by the Swiss diplomat Heidi Tagliavini published a thousand-page report which corroborated the initial reports.[55] Civil Georgia summarized the findings of the committee as follows:

- It is impossible 'to assign overall responsibility' to one side alone.
- Open hostilities began with Georgia's shelling of Tskhinvali.
- Some Russian forces other than peace troops were in South Ossetia prior to Georgia's attack.
- Georgia's use of force was unjustifiable.
- Russia's use of force beyond South Ossetia was also unjustifiable.
- The Georgian intention to carry out genocide 'could not be proven'.
- Ethnic cleansing was carried out against Georgians.[56]

This confirmed leakages to the German magazine *Der Spiegel*, which had predicted that the EU report would put the blame for the beginning of the fighting on Georgia, while also criticizing Russia for an exaggerated counter-reaction.[57] The Georgian government tried to

strike back by accusing *Der Spiegel* of getting its information from
the Russian Secret Service and being owned by Gazprom.[58]

The EU report was embarrassing not only for the warring parties,
and most of all for Georgia, but also for some Caucasus experts
and Western politicians who had put all the blame on Russia and
relieved the Saakashvili regime of guilt. Only a month before the
EU report the Swedish Caucasus expert Svante Cornell (together
with Frederick Starr) published a book on the Ossetia War which,
despite containing several balanced and factual contributions by
experienced journalists and scholars, delivers a unilateral accusation
in its subtitle: 'Russia's war in Georgia'. In their introduction Cornell
and Starr make the unqualified assertion that 'for the first time since
1979 the Russian military crossed national borders to *attack* [my
emphasis] a sovereign state'.[59] The main conclusion is that the West
must 'respond to Russia's revival of a classical modern, Realpolitik
culture of security'. Or in other words – a new cold war!

There is no indication that this book has been supported by the
Swedish Ministry of Foreign Affairs, as have other studies on the
Caucasus by Cornell's institute.[60] Nevertheless the situation became
rather piquant because during the period from July to December 2009
the presidency of the European Union was held by Sweden, whose
minister of foreign affairs, Carl Bildt (a conservative), is a well-known
hawk on Russia, and started his political career in the 1980s by orches-
trating violent accusations against Russia for having sent submarines into Swedish waters. However, Bildt's credibility has been badly
hurt by recent investigations, according to which most of the alleged
submarines were diving animals – or submarines from NATO, testing
the Swedish defence system![61] At the end of August 2009 he was also
criticized in a cover story of the Swedish newsmagazine *Fokus*, under
the title 'Left behind in the cold war – Carl Bildt is making his own
race, which splits the EU and gives him many enemies'. One reason
for Bildt's difficulties in trying to unite the European Union behind a
common policy, the article asserts, is that he:

> made a mistake when by extremely harsh words he condemned
> the Russian invasion of Georgia ... making parallels to Nazi
> Germany ... furthermore many observers are of the opinion that
> the Georgians started the shooting, which has not strengthened
> the position of Bildt in France and Germany, which have many
> good relations with Moscow.[62]

As a matter of fact no comment on the Tagliavini report by Carl

Bildt could be found by November 2009 on the website of the Swedish Minister of Foreign Affairs, that of the Swedish EU presidency, or on his own blog.

In a first reaction the Georgian government tried to interpret the report in its own favour, although it complained 'that the report did not contain direct wording about Russian military aggression'. The Russian Foreign Ministry also raised some objections but on the whole was satisfied with 'the major conclusion about Tbilisi's fault for unleashed aggression against peaceful South Ossetia'.[63]

At the EU-Georgia Association Council on October 26, 2009, in Tbilisi, there was no criticism by the EU delegation, led by Carl Bildt, against Georgia because of the findings of the Tagliavini report, a fact that surprised the *Georgian Times*, which in an analytical article stated that 'the EU gave encouragement to the Georgian government that the opposition calls authoritarian. Remarkably, the Europeans paid compliments for freedom of mass media that the independent TV channels and newspapers in Georgia don't quite feel.'[64] However, according to some sources EU diplomats at the sidelines of the official EU–Caucasus summit declared that 'Georgia no longer enjoys front-runner status in the region', mainly because 'political reforms have been moved to the back burner, as the country's increasingly restrictive president, Mikheil Saakashvili, has accumulated an estimated 200 political prisoners and taken over the country's most influential media outlets'.[65] It is uncertain whether the Tagliavini report will contribute to a solution of the conflicts. While the representative of South Ossetia at the Geneva four-party talks believed that the report would lead to a breakthrough,[66] the Russian General Staff warned of renewed Georgian efforts to solve the conflict by military means;[67] and president Saakashvili appointed as his seventh minister of defence in six years a notorious hawk, 28-year-old Batcho Akhaia, who at his previous post as general director of the prison system has displayed utter neglect for humanitarian principles.[68] In a speech to students Saakashvili emphasized that one of the cornerstones of modern Georgia is 'military-patriotic education'.[69]

However, signs appeared that more and more people in the area are not satisfied with the official efforts to find solutions. One example was a meeting in November between the Orthodox Patriarchs of Russia and Georgia in Baku, where the two men promised to make huge efforts to restore good neighbourly relations between Russia and Georgia.[70] Another example was the 'private' visit by one of the many former prime ministers of the Saakashvili regime, Zurab Nogaideli, to the Kremlin, where he had talks at the Ministry of Foreign Affairs.[71]

The repercussions of the Ossetian War will persist for a long time. At the end of 2009 still tens of thousands of displaced persons have not been able to return to their homes and skirmishes erupt every now and then along the borders of the seceded statelets. Nevertheless there are signs that more and more people have learned a lesson and understand that Georgia's problems cannot be resolved only by support from outsiders, but also require the establishment of normal neighbourly relations in the Caucasus region.

NOTES

1   <www.iwpr.net>. According to its home page, 'IWPR maintains a diverse international base of private foundations, individuals and government agencies to avoid dependence on any single source.' Among dozens of supporters are the British Council and the Swedish International Development Agency, SIDA.

2   *Caucasus Reporting Service*, 'How the Georgian war began', report no. 456, August 22, 2008.

3   *Svobodnaya Gruzia*, 'Overview of the armed conflict', August 2008.

4   International Crisis Group, 'Russia vs. Georgia: the fallout', Europe Report no. 195, August 22, 2008.

5   *Kommersant*, March 7, 2008.

6   *Kommersant*, April 17, 2008.

7   *Nezavisimaya Gazeta*, August 7, 2008.

8   *Caucasus Reporting Service,* no. 452:1, July 25, 2008.

9   *New York Times*, November 6, 2008.

10 AFP, August 7, 2008.

11 Arkadij Babtjenko, *Bilder av ett litet krig* (Pictures of a small war, translated from Russian), Ersatz, Stockholm, 2009.

12 Statement by the Green Parties in Georgia and Azerbaijan, February 25, 2008.

13 *Sydsvenska Dagbladet*, August 30, 2008.

14 Ove Bring, professor of international law at the Swedish National Defence college and Said Mahmoudi, professor of international law at Stockholm University, in the radio newsreel *Dagens Eko*, August 27, 2008.

15 Independent International Fact-Finding Mission on the Conflict in Georgia, *Report, Volume I*, p. 17. The report refers to the *uti possidetis* principle and also takes Russia's refusal to accept the independence of Kosovo as an argument against its recognition of Abkhazia and South Ossetia.

16 *Kviris Palitra*, August 11–17.

17 EUOBSERVER, August 11, 2008.

194

18 Independent International Fact-Finding Mission on the Conflict in Georgia, *Report, Volume I*, p. 5.
19 Report by Amnesty International, November 2008; Report by Human Rights Watch, August 18, 2008.
20 Marie Anne Isler Beguin, 'Report from the chair', European Parliament, Ad Hoc Delegation to Georgia, August 12–17, 2008, EURO/SP/sw/19.08.2008.
21 *Interfax*, August 12, 2008.
22 European Parliament Resolution of September 3, 2008 on the situation in Georgia, P6_TA-PROV(2008)0396.
23 PACE resolution on the consequences of the war between Georgia and Russia, adopted on October 2, 2008.
24 *Nezavisimaya Gazeta*, August 22, 2008
25 Ali Abunimah, 'Tel Aviv to Tbilisi: Israel's role in the Russia-Georgia war', *The Electronic Intifada*, August 12, 2008.
26 Centre for Research on Globalization, August 10, 2008.
27 *Nezavisimaya Gazeta*, 'When does the tiger jump?' (in Russian), March 1, 2006; *Novy Region,* 'South Ossetia awaiting the tiger jump' (in Russian), March 22, 2008.
28 Mikhail Leontiev and Dmitrij Zhukov, *'Nezavisimaya' Gruzia – bandit v tigrovoj shkure* ('Independent' Georgia – a bandit in a tiger's hide), Yuaza Press, Moscow, 2008.
29 *Daily Telegraph,* September 9, 2008.
30 *International Herald Tribune*, 'US Congressman defends Russia in Georgia conflict', September 12, 2008.
31 BBC (in Russian), December 20, 2008.
32 *Civil Georgia*, December 24, 2008.
33 *Civil Georgia*, 'Time for tough question has come', September 4, 2008.
34 Pavel Felgenhauer, *Novaya Gazeta,* August 14, 2008.
35 Andrei Illarionov, 'Kto byl pervym?' (Who was first?), <www.illarionov.livejournal.com>, February 20, 2009.
36 Blanka Hancilova and Magdalena Frichova, *CACI Analyst,* August 20, 2008.
37 *Der Spiegel*, August 25, 2008. The expression 'chicken race' originates in a car game popular in the United States in the 1950s (according to the James Dean film *Rebel Without a Cause*) where two cars drive as fast as possible towards an abyss and the driver who first diverts is considered the loser and a coward (a chicken). The expression is also used in a figurative sense, for political and diplomatic activities.
38 Uri Avnery, *Gush Shalom,* email article, August 30, 2008.
39 Albrecht Rotbacher, *Stalins langer Schatten, Medwedjews Russland und der postsowjetische Raum* (The long shadow of Stalin, Medvedev's Russia and the post-Soviet area), Ares Verlag, Graz, 2008.
40 Anna Jonsson and Carolina Vendil Pallin, *Ryssland: Politik, samhälle och ekonomi* (Russia: politics, society and economy), SNS, Stockholm, 2009.
41 Vladimer Papava, *Harvard International Review*, spring 2008.

42 *Rossijskaya Gazeta*, no. 3491, June 2, 2004.
43 *The Financial* (website), August 25, 2008.
44 *Civil Georgia*, September 4, 2008.
45 Stephen Blank, US Army War College, *CACI Analyst*, August 20, 2008.
46 Russian website, August 23, 2008.
47 <www.cacianalyst.org/?q=node/4914>.
48 *Caucasus Reporting Service*, no. 467, November 6, 2008.
49 Central Asia-Caucasus Institute and Silk Road Studies, 'The Russian–Georgian War: political and military implications for U.S. policy', February 2009.
50 Marshall T. Poe, *Den ryska tiden i världshistorien* (The Russian time in World history), SNS, Stockholm, 2005.
51 *Izvestia*, August 10, 2009.
52 *Novaya Gazeta*, August 21–24, 2008.
53 Interview with Zurabishvili in Russian language web news agency GHN, August 21; with Burjandaze in Russian language Kavkazweb August 19, and *Vzglad-Delovaja Gazeta*, August 22.
54 *Le Monde Diplomatique*, April 2009.
55 Independent International Fact-Finding Mission on the Conflict in Georgia, Report Vol. I-III, September 2009.
56 *Civil Georgia*, September 30, 2009.
57 *Der Spiegel*, 'Kaukasus-krieg, zerschmetterter Traum' (The Caucasus war – a crushed dream), no. 25, June 15, 2009.
58 *Der Spiegel*, 'Krieg der Informationen' (War of information), no. 33, August 10, 2009.
59 Svante E. Cornell, and Frederick S. Starr, *The Guns of August 2008: Russia's war in Georgia*, M.E. Sharpe, New York, 2009.
60 See Chapter 1 of this book, note 26.
61 Mathias Mossberg, *I mörka vatten – hur svenska folket fördes bakom ljuset i ubåtsfrågan* (In dark waters – how the Swedish people was deceived about the submarines), Leopard, Stockholm, 2009. Mossberg is an ambassador and was the secretary of the last official investigation into the issue of alleged Soviet submarines. See also 'Militären vilseledde regeringen om u-båtar' (The military misled the government about submarines), by Svante Nycander, former editor-in-chief of *Dagens Nyheter*, in *Dagens Nyheter,* July 5, 2009, and 'Carl Bildt vilseleder allmänheten om ubåtarna' (Carl Bildt misleads the public about the submarines), by Sune Olofsson, former military reporter of *Svenska Dagbladet,* in *Dagens Nyheter*, July 6, 2009.
62 *Fokus*, no. 34, August 21–28, 2009.
63 *Civil Georgia*, September 30 and October 1, 2009.
64 *Georgia Times*, October 27, 2009.
65 <georgiamedi, http://georgiamediacentre.com/category/tags/carl_bildt>, October 26, 2009.
66 GHN, November 7, 2009.
67 GHN, November 5, 2009.
68 Caucaz.com, 'Géorgie: Saakachvili augmente son contrôle sur l'armée'

(Georgia: Saakashvili increases his control over the army), October 29, 2009.

69   *Civil Georgia*, November 6, 2009.
70   *Svobodnaya Gruzia*, November 7, 2009.
71   <www.georgica.net/analitic/?page=ru&id=300>.

13

AFTER THE WAR: RENEWED POLITICAL CLASHES

After a short political truce during and immediately after the war, the protests against the Saakashvili regime restarted with reinforced vehemence. The president tried to counterbalance the popular dissatisfaction by promises and dismissals of scapegoats. In a speech to the parliament on September 16, 2008, he declared that 'our aim is to create a stronger parliament, guarantee the inviolability of private property, make the media more free and unbiased and the courts more just and independent'. These commitments were seen as a covert reply to a remark by NATO general secretary Jap de Hoop Scheffer the day before, which suggested that Georgia's best route to membership of the alliance would be to undertake democratic reforms. In his speech Saakashvili also announced that he wanted more multiparty debates on the public television channels. But the opposition was not satisfied. One of the critics was the ombudsman, Sozar Subari, who stated, 'We can only dream of the quality of democracy which we had before the Rose Revolution during Shevardnadze's rule.'[1]

The first major demonstration against the Saakashvili regime after the Ossetia War was held on November 7, the first anniversary of the worst political turmoil after the Rose Revolution. Between 10,000 and 15,000 people gathered to shout 'STOP RUSSIA, STOP MISHA'. At the end of November the International Crisis Group concluded that 'a failed war and a worsening economy present severe challenges to state authority in Georgia,' and predicted that 'although President Mikhail Saakashvili's position is secure for the moment, his administration will be severely tested politically and economically in the winter and spring ahead'.[2] According to the Freedom House index on Freedom in the World 2009, Georgia is only 'partly free', with a downward trend. Out of seven indicators, three (electoral process, civil society and national democratic governance) have deteriorated, and none has improved.[3]

Another indication of the seriousness of the Georgian crisis is the 'failed states index' for 2009, which shows that Georgia has been deteriorating rapidly since the death of Zhvania. If Georgia in 2006 barely qualified to be included among the 60 failed states of the world (it was number 60, where number 1 indicates 'most failed'), it started to fall the following year, to number 58, then to number 57 in 2008, and took a big jump downwards in 2009 to number 33.[4]

In November Mikheil Saakashvili appointed his fourth prime minister since he was first elected president in January 2004, the diplomat Grigol Mgaloblishvili, who was to remain in office only about three months.

A new minister of foreign affairs, Grigol Vashadze, was also appointed. He was the sixth holder of that office since the Rose Revolution. In addition he was a citizen not only of Georgia, but of its main foe, the Russian Federation, which in the eyes of many Georgians was an incomprehensible paradox. The Green Party asked for clarification about Vashadze's activities in the 1980s when he worked in the Space and Nuclear Armament division of the Ministry of Foreign Affairs of the USSR, which, it was underlined, 'as a rule was staffed by high-ranked specialists from the Russian KGB and GRU'.[5]

The effects of the war continued to hit the headlines many months after the actual fighting. An official parliamentary report, while blaming Russia for 'aggression', also admitted 'significant failures of the Government of Georgia, National Security policy perform-ance and management and military management'. Most serious, it concluded, was that 'despite sound intelligence data, the Govern-ment of Georgia did not expect and was not ready for the aggression on as large a scale as was conducted in August 2008'.[6] This has resulted in accusations against Saakashvili for having gambled with the fate of the nation, taking a chance that the Russians would not intervene. Others have drawn the conclusion that 'somebody' must have lured him into a trap.

One effect was that the military build-up that had taken an increasing part of the state budget since the Rose Revolution, with the double aim of preparing for the reconquest of Abkhazia and South Ossetia and at the same time displaying compatibility with NATO requirements, had been revealed as highly unsatisfactory. In addition, most of what had been achieved had been destroyed by the Russian forces. Georgia had lost equipment worth US$400 million. However, worse than the material damage was the loss of confidence in the army and the resulting decline of morale among military personnel. From having been the heroes of the nation, the professional US-trained soldiers, after the humiliating defeat, numerous desertions and reports of misbehaviour against civilian Ossetians, lost much of their good reputation in the public perception.

One more lingering effect of the war was the refugees. It was estimated that around 130,000 Georgians had been displaced. While many of them were able to return to their homes after just a few months, tens of thousands were still sheltering elsewhere for a long time. In September 2009 I visited some refugee families who together with hundreds more had been settled in former Soviet military barracks outside Tbilisi, without much hope of ever being able to return to their homes in South Ossetia.

An article by a former Georgian MP, living in the United States, which was reprinted in the *Georgian Times* at the beginning of April 2009, gave a bleak picture of the situation: 'Political prisoners rot in the filthy jails. The best and the brightest have escaped to other countries seeking political asylum, and unemployment in Georgia is at the highest level in the Caucuses. The country is on the brink.'[7]

On April 9, 2009 mass demonstrations of at least 30,000 people gathered on Rustaveli Avenue to demand Saakashvili's resignation and early presidential elections. One of the opposition leaders, Irakli Alasania, declared that he was prepared to 'engage in negotiations' with the regime. Alasania was presented by some media as the main leader of the opposition, since he had received two-thirds of the votes in a poll among the readers of a weekly Georgian magazine.[8]

However, Alexander Rondeli, president of the Georgian Strategic and International Research Foundation, was of the opinion that negotiations would be of no avail because 'a step towards a compromise is viewed by our society as a weakness'.[9] According to GYLA, 'repeated attacks and physical violence were used against peaceful demonstrators' on April 9.[10] Three weeks later GYLA condemned 'the increased acts of violence committed against citizens and journalists'.[11]

ATTEMPTED COUP – OR FAKE?

A NATO exercise in Georgia, from May 6 to June 1, 2009, contributed to increased tension and escalation of the confrontation between the regime and the opposition, not because the opposition was against cooperation with NATO, but because the regime repeatedly accused the opposition of cooperating with Russia. There were protests by Russian officials, but Georgia emphasized that the exercise was to be unarmed, comprising only desk-type operations, and blamed Russia for being 'hysterical'.[12]

During the continued demonstrations the opposition set up mock prison cells outside the parliament and government buildings to show what they claimed was the reality of Saakashvili's rule. There were repeated violent clashes which left several opposition leaders and protesters injured, as well as three journalists. The television news showed blood seeping from wounded opposition politicians.

It was announced that the main highways connecting Tbilisi with the rest of Georgia would be blocked by protesters on May 6. However, one day earlier the regime declared that it had thwarted a military coup at the Mukhrovani military base 30 kilometres outside Tbilisi, and accused Russia of being behind it. While some commentators in the West seem to have been fooled by this obvious manoeuvre by the government to divert attention from the internal clashes when receiving thousands of guests from the coveted NATO, the Georgian opposition was not. Neither was former minister, General Davit Tevzadze, who publicly refuted the claim about a mutiny or coup.[13] Salome Zurabishvili declared that the opposition was ready to meet with Saakashvili 'to tell him that the country can be saved only if he leaves.'[14] Finally, a meeting between representatives of the government and the opposition took place on May 8 in Tbilisi. While the

During three months, from April to July 2009, mock cells established by the opposition on Rustaveli Avenue transformed the main street of the Georgian capital into a pedestrian area, and also annoyed quite a few city dwellers

leader of the government delegation, speaker David Bakradze, made a positive evaluation of the meeting, Tina Khidasheli of the opposition was less satisfied, although she declared that she was prepared to participate in future talks.

It was demonstrated that not only the government had problems with the prolonged strife when Nino Burjanadze found it necessary to make a public apology to the residents of Tbilisi for the blocking of roads by the opposition demonstrations.[15] An indirect motive for Burjanadze to make an apology may have been that a rumour she had been chosen by Russia as the leader of a new pro-Russian regime, had been spread by Russian-language media.[16] When this and other insulting accusations were repeated by President Saakashvili, Burjanadze replied with utter anger and threatened to open a judicial procedure for public offence against the president.[17]

At the same time the difficulties for Georgian mass media in dealing with the situation were illustrated when the opposition turned against some of the television stations and formed a 'corridor of shame' outside the office of the Georgian Public Broadcasting, through which the staff were forced to walk to reach their workplace. The GPB declared that the picketing was an offence against its personnel and refused to cover the incident as a news item, a policy which, in an act of solidarity, was followed by several other television stations. *Georgian Times* commented that this 'once again revealed the deep-rooted problems existing in the heavily politicized Georgian media'.[18]

The government offered some moves to approach the demands of the opposition, including a commission for constitutional change on a parity basis with a chair appointed by the opposition. However, initially the reaction by most opposition leaders was negative, because they did not believe in the sincere intentions of the president.

In the middle of May a congress for the Assembly of the Peoples of Georgia, gathering participants from 20 countries, was held in Sochi in Russia. In the inaugural speech the president of the organization, Gocha Dzasokhov, an ethnic Ossetian, expressed his conviction that the 'fall of the bankrupt regime' in Tbilisi was imminent.[19] This made the Georgian government denounce the Assembly as a creation of the Russian intelligence bureau FSB, especially when an infamous St Petersburg multibillionaire and oligarch of Georgian origin, Alexander Ebralidze, declared himself while addressing the congress to be a candidate for the presidency of Georgia. A week after the Assembly's congress, Givi Targamadze, an influential lawmaker from the ruling party, claimed that the failed Mukhrovani mutiny had been sponsored by Ebralidze.[20]

In May 2009 the European Union's new Eastern Partnership, comprising six former Soviet Republics, (Azerbaijan, Armenia, Georgia, Ukraine, Moldova and Belarus), irritated Russia. President Medvedev, at the end of the Russia-EU summit in Kharkov on May 22, stated that 'the Eastern partnership must not become a partnership against Russia'. However, he added that 'if the Eastern Partnership develops as a normal economic cooperation there will be no opposition from Russia'.[21]

During the summer of 2009 protests and clashes continued unabated. One bizarre, paradoxical and 'typically Georgian' incident was when Saakashvili offered Salome Zurabishvili the post of deputy minister of the interior, in order to let her check from within how the police handled public protests. However, the offer was withdrawn when Zurabishvili accepted, but emphasized that she intended to remain part of the opposition and continue to demand the resignation of the president.

The opposition signed a 'charter of commitments' to adhere to democratic principles after having taken over power. The main opposition candidate at the presidential election, Levan Gachechiladze, had a meeting with Saakashvili, without result. Saakashvili appointed a commission for constitutional reform with some representatives from the tiny parliamentary opposition. The nonparliamentary opposition, however, refused to participate. The pro-Western leaders of the opposition continued to accuse the West of having 'fallen into Saakashvili's trap'. Nino Burjanadze even alleged in an article in an American magazine that Saakashvili was establishing a 'Soviet-style regime'.[22]

REPRESSIVE TOLERANCE

When I visited Tbilisi in the middle of July 2009 a camp of fake prison cells was still blocking Rustaveli Street, as it had done for the previous three months. One good result of this was that the main street of Tbilisi had been transformed into a pedestrian area. But at the same time it is likely that the image of the opposition had been tarnished. The level of activity in the camp had sunk to close to zero. Most cells were empty. Altogether only two dozen representatives of the opposition were present in the area, in or outside a few cells, playing cards, eating or chatting. Most of the time there was no political activity whatsoever going on, which was easy to observe for all the common inhabitants of the city who had to pass the place on their everyday business. One evening there was a rally with maybe a hundred listeners. The impression was that the organizers had lost their fighting spirit, were tired and exhausted.

Why had the regime allowed this to go on for so long? If a similar action had been attempted in Stockholm, something that would block all traffic on one of the main streets of the city, it would have been cleared by the police in less than an hour. And almost everybody would have appreciated it. Neither the authorities, nor the common people would have accepted something blocking the traffic for political motives for more than a symbolic few minutes. So why did the Saakashvili regime allow this to go on for three months? The general secretary of the Greens, Gia Gachechiladze, did not mince his words when he explained to me why his party did not participate: 'Never, it is a set-up by Saakashvili, to delegitimize the opposition.' He was right, of course. The permission to block the main street for months was a classical example of 'repressive tolerance', a famous method used by ingenious rulers to disarm a protest movement by letting it exhaust itself, and in addition make it look stupid in the eyes of a large section of the public. Obviously Saakashvili had learned from his serious mistakes in November 2007, when his harsh methods cost him sympathy both abroad and at home.

My impression during visits to Georgia in July and September 2009 was that more and more of the opposition representatives understood that they had to reconsider their strategy. That is why they accepted the order to clear the Rustaveli Avenue before the arrival of the US vice president Joe Biden at the end of July. At the same time it seems that Saakashvili had learned something from the struggle with the opposition. In a speech on July 20 he invited opposition leaders to take part in the National Security Council, and promised to give more powers to parliament and the courts, secure the freedom of the press, bring forward local elections from autumn to spring 2010, and introduce a directly elected mayor of Tbilisi. However, the opposition rejected the proposals as window-dressing, which made Vladimer Papava, himself a critic of Saakashvili, accuse the opposition of lacking 'a clearly worked out vision on the main questions'.[23]

In an opinion poll among Tbilisi residents in the middle of April 2009, 50 per cent of the respondents saw the resignation of the president as an unavoidable prerequisite for a solution to the political crisis.[24] Nevertheless, in August the Caucasus Reporting Service asserted that 'post-war opposition protests have strengthened the Georgian president'.[25]

On November 7, 2009, in memory of the upheavals exactly two years earlier, the opposition took to the streets again and promised a renewed campaign against the regime, sending demands to the United States and the European Union to stop all financial support to Georgia until 'democratic reforms' have been introduced. The harsh words were back in the air, Levan Gachechiladze accusing the regime of 'treason' and Salome Zurabishvili talking about its 'criminal actions'.[26] These accusations were partly supported by international watchdogs, such as the International Federation for Human Rights, accusing the Georgian authorities of holding political prisoners,[27] and International PEN, at its congress in Linz, Austria, from October 19 to 25, claiming that Georgian media are subject to 'strict censorship'. At the same time, however, there were signs that at least some parts of the opposition were changing strategy. Irakli Alasania was only one of several prominent opposition figures who announced his intention to campaign for the mayoralty of Tbilisi at the direct election, set for May 2010, thereby possibly getting the same important platform for further ascension as Saakashvili had had in 2000–03.

Whether President Saakashvili will manage to remain in office until the end of his legal term in 2013, or whether his political career will end in the same way as that of all his predecessors in independent Georgia, I dare not guess. But I believe that in some way the political struggle in Georgia reached a new stage in the summer of 2009.

NOTES

1   *Caucasus Reporting Service*, no. 466, October 30, 2008.
2   International Crisis Group, 'Georgia: the risks of winter', November 26, 2008.
3   <http://www.freedomhouse.org/template.cfm?page=363&year=2009&country=7612>.
4   <www.foreignpolicy.com>.
5   Green Party of Georgia, press release, December 2008.
6   Home page of the Georgian Parliament, December 18, 2008.
7   Tsotne Bakuria, former member of the Georgian parliament, *Georgian Times,* April 8, 2009.
8   *Nezavizimaya Gazeta,* April 21, 2009.
9   *Caucasus Reporting Service*, no. 489, April 17, 2009.
10   GYLA, April 11, 2009.
11   GYLA, April 29, 2009.
12   *Caucasus Reporting Service*, no. 490, April 24, 2009.

13 *Georgian Times*, May 18, 2009.
14 *Caucasus Reporting Service*, no. 492, May 8, 2009.
15 *Interpressnews*, May 21, 2009.
16 Published by the Georgian newspaper *Georgia XXI* and spread by Russian-language websites, May 11, 2009.
17 *Civil Georgia*, May 20, 2009.
18 *Georgian Times*, May 18, 2009.
19 *Svobodnaya Gruzia*, May 18, 2009.
20 *Civil Georgia*, May 23, 2009
21 <www.regnum.ru/news/1167047.html>, May 22, 2009.
22 Nino Burjanadze, *The National Interests* (published by Washington-based Nixon Center), *Civil Georgia*, June 2, 2009.
23 *Caucasus Reporting Service*, no. 503, July 27, 2009.
24 Tbilisi residents polled on current situation in Georgia, 16 April, 2009, Georgian NGOs Initiative – Civil Manifesto, Tbilisi, Georgia.
25 Dmitry Avaliani, 'Saakashvili the survivor', *Caucasus Reporting Service*, no. 505, August 7, 2009.
26 Gruziaonline, November 9, 2009.
27 *Caucasus Reporting Service*, no. 517, October 30, 2009.

14

GEORGIA AND RUSSIA, THE PRODIGAL SON AND THE BIG BROTHER

Two weeks after the Ossetia War a Russian newspaper carried a piece of news announcing the opening in Yekaterinburg of an exhibition of Georgian avant-garde art with the title 'In the world of fantasy'. The organizers were keen to emphasize that the exhibition had been planned long before the war, thus 'there is no political allusion whatsoever'.[1] However, the exhibition was not cancelled. This is but one of a great number of indications that the relations between Russia and Georgia are not as hostile and frozen as might be believed.

In June 2009 a Russian website announced that there would be a Russian–Georgian poetry conference on the Georgian Black Sea coast, officially blessed by the Georgian and Russian Orthodox Churches because of its assumed positive impact on 'the development of brotherly relations between the peoples of Georgia and Russia'. Among the participants were the editors of the literary magazines *Novy Mir* (New World) and *Literaturuli Sakartvelo* (Literary Georgia). A round table was held about 'the Russian language and the Russian literature as factors for rapprochement between national cultures'.[2]

One of the stars of Russian television, Georgian-born Tina Kandelaki, is one the hundreds of thousands of Georgians in Russia who have been squeezed by the conflict between their dual loyalties to the two states. When only a couple of days after the ceasefire in August 2008 she was asked by the Russian newspaper *Trud*, 'How do you feel today, like a Georgian or a Russian?' she promptly replied: 'Of course I feel like a Georgian!' But she added, 'In the present Russian society, this does not prevent me from feeling like a full-fledged Russian!'[3] According to her homepage, Tina Kandelaki, born 1975 in Tbilisi, left for Moscow in the middle of the 1990s to be able to pursue a brighter career as television star and artist than was possible in Georgia, but also because 'Georgia is a patriarchal society and the independent Kandelaki, aiming at success, had already broken outside the framework of what was expected by a woman in Georgia'.[4] Her clear statement that she felt Georgian did not stop accusations against her by some nationalist Georgians for being a traitor. In a videoconference in early 2009 she admitted having lost faith in Saakashvili and hoping for another Georgia under the presidency of Burjanadze or Alasania, and also made herself a spokesperson for the large number of Georgians living in Russia:

> Very few of them are citizens of the Russian Federation. All the others are representatives of Georgia outside their country. Nobody paid attention to this part of the Georgian people. They were left without any consideration. The president should think of them also when taking such a step [as the Ossetia War], don't you think?[5]

Tina Kandelaki in many ways personifies an aspect of the Russian–Georgian relations that is unknown or not well understood by many Western commentators: the fact that Russia, at least in its big cities, is a richer, more developed and even more modern society than Georgia. While between a quarter and a fifth of the population of Georgia have emigrated since independence, probably at least as many have had plans or dreams to do the same. Thus, when Georgians are thinking about their personal future, the possibility of emigration plays a major role. And in such dreams Russia has for many reasons taken the first place. Undoubtedly the younger generation today might see London or Paris as their future workplace, more often than Moscow and St Petersburg, but for practical reasons Russia has been and will probably remain the major recipient of Georgian emigrants.

Russia may need Georgia for some rather vague imperial purposes, but Georgia needs Russia much more, for trade, economic relations and a destination for migration. The very practical role of Russia for the social and economic welfare and development of Georgia and the Georgians cannot be replaced by US military advisers or membership of NATO. It is both a mystery and a tragedy that Russian leaders have not understood this, but on the contrary seem to do their utmost to push Georgia into the Western camp.

RUSSIA'S WHIPLASHES

Despite the conflicts over Abkhazia and South Ossetia, official relations between the Russian Federation and independent Georgia did not start badly. Diplomatic relations were established on July 1, 1992. Since then, about 100 agreements on political, economical, military, cultural and humanitarian cooperation have been signed. Even after the Rose Revolution prospects for cooperation were not immediately too bleak. Mikheil Saakashvili made his first visit abroad as president to Russia, in February 2004.

Russian–Georgian economic relations have been based on a free trade agreement of 1994. During the rest of the 1990s, as described in previous chapters, relations were complicated but not cata- strophic. However, in December 2000 Russia imposed visa require- ments on Georgians, supposedly as a reprisal for Georgia's refusal to let Russian troops pursue Chechen guerrillas into Georgian terri- tory in the Pankisi valley, where thousands of Chechen refugees have remained since the First Chechen War of the early 1990s. In June 2001 Russia started to issue Russian passports to Abkhazians and South Ossetians, a policy that after some time made the majority of the population of the two regions into Russian citizens. From 1999 to 2002 Russian warplanes infringed on Georgian airspace at least 25 times. In Russian eyes, Georgia proved by its handling of the Pankisi issue that it was not serious about fighting separa- tism, at least not if it was directed against Russia. In Georgian eyes the Russian behaviour was proof that Moscow did not respect its sovereignty.

In 2004 a briefing document of the European Parliament recapitulated the Georgian issues that Russia was supposed to be unhappy about: its close links with the European Union and NATO, its membership of GUUAM (a grouping of Georgia, Ukraine, Uzbekistan, Azerbaijan and Moldova), its refusal to support Russia on Chechnya, the plans to close Russian military bases and its support for the BTE pipeline. Russia was believed to be aiming at ensuring Georgian membership of the Eurasian Economic Community and the CIS customs union, neutrality on Chechnya and the postponement of the dismantling of the military bases.[6]

After the Rose Revolution tensions between the two neighbouring states increased, and they reached a peak in 2006. On January 26, 2006, explosions in the Caucasian region of Russia broke off gas and electricity deliveries to Georgia. The Georgians accused Russia of deliberately sabotaging the country's energy supply, while Russia blamed terrorists and dismissed the Georgian accusations as absurd and hysterical. In March the chief doctor of Russia claimed that 44 per cent of Georgian wine imported to Russia contained pesticides and ordered a total ban, which hit 80 per cent of Georgia's wine exports. A month later similar accusations were directed against Georgian mineral waters, 35 per cent of which were exported to Russia.

It is worth mentioning that a Georgian minister publicly declared that a lot of the Georgian wine was of such low quality that it could not be sold in Europe, but to Russia 'even faeces' could be exported! And it was a well-known fact that there had been cases of mineral water bottles refilled with water from any tap and falsely sold as the famous Borjomi table water.[7]

Nevertheless, no other country banned Georgian wines and mineral waters. And the fact that the wine ban also hit Moldova, another former Soviet republic with problems with a Russian-supported secessionist region, Transnistria, gives credibility to the Georgian conviction that the Russian measures had little to do with health requirements but were purely political instruments of pressure.

According to Michael Menteshashvili, a member of parliament of the ruling party and old colleague of Zurab Zhvania, whom I met in May 2006 in Tbilisi, the wine boycott hit 400,000 persons in Kahketi province. And now everybody feared that Russia would expel most of the hundreds of thousands of Georgians working in Russia. He said that Georgia hoped to be independent of Russian energy in three years, and asked for help from the European Union and NATO. But at the same time he sighed, 'We cannot keep Russia out for ever!'

ESCALATION

On September 27, 2006, the chain of events escalated further when four Russians were arrested on suspicion of espionage and extradited one week later. According to the website of the Russian embassy in Tbilisi this 'spy scandal' was the starting point for a deterioration in relations, which continued when 'Russia introduced measures to restrict the direct bilateral air and post connections and stopped issuing visas, except for humanitarian reasons'. However, an alternative explanation has been presented by Vladimer Papava, who has suggested that 'everything began much earlier', when it was announced that the Georgian government was planning to sell its main gas pipeline, connecting Russia to Armenia via Georgia, to the Russian giant Gazprom. This deal was stopped by the Americans, who 'not only disrupted negotiations, but demanded that Georgia stop talks altogether on the issue'.[8] According to Papava this was the real reason for the Russians striking back so violently.

In November 2006 the minister for Euroatlantic integration, Gia Baramidze, told me in his office in Tbilisi that 'Russia wants to make us into slaves, to crush us'. And he was extremely critical of some European politicians, such as the former German chancellor Gerhard Schröder: 'they are bought by the Russians'. However, he was satisfied with the new Swedish minister of foreign affairs, Carl Bildt. He also asserted that 'we do not intend to start a war'. Nevertheless he underlined that 'we don't promise not to do it irrespective of what happens; the other side must not be too sure.' The most sensational thing he said, if seriously meant, was that 'we can abstain from NATO as a compromise'. However, after some thought he added, 'But it is impossible to trust Russia, so it will never be on the agenda to abstain from NATO.'

Half a year later, on March 26, 2007, the Georgian government lodged a complaint against the Russian Federation at the European Court of Human Rights, accusing Russia of infractions of several paragraphs of the Convention on Human Rights. The Georgians were particularly upset by the detention of 2,380 Georgians in Russia under deplorable conditions, and the collective expulsion of thousands of Georgians from Russia, which 'involved systematic and arbitrary interference with documents evidencing a legitimate right to remain'. The Russians considered the Georgian action a proof of the unfriendly intentions of the Saakashvili regime.

The immediate effects of the 2006 Russian blockade could be seen in the rapid fall in the volume of Georgian exports to Russia, from US$158 million in 2005 to $69 million in 2007, while Russian exports to Georgia steadily increased, from $353 to $586 million, resulting in a growing trade deficit for Georgia, which reached $517 million in 2007. Russian investments in Georgia have been increasing, despite the tension, from $43 million in 2003 to $93 million in 2007. Russian ownership is especially great in the energy sector, with Russian firms owning 75 per cent of the major electricity distributor Telasi, 100 per cent of Mtkvari Energy and 50 per cent of Transenergy. According to an agreement between the Russian Inter RAO EEC and the Georgian government, the Russian firm is planning major hydropower installations on the River Khrami. The Russian Lukoil has about 25 per cent of the Georgian diesel and petrol market. There is also major Russian participation in the Georgian financial, metallurgy, chemical and mobile telephone sectors.

In January 2007 the Russian ambassador returned to Tbilisi, which by some was interpreted as a new beginning to friendly relations, while others saw it more as a tactical move by Russia to avoid being censored by the OSCE. Vladimir Putin publicly commended Georgia for its agreeing to purchase gas from Gazprom at market prices, and Mikheil Saakashvili admitted on Russian radio that 'both sides' had committed mistakes.[9] However, apart from the unresolved issues of the Russian support for Abkhazia and South Ossetia, the economic blockade and the visa regulations, there were several on-going conflicts, such as Georgian accusations against Russia for allowing uranium to be smuggled into Georgia, Russian allegations that Georgia still harboured Chechen fighters in the Pankisi gorge, and not least, Georgia's threat to stop Russia's entry into the World Trade Organization.

On March 11, 2007, Russian military helicopters supported a ground-to-ground rocket attack by Abkhazians on the Georgian-held part of Upper Abkhazia. And on August 6 an air-to-surface missile, which failed to detonate, was dropped near a Georgian military radar station, in the vicinity of South Ossetia. Russia denied involve-ment, which was partly accepted by international organizations. This caused the Central Asia-Caucasus Institute to blow the alarm whistle and claim that 'the international reaction to the incident – particu-larly on the part of multilateral organizations such as the OSCE and EU – remained grossly inadequate'.[10] Did these incidents indicate growing aggressive intentions by Russia towards Georgia? It is not clear, because at about the same time quite another development was under way, the evacuation of the last Russian troops from Georgia.

During the first post-Soviet period Russia in full agreement with Georgia had kept troops in the country (in 1993 about 15,000 of them), along the border with Turkey and at four military bases, Vaziani (near Tbilisi), Batumi (in Adjara), Akhalkalaki (in the Arme-nian-populated Javakheti) and Gudauta (in Abkhazia). It was agreed at the OSCE meeting in Istanbul in November 1999 that Vaziani and Gudauta should be evacuated by Russian troops on July 1, 2000. The future of the remaining two bases was to be decided before the end of 2000. This did not happen. Talks were delayed but reopened in 2005. An agreement was reached on May 31, 2005, that Batumi and Akhalkalaki should be evacuated by 2008. Nevertheless, Vaziani was evacuated in 2001. On June 27, 2007, 196 buildings and a combat training range in Akhalkalaki was handed over to Georgia, despite strong opposition among the local ethnic Armenian population, who had appreciated the Russian military presence both as a shield against Turkey and as a source of work and income. The Batumi base was evacuated on November 13, 2007. Concerning Gudauta, Russia claimed that it was evacuated according to the agreement and that the remaining Russian military personnel and facilities belonged to the CIS peacekeeping forces. The Georgians doubted this and called for international monitoring.[11]

NO ANTI-RUSSIAN FEELINGS

One night during the peak of the tension in the autumn of 2006 I met Georgian friends in one of the Soviet-style multistorey buildings on the outskirts of Tbilisi, which from its exterior gives the impression that it is about to crumble, but internally could be situated in any well-to-do West European suburb. We had *khatchapuri, khinkali, mtsvadi, kebab* and all the other ingredients of Georgian cuisine that are reminders that the country lies between Russia and the Orient, Christianity and Islam, West and East. On the table stood bottles of the same type of wines and mineral waters that had until recently been items of everyday consumption even north of the Caucasus mountain range. After the Russian ban on the importing of Georgian beverages, restrictions on communications and financial transfers had followed. The Russian actions had substantially affected everyday life for most Georgians in a negative way. In this situation it would not have been unnatural if everything Russian had been avoided and even hated by Georgians.

Nevertheless most of my Georgian friends in their conversations with me preferred to use their fluent Russian rather than their halting English. And when one of them started to play on his guitar and sing a song it was in Russian. It is striking that when the Russian newspaper *Izvestia* some months later sent a special team to Georgia to investigate 'how Georgians live under the rule of Saakashvili', one of its first discoveries was that 'in Tbilisi people sing in Russian'.[12]

There have been many reports about a decline in the Russian cultural presence in Georgia. Undoubtedly there is a difference between the generations. The English language and Western ideals and customs are gaining terrain among the youth. The website of the Russian Embassy in Tbilisi – closed since September 2008 – complains that 70 per cent of all Russian language teachers are unemployed because of the limitation of education in Russian in Georgian schools. At the same time in 2004 it was estimated that 130,000 people in Georgia had Russian as their mother tongue, 1.7 million could use it fluently, 1 million had passive knowledge and only 1.8 million said they did not know it at all. In 2008 a Gallup poll showed that the proportion of Georgians who estimated that knowledge of Russian was very important had increased from 43 to 64 per cent since the previous poll, a result that was interpreted by *Nezavisimaya Gazeta* as a sign that the population 'is not prepared to support the anti-Russian rhetoric of president Saakashvili'.[13]

Signs that the Russian cultural presence is far from eradicated are visible everywhere in Georgia. At least 75 per cent of all books displayed by street sellers in Tbilisi are in Russian, maybe 15 percent in Georgian and only a few in English. In the DVD and CD shops there are overwhelming numbers of Russian discs and films. I have seen Russian politicians being interviewed on Georgian television without either written or spoken translation. In July 2009 at the home of my friend Nato Kirvalidze I found that out of the 50 television channels she could receive, 25 were in Russian, ten in Georgian and only three in English, the rest being in Azerbaijani, Armenian, German, French or Italian.

At a scientific conference in January 2008 on the status of the Russian language in Central Asia and South Caucasus, Dr Dan E. Davidson, president of the American Councils for International Education, claimed that the decline of Russian in most former Soviet republics is an illusion. In fact, he maintained, 'Russian proficiency is not decreasing'. He explained that Russian is still considered an important gate-opener for social advancement and higher status, which is of course connected with Russia's position as the major economic power and the largest recipient of immigrants from the area. Why then the common impression that proficiency in Russian is declining? Davidson's explanation is that urbanization is bringing less well-educated people with deficient knowledge of Russian to the big cities, which creates a flawed impression of a general decline in the status of Russian.[14]

A sometimes forgotten fact is that there are numerous personal relations between Russians and Georgians. One of my Georgian friends frequently resorts to whole sentences in Russian while talking Georgian with other Georgians. When I asked her why, she reacted with astonishment. 'My mother is from Moscow, Russian is just as close to my heart as Georgian. And everybody understands!'

Despite decades of Georgian struggle for national liberation and years of tension and Russian anti-Georgian policies, it is difficult to detect any general anti-Russian sentiment among Georgians, even after the Ossetia War. Most Georgians make a distinction between the present Russian state, led by the Putin–Medvedev regime, and Russian language and culture. A sign of this is the exhibition concerning 70 years of occupation. It is explicitly aimed at the

Soviet rule from 1921 to 1991, not at the previous long Russian supremacy.

The first minister of foreign affairs in Shevardnadze's government for independent Georgia, the experienced Soviet diplomat Aleksandr Chikvaidze, wrote his memoirs some years after the Rose Revolution. While he was highly critical of Russia's policy against Georgia, he emphasized that Georgia could not allow itself the 'luxury of trusting that its future would remain an integral part of the self-interest of the USA'. Even if it was correct to move closer to the West, he asserted, 'Russia cannot be driven out of the Caucasus region'. Thus, he wrote, we must organize our relations with the United States and Europe in a way that avoids creating suspicion among our closest neighbours. 'Our direction should not be pro-Russian or pro-American or pro-European, but pro-Georgian.'[15]

RUSSIANS AGAINST ANTI-GEORGIAN POLICY

The tough anti-Georgian policy by the Putin regime, especially from 2006, has of course had support from some groups in Russia. One example of a not uncommon way of reasoning was an article on a Russian website which claimed that basically the Russian–Georgian tension was a 'cultural war' between different ideologies, but hardly in the way a Western observer, affected by the Huntington hypothesis of 'the clash of civilizations', would assume. To the writer the Georgians in general are extremely narrow-minded nationalists, a theory he tried to prove by recapitulating some statements by Georgians from the early 1990s. Then a professor had demanded the obligatory sterilization of non-Georgians. Another professor had proposed the expulsion of non-Georgians who dared to have more than two children. A future parliamentarian had expressed contempt for the languages and cultures of the non-Georgian minorities.[16]

However, this type of extremely biased view of Georgians is not shared by all Russians. On the contrary there have been an abundance of expressions of dissatisfaction with the anti-Georgian policy. When it was rumoured, during the crisis in 2006, that there had been a decree distributed to all schools in Russia to register all children with Georgian names, it was emphatically denied by officials and politicians. The weekly *Moscow News* presented arguments to prove that the decree must have been an invention by provocateurs who wanted to damage the image of Russia abroad. The same publication also recalled the old cultural bonds, by publishing a full page of

Georgia-praising texts by most of the well-known Russian authors of the last 200 years.[17] Some Tbilisi editions of major Moscow newspapers contained apologetic articles where Georgians were commended for their hospitality and ability to distinguish between politics and people, and their unwillingness to pay the Russian government back in its own coin.

In *Sovershenna Sekretno* a reporter described how Russia 'since the iron curtain fell between our countries' had granted only a few emergency visas for very deserving cases, such as persons who absolutely needed an operation in Moscow. Nevertheless, when the reporter himself arrived at Tbilisi airport, via Baku, he was given a visa 'just as in earlier years' in ten minutes, without having to show any special reasons. He terminated the article with an account of his being invited to a wedding by a friend. 'I felt ashamed. And the more toasts that were proposed in favour of the continuation of the friendship between the Russian and Georgian peoples, the more I felt ashamed, despite the fact that I personally haven't done anything shameful against Georgia!'[18]

Replying to my question how she would have handled the Russian–Georgian crisis of 2006, Salome Zurabishvili exclaimed, 'In the first place I would not have provoked it.' Taking into consideration that many Georgians would agree with that statement, it is very strange that the Russian leadership has not been able or willing to exploit the growing dissatisfaction in Georgia with the Saakashvili regime in a constructive way. Maybe Julia Latynina of *Novaya Gazeta* caught the explanation when some time before the Ossetia War she accused the Putin regime of having made Russia into a copy of the Mongols, which after their rule left nothing but desert behind. Why not behave like the Romans or British, which maintained an enormous cultural and ideological influence long after the dissolution of their empires? When the Soviet Union of Jagoda and Beria was gone, the Russia of Dostoyevsky and Pushkin still had a chance, she wrote.[19]

IS A RUSSIAN CARROT IMPOSSIBLE?

At the beginning of 2008 there was some hope for an improvement in Russian–Georgian relations. In the wake of the CIS summit in March great hopes were expressed that presidents Putin and Saakashvili would be able to solve a lot of problems in a personal meeting. As a matter of fact it was reported that they had agreed to restore the direct air and postal connections and resume the Georgian export of wine and agricultural products to Russia. However, Georgian hopes, expressed by several commentators, that the CIS summit would be a starting point for a general 'thaw' did not come true.[20]

A major reason was of course the NATO meeting in Bucharest in April which, although it did not give Georgia the Membership Action Plan (MAP) it wanted, nevertheless expressed a commitment to grant Georgia membership at some undefined time in the future. The Georgian minister of foreign affairs expressed disappointment, calling the result 'a strange animal', and said that 'it was a mixed signal and was seen in Russia as a mixed signal'. However, it was not too mixed to be able to convince Russia that the possibility that Georgia would become a NATO member was increasing.[21]

As has been shown above, the growing Russian financial and economic presence in Georgia does not seem to have been slowed down even by the Ossetia War. A typical example was a speech by President Saakashvili on the 88th anniversary of the Soviet occupation, February 25, 2009, at the Museum of Occupation, when his main subject was the eternal threat from Russia. Nevertheless he was keen to emphasize that Russian business, Russian investors and Russian tourists are always welcome in Georgia.[22] This was a remarkable acknowledgement of Georgia's strong need for functioning working relations with its Big Brother.

Unfortunately a positive Russian reaction has not been forthcoming. In a television interview in the middle of June 2009 President Medvedev claimed that he was ready to discuss 'issues related to stability in the Caucasus with Western powers', but that there were two red lines concerning Georgia: the recognition of Abkhazia and South Ossetia, which he defined as 'irreversible', and the current regime in Tbilisi, which he described as 'criminal', a regime 'we will have nothing in common with'. In fact he called on the Georgian people to elect a new leadership.[23]

Does this mean that Medvedev will continue the inflexible Big Brother tradition of his predecessors? If so, it implies, according to a formulation by a German specialist on Georgia, that while the Americans use the carrot to draw Georgia closer, Russia keeps using the stick.[24] That tactic is incomprehensible from a rational point of view, when calculating the large amount of economic, cultural and other trumps that Russia has, which could constitute the basis for much more of a carrot strategy.

NOTES

1   *Nezavizimaja Gazeta*, August 23, 2008.
2   <http://olegpanfilov2.livejournal.com/892833.html>.
3   *Trud*, August 14, 2008. For the record: she did not use the word *russkaya* (ethnically Russian), but *rossiyanka* (citizen of Russia).
4   <www.tinakandelaki.ru>.
5   <http://www.tinavssaaka.ru/2008/12/video-konferenciya-tiny-kandelaki-ch1>.
6   EU Directorate-General for External Policies, Information note on the political and economic situation in Georgia and its relations with the European Union, Luxembourg, August 24, 2004.
7   Russian Wikipedia.
8   *The Messenger*, 'Nobody speaks about the real reasons behind the sanctions', Friday, November 17, 2006.
9   Economist Intelligence Unit, 'Georgia, Country Report March 2007', <www.eiu.com,>, 2007.
10 'The August 2007 bombing incident in Georgia: implications for the Euro-Atlantic region', Silk Road Paper, Central Asia-Caucasus Institute and Silk Road Studies Program, Johns Hopkins University, Baltimore, Md., 2007.
11 Kornely K. Kakachia, 'An end to Russian military bases in Georgia? The implications of past withdrawals', PONARS Eurasia Policy Memo no. 24, Tbilisi State University, August 2008.
12 *Izvestia*, 'Kak zhyvut gruzini pod vlastiu Saakashvili?' (How do Georgians live under the power of Saakashvili?), February 13, 2007.
13 *Nezavizimaya Gazeta*, October 28, 2008.
14 'Directions in Language Policy and Practice in Central Asia and South Caucasus', A discussion hosted by the Central Asia Caucasus Institute, January 22, 2008, <http://www.sais-jhu.edu/media/caci/January08/DirectionsInLanguagePolicy1-22-08.mp3>.
15 Alexandr Chikvaidze, *Na izlome istorii* (At the fracture of history), Mezhdunarodniye Otnosheniya, Moscow 2006.
16 Valerij Perevalov, 'Kulturnaya voina' (Cultural war), October 12, 2006, <www.kreml.org>.
17 *Moskovskie Novosti*, no. 40 , October 20–26, 2006.
18 *Sovershenna Sekretno*, no. 11, November 2006.
19 *Novaya Gazeta*, May 8, 2008.
20 <www.ghn.ge>, February 16, 2008.
21 CACI Forum, 'Recent Russian policies in Georgia: how should the West respond?' April 22, 2008.
22 *Civil Georgia*, 'Saakashvili on ties with Russia', February 26, 2009.
23 *Civil Georgia*, 'Medvedev speaks on Russia's red lines on Georgia', June 15, 2009.
24 Silke Kleinhanss, *Die Aussenpolitik Georgiens – Ein failing state zwischen internem Teilversagen und externen Chancen* (The foreign policy of Georgia – a failing state between internal part failure and external possibilities), LIT Verlag, Münster 2008, p. 65.

15

GEORGIA'S FUTURE: CAUCASIAN, EUROPEAN AND NONALIGNED

'I am Georgian and therefore I am European,' exclaimed Zurab Zhvania when on January 27, 1999 he addressed the Parliamentary Assembly of the Council of Europe. In his lectures to Georgian students from 2001 to 2003 (see Chapter 10), he repeats his own expression, but adds, 'However European we may feel inwardly, we will always remain Caucasians.' This goes without saying. Nevertheless, Zhvania found it necessary to say it to his young listeners, which is worth considering. As a matter of fact not all Georgians, especially not all Georgian politicians, seem to have realized this obvious truth. Quite a lot of Georgian politics is characterized by an illusion that further integration with the West, especially NATO and the United States, is the solution for all problems. But neither NATO nor the United States can in any way replace Russia as a market for Georgia's commodities and labour, and a source of investment and energy.

However, the European Union could, at least to a certain extent. But even with the European Union as its major economic partner, as Zurab underlined, Georgia would still be a Caucasian country with an urgent need to resolve the conflicts with its minorities and neighbours, not least with Russia.

NATO: NO SOLUTION

As I have shown in Chapter 4, the usual Georgian opinion that the origin of the secession of Abkhazia and South Ossetia lies in Russia's refusal to accept Georgia's independence is a gross simplification. There have been well-motivated apprehensions in the two regions about certain brands of Georgian nationalism, as well as legitimate ambitions for national liberation and self-rule. Nevertheless, there is no doubt that important groups in Russia have exploited the conflicts for their own purpose.

From a Georgian point of view membership of NATO is often presented as a means of achieving security. But recent history has shown that NATO is not keen to receive a new member which does not already have a reasonable degree of security. NATO is not prepared to risk being drawn into a war to defend a member state which has brought old conflicts with it into the organization. This has finally been proven by the Ossetia War. It is an illusion to believe that the United States and NATO are ready to take serious risks to help Georgia achieve its coveted territorial integrity, despite all the nice words, for example as expressed by vice president Joseph Biden on a visit in Tbilisi in July 2009.[1]

It is likely that NATO honestly wants to have Georgia as a member, but not for Georgia's sake, and not in order to defend Georgia's security or interests. No, NATO wants Georgia as a member to strengthen its own security, by using Georgia as a link in the chain that is being assembled to surround Russia. And what Russia and most Russians cannot accept is not Georgian independence per se, but a Georgia that is part of a hostile strategy that is aimed at containing Russia. Thus, Georgia's ambition to become a member of NATO is counterproductive.

A Georgian declaration of nonalignment would not solve all problems automatically, especially not after the Ossetia War and the Russian recognition of Abkhazia and South Ossetia. Nevertheless, an official Georgian declaration that NATO is no longer an option would profoundly change the situation. At the same time such a policy is not more mysterious, not more deviant or 'anti-West', than the official policy of several EU member states, including Sweden.[2]

Theoretically an alternative to Georgia remaining outside NATO could of course be Russia joining it. In the spring of 2009 the president and vice president of the respected International Crisis Group suggested that NATO leaders should 'make a very clear statement that NATO is an alliance of the free nations open for membership by all countries on the European continent, including Russia itself'.[3] While this proposal is based upon a critical evaluation of the policy of surrounding Russia with NATO members, it is basically illogical. As NATO was established to contain the USSR and has been resuscitated only by constructing the Russian Federation as a similar threat, the logic of the idea of Russian membership is of course to dissolve the alliance.

In a situation where European states are already united in the

Council of Europe, OSCE and the European Union, there is no need for NATO's alleged 'positive cooperation', not even for those who want organized cooperation with the United States, as the United States is already a member of the OSCE. Thus, there is no point in the existence of NATO without a Russian threat, real or invented.

It is true that NATO is seeking new enemies, such as 'international terrorism', in order to motivate its continued existence. It is a well-known disease of all organizations, small and large, to refuse to accept that their purpose has vanished. A lot of vested interests make them attempt to prolong their life by all means. But unless the original rationale is still valid, such efforts usually fail. I am convinced that the NATO leaders have understood that the catastrophic war in Afghanistan will not prolong the organization's survival, but rather contribute to its demise. That is one important reason for the strategy of treating Russia as if it were a reincarnation of the USSR.

WHY NOT A FINNISH OPTION?

In an article published in early 2009, Vladimer Papava and Argichil Gegeshidze tried to find a prototype that Georgia could learn from while searching for a new strategy after the defeat in the Ossetia War. They discuss Finland, Serbia and Cyprus, which all in relatively modern times have had to cope with defeats in war that resulted in loss of territory (Karelia 1940, Kosovo 1999 and North Cyprus 1974). The approach is extremely interesting, but the result of their analysis rather discouraging, because they immediately destroy their own attempt at fresh thinking by stating bluntly that neither the Finnish nor the Serbian examples could be followed by Georgia 'for reasons of mentality and historical memory'. Instead they find Cyprus more relevant, because for 35 years the Republic of Northern Cyprus has been recognized only by Turkey, and there is a peace process in progress that may reunite the two parts of the country.[4] The logical implication of this is that Georgia should wait for decades with the conflict frozen and hope that finally, as is happening in Cyprus, the population of the breakaway regions as well as their patron would be convinced that reunification is in their best interest. Unfortunately the authors have missed several important details, the consideration of which may lead to another conclusion.

In the case of Finland it was not only a matter of the country being forced by Soviet brutal might to accept the territorial loss. Finland did make an attempt to regain Karelia by military force together with Nazi Germany in 1941, which led to a loss of much of the moral support the country had received because of the Soviet assault in 1939. Without the 'Continuation War', the outcome may have been different, something that Georgia might learn from. Fifty years later, after the dissolution of the Soviet Union, Finland was invited to buy back its lost territory, but in 1992 President Koivisto declined because the links had been broken for too long and it would have cost too much to bring the area up to contemporary Finnish standards.[5]

Scandinavia is full of similar examples. I myself live in Scania, an area which was part of Denmark until 1658. It is true that during the first Swedish decades there were several revolts, even organized guerrilla resistance. But from about 1700 Scania has been an integral part of Sweden, and there has never been any broad popular movement demanding reunification with Denmark. For many centuries it has not mattered in practical everyday life to which state the province belongs; the borders have been open for a long time and Copenhagen has remained a centre for Scania despite its being in another state.

In 2009 there were celebrations – or rather ceremonies of reminiscence – in Sweden and Finland because it was the 200-year anniversary of the Russian conquest of Finland, which before that had been an integral part of the Swedish kingdom for at least 600 years. Today nobody in Sweden regrets that Finland is an independent state and not a province of Sweden. As a matter of fact Sweden decided just a few years after the defeat in 1809 to accept the loss and 'win Finland back inside the borders of Sweden', as it was formulated by the national poet Esaias Tegnér.[6] The Finns were rather satisfied with the relative autonomy they were granted as a Grand Duchy inside Russia, until they opted for independence after the Russian Revolution.

Today most people in the West, including Papava and Gegeshidze, seem to take for granted that Serbia must react in the same way as Sweden after 1809 and Finland after 1945 and accept the loss of Kosovo. So why should a mere discussion about Georgia choosing the Finnish option be taboo?

Papava himself in another article has described how time is running out.[7] If no more states recognize them than Russia, Nicaragua and Venezuela, which seems possible, Abkhazia and South Ossetia will be temped to seek entry into the Russian Federation and that would seal the matter for the foreseeable future. If, some day, as 'independent' states, they choose some kind of reunification with Georgia, it would be difficult for Russia to stop it. However, if they are a form of province of the Russian Federation the situation would be different.

So why not go for the Finnish (or Swedish or Danish) model where the lost territories will remain formally outside the 'mother state', but be open for all types of contacts and close relations? Then practical issues, like the return of refugees or compensation for lost property, could be dealt with as in many other cases, such as for example concerning Germans who after the Second World War were forced to leave territories which today belong to Russia, Poland and the Czech Republic. As a matter of fact such a strategy of not changing borders but making them soft, unimportant, transparent, is one of the basic principles of the united Europe most Georgians want to be a part of.

When I put forward ideas like these, people keep telling me, 'The Caucasus is not Scandinavia!' Of course, I know very well that the Caucasus is not Scandinavia. But Caucasians are human beings like Scandinavians, with the same need for peace and security.

Nevertheless, I admit that it is not easy. When I was rapporteur of the European Parliament for South Caucasus I once visited Nagorno-Karabakh and met its president, Arkadi Ghukasyan, in Stepankert. I told him about Åland, the purely Swedish-speaking archipelago in the Baltic Sea between Sweden and Finland, which wanted to join Sweden when Finland received its independence from Russia in 1918. After some time, however, it was internationally decided that Åland should remain part of Finland, but with a very high degree of autonomy. Both Ålanders and Swedes accepted the solution, and since the 1920s it has been a non-issue. Most Ålanders have more practical relations with Sweden than with Finland, but they are citizens of Finland and nobody bothers. My interlocutor got very interested. A year later I met him again, in Yerevan. He told me that he had visited Åland. He was now ready to accept the same status for Nagorno-Karabakh – inside Finland!

Maybe Papava and Gegeshidze are right, maybe 'history bulimia' and other factors make compromise and smooth 'Scandinavian' models impossible. It is not for me to decide, it is up to the Georgians to decide by themselves.

CYPRUS REPEATED IN THE CAUCASUS?

Nevertheless, let us look at the Cyprus model. First, Cyprus, since it became independent, has chosen nonalignment as basis for its foreign relations. Cyprus is situated in a conflict-ridden area, close to both Israel and Arab countries. That it should remain outside major blocs and conflicts has been understood by most Cypriot politicians as a basic precondition for a restoration of internal, national unity. Second, there has been, as Papava and Gegeshidze admit, an extensive use of carrots. The North Cypriots have been able to see how the Southern part has had a more prosperous development and been accepted as member of the European Union. Its patron, Turkey, has been offered, at least in principle, the prospect of membership of the European Union.

In order to repeat the Cyprus model for Georgia the first condition would be to make Georgia attractive for Abkhazians and Ossetians. How could that be achieved? First and basically it is a question of Georgia's internal development, politically, economically and socially. Will Georgia convincingly prove to be a profoundly multicultural society without any remnants of the ethno-religious type of nationalism that has been so scaring for minorities? Will Abkhazians and Ossetians feel that they would be regarded as just as equal citizens in Georgia as they are in their own mini-states or even if they lived in provinces of the Russian Federation? To achieve this there is a need for very imaginative ideas about the future relations between Georgia and the breakaway regions, of the type Zurab Zhvania was pondering when he proposed to Ardzinba that the Abkhazians should have a right of veto, and to appoint a president of a common senate (see Chapter 10). Will the economic and social development make Georgia more attractive than Russia? Could a pensioner in Abkhazia or South Ossetia feel secure that abandonment of their Russian passport and becoming a Georgian citizen would not cost them 90 per cent of their pension? And will the populations of the two regions be convinced that their important relations with Russia will not be hampered?

To achieve this Georgia would have to reconsider its decision to leave the CIS, a move that was of course understandable at a time when Russian troops were attacking Georgia proper and nobody knew whether they were going to assault the capital. Nevertheless the decision is undoubtedly counterproductive not only for the relations between Tbilisi and the breakaway regions, but also for Georgia itself. Even in Georgia some critics have drawn attention to the fact that belonging to the CIS would not involve just a bilateral Georgian–Russian relationship, but be a framework for Georgia's relations with all other former Soviet republics, except the Baltic States. For example, Georgia has enjoyed a visa-free regime as well as a preferential customs and duties regime with all the other ten CIS countries even after Russia's introduction of visas and imposition of economic sanctions. The main loser from Georgia's exit from the CIS will be Georgia, while the effect for other CIS members will be marginal.[8]

A retreat from the CIS, while psychologically understandable, recalls an example of similar counterproductive Georgian thinking, which was mentioned and ridiculed by Zhvania in his lectures. During one of the many crises with Russia some Georgian politicians suggested that Georgia as punishment should impose sanctions on Russia by stopping the export of Georgian wine and mineral water!

The conclusion of this is that rationally, even if it has a bitter taste after the Ossetia War, Georgia's future is not to severe relations with Russia and other former Soviet republics, but on the contrary to contribute to more cooperation in the whole of the Caucasus–Caspian region, including Russia, Abkhazia and South Ossetia.

WHAT CARROT FOR RUSSIA?

In addition, Russia would also need a carrot (just as Turkey has been offered by the prospect of EU membership). What would Russia get for letting Abkhazia and Ossetia go back to Georgia? Here the European Union could and should play a role. To match the Cyprus example Russia should be offered membership of the European Union. One of my first political actions as a new member of the European Parliament directly after Sweden's entry in 1995 was to propose an amendment that Russia has the same right as all European countries to become a member of the European Union, provided, of course, that it fulfils all the conditions, the so-called Copenhagen criteria. Russia is just as much a part of Europe as Turkey, an opinion that was officially confirmed when Russia was accepted as a member of the Council of Europe in 1996. Nevertheless my proposal was rejected by an overwhelming majority, which was a pity. I do not believe that Russia would have been a member of the European Union today if my proposal had been adopted, but in the 1990s there was serious sympathy in Russia with the idea of joining the European Union. In the beginning of the twenty-first century that option is of course not on the agenda of the rulers in the Kremlin (just as it is not on that of the leaders in Brussels). That might, however, change, with new rulers and circumstances.

I believe that it is a tragedy and a major mistake that the West missed the opportunity in the 1990s to integrate Russia into a 'common European House', as it was formulated by Gorbachev. Why was the same logic not followed for Russia after its defeat in the Cold War as for Germany after its defeat in the Second World War? For Germany, European politicians were keen not to repeat the disastrous policy of punishment and isolation of the period after the First World War, which lead to the emergence of Hitler. Today the European Union is often presented as a body of peace that has bound the age-old enemies, France and Germany, in the same framework. But for Russia it seems that many European politicians are prepared to administer the same medicine that was so disastrous for Germany in the 1920s. Many veterans of the Cold War have remained unable – or unwilling – to reverse their basic attitudes and substitute friendship for the well-known hostility towards the 'Russian bear'.

There is unfortunately a basic conflict of interests in a world where the struggle for scarce resources is growing, and a level of consumption and waste like the American lifestyle is possible only by forceful acquisition of much more than one's legitimate share of the common 'environmental space'. Either we cooperate and establish a sustainable level of consumption for everybody, or we compete and fight. Whatever Russia's flaws and sins have been, by not offering Russia a realistic model of integration into a common project the West made a fateful choice. The Russian bear has been driven into a corner, and like any surrounded beast, it strikes back.

However, there are many other forms of cooperation than EU membership that could be offered to Russia. Probably the most efficient offer would be to prove that the European Union does not take part in any policy of surrounding and destabilizing, even dissolving, the Russian Federation. There are some hopeful signs that this is at least partly going on. According to a booklet by the European Council on Foreign Relations (ECFR), 'the EU has established itself as the main diplomatic broker in the conflict between Russia and Georgia'. As a matter of fact the European Union has sent 350 people, including 220 observers, to the conflict area after the Ossetia War. The European Union is also, together with OSCE, the United Nations, the United States, and the parties of the conflict – Georgia, Russia, Abkhazia and South Ossetia – a participant at the Geneva peace discussions which were established according to paragraph 6 of the Medvedev–Sarkozy agreement after the war.

ECFR gives the advice that 'instead of focusing on short-term sanctions against Russia, the EU should move quickly to raise its profile in the Eastern Neighbourhood and to help stabilize other conflict regions'.[9] The recommendation to the European Union to abstain from sanctions against Russia is of course motivated by the too hasty threat by the acting EU president, the French minister of foreign affairs Bernard Kouchner, directly after the Ossetia War, to do just that. A Russian observer listed all imaginable sanctions that might be introduced against Russia: blocking of its membership to the World Trade Organization (WTO) and OECD, exclusion from G-8, no new cooperation agreement with the European Union, and exclusion from the NATO-affiliated Partnership for Peace. But all this, concluded the observer, would probably be more damaging to the United States and/or the European Union than to Russia.[10]

In any case, the option of sanctions against Russia was rapidly deleted from the EU agenda. In February 2009 the EU foreign policy spokesperson Javier Solana told Russian media that 'we opted for dialogue and negotiation rather than sanctions as the best means of passing on our messages and defending our interests'.[11] During the first half of 2009 the EU troika visited Moscow, the European Commission met the Russian government in Kremlin for the first time in three years, talks on a new partnership agreement were resumed and an EU–Russia summit meeting took place.

Nevertheless, it is legitimate to ask what motives the European Union has for becoming engaged in the Caucasus–Caspian region. Is it about the well-being of the peoples of that area and world peace? Or is it more about narrow European interests? According to an EU policy plan for Georgia, the four priority areas are:

- support for democratic development, the rule of law and governance
- support for economic development
- support for poverty reduction and social reforms
- support for peaceful settlement of Georgia's internal conflicts.[12]

That sounds rather altruistic. However, in a chapter on 'Strategic objectives of EU/EC cooperation with Georgia', it is admitted that one aim of the European Union is to 'promote a ring of well governed countries to the East of the European Union ... with which we can enjoy close and cooperative relations'. Georgia is also defined as a central part of the European Union's strategy for 'security and diversification of energy supply', as 'a strategic alternative energy corridor'. This sounds less altruistic, more like the old-fashioned great power politics of the Great Game.

The Eastern Partnership, established in March 2009, leaves a similar ambiguous impression. The European Union gives a promise to 'promote mobility of citizens of partner countries through visa facilitation'. At the same time it is underlined that 'the Eastern Partnership aims to strengthen the energy security cooperation of all participants with regard to long-term energy supply and transit'.[13] In all, there are stated ambitions by the European Union to support Georgia's political, social and economic development, but there is also an openly admitted intention to exploit the strategic position of the country for European strategic interests, especially concerning energy.

The crucial question is of course, if it were to emerge that the two aims are not compatible, that there is a contradiction between Georgia's own interests and its role as a transit country for energy in the interest of the West, how would the European Union react? And what conclusion would Georgia draw? It is not unlikely that it will prove to be in Georgia's interest to not use its position as a transit country as a weapon in the Great Game against Russia. This will not necessitate the closure of any existing route, but it might imply that Georgia should not always give priority to new routes that circumvent Russia.

RUSSIAN NEOCOLONIALISM – OR JUST GLOBALIZATION?

The future of Georgia and other South Caucasus states does not of course lie in reverting to being a kind of Russian satellite. That option is probably not even on the agenda of serious Russian politicians. At least, there is no Russian intention to infringe formally on Georgia's independence. A different question has to do with real economic independence. Here the theory proposed by Vladimer Papava and supported by the Georgian Greens, that there is a premeditated Russian strategy to regain control over Georgia through investments by Russian capital, is worth taken seriously. It is a fact that Russian capital is astonishingly strong in Georgia and that its presence is surprisingly well accepted by the ruling regime in Tbilisi. Does this mean that there is a Russian political strategy to create a 'liberal empire', as formulated by Papava, or even some kind of collusion between Russian Big Capital and the Saakashvili regime, as some oppositional Georgians claim?

The situation brings to mind a wide debate about 'neocolonialism' after the large decolonization of European empires in the first decades after the Second World War, when scores of new 'independent' states were established in Africa, Asia, South and Central America, and Oceania. Very soon left-wing critics revealed that although all these new states had their own presidents, parliaments, flags, anthems and armies, the bulk of their economies were controlled by capitalists from the former 'mother countries'. Even today, when many of these 'independent' states have been members of the United Nations for 40 or 50 years, the economic influence of capital from the former colonial centres is great. This very rarely has anything to do with either covert plans by the governments of Britain, France, Belgium, Spain and the rest, or collusion between them and local leaders to sabotage political independence. Rather such phenomena are effects of international capitalism and globalization. If a country wants to be a loyal partner of world capitalism and lay itself wide open to foreign investments, it is no wonder that most of the investments come from capitalists who know the country, which usually means capitalists from the former colonial centre. This is no different for former 'colonies' of Russia than for former British, French and similar countries' colonies.

Under labels such as 'Arab socialism' and other left-wing slogans, factories and properties of the colonial powers were 'nationalized' in the second half of the twentieth century in order to add economic independence to political autonomy. Is the conclusion that Georgia must cut off, legally and brutally, the possibilities for Russian capital to act in the country?

I think such a policy would be very difficult to implement in our time. First, 'freedom nationalizations' in Asia, Africa and Latin America have not always had the intended result. The outcome has varied, from success to catastrophe. To nationalize a foreign activity risks the outcome that its efficiency is reduced, that independence does not increase but rather decreases. Second, the global ideological climate today is different from the 1960s and 1970s. Then it was quite accepted that after a liberation or popular revolution came nationalizations. Today such activity is often considered to be theft, and causes reactions from international financial institutions and international capital. Third, there are no signs that nationalization or more strict control over investments is part of any political programme of any major political party in Georgia. The ruling elite of the Rose Revolution and the overwhelming majority of the opposition agree on a neoliberal, free-trade agenda, just like all the major supporters of Georgia, such as the United States and the European Union.

The only possibility, if there were a wish by Georgia's political leaders to decrease the economic dependence on Russia, would be to claim that there is a state of war between Georgia and Russia which gives Georgia the right to intervene against Russian interests in the country. Such a strategy might have a chance of being accepted by the West, but not without hesitation and debate. However, what would the direct effect for the Georgians be? Could Russian capital, supplies and commodities be replaced rapidly enough to not make the price unacceptably high?

The problem is of course, that it is even more difficult today than it was in the twentieth century, to take the most infinitesimal step away from the global free market and try to establish a minimum of national self-sufficiency and control over the national economy. One reason is the growing strength of the neoliberal global institutions, like the WTO, the International Monetary Fund (IMF) and the World Bank, which immediately punish every country that tries to make its own decisions about its own economy. Another reason is probably objective. The technological development and specialization is so rapid that not even very large countries have a chance to be on the top if they are not integrated into the world market. If smaller countries try to become independent not only politically but also economically, they usually have to pay a price in the form of lower economic standards (as happened in Cuba).

In a world where a continued increase in the consumption of energy and raw material is not sustainable, this should be a decreasing problem. However, in real politics it is very difficult for one country to maintain such a policy unilaterally without having to limit political freedom. That is why most environmentalists are opting for international and global strategies rather than trying to create national 'Green islands' in the global sea of overconsumption. With a historical comparison, it could be said that the global Green movement does not believe that a Green revolution in one country is possible. Modern Greens are strategic 'Trotskyites', with the crucial difference of course that Greens fundamentally are both democrats and pacifists.

OPTIONS FOR GEORGIA

Based upon this reasoning, I see three options for Georgia:

- To go on as hitherto, which means a growing chasm between a political conflict with Russia and economic dependence on

Russia. This is a risky business, because suddenly the Russian leadership, autocratic as it is, may choose to interfere with the 'free market' and try to use its economic leverage to forward its national interests in the unresolved political conflict.

- To try a kind of 'national socialism', including nationalization or regulation of Russian firms and capital. This option would entail more self-sufficiency and less dependence on the world market. From an ecological point of view probably this is a direction the economic development must take, sooner or later, in combination with renewable energy. However, in the present globalized world with its dominating neoliberal ideology such a strategy would, as I have argued above, be very difficult to implement.

- To try to come under a common political umbrella with the capital interests that are undermining the political independence. This is the logic of the European Union, and the explanation why so many left-wingers and Greens have changed from being opponents of the European Union to trying to use the European Union for progressive politics. They do not believe that small nations are unilaterally capable of controlling the capitalists without having to pay a price that most inhabitants cannot accept. Thus they go for such controls on the EU level.

For Georgia this means that the only remaining way of counteracting the influence of Russian capital is by common political action with Russian politicians who have similar goals. In the short run it could be in the framework of the CIS or Eurasian Economic Community (EAEC). In a longer perspective it might be in the framework of the European Union, with Russia, Georgia and other CIS states as full or associate members. In a recent book about Russia's future until 2050, the mayor of Moscow, Jurij Luzhkov, who is neither liberal nor a friend of the West, nevertheless proposes a kind of merger between the European Union and the Russian-led structures into a Eurasian Union as the only solution for a common future in the world of global capitalism.[14]

My point here is that Georgia has very little chance to counter what Papava has called the establishment of a Russian economic 'liberal empire' through actions against Russia, but only through cooperation with Russia under some supranational umbrella. This is a reason why Georgia should of course not veto Russia's entry into the WTO but promote it. With all its well-known flaws, especially from a Green point of view, the WTO is in fact a supranational body imposing the same rules of the game upon all member states. Georgia has a strong interest in having Russia's trade behaviour come under international scrutiny. If Georgia does not understand that its future depends on a positive and cooperative international-ism, including all the countries that are able to influence its fate, one of which is Russia, the country risks becoming a powerless pawn in the new Great Game.

THE NEED FOR ALTERNATIVE POLICY

The ultimate Georgian paradox is that despite a fierce political battle, which has been going on in Georgia for many years, where one after another the president's colleagues have defected and joined the opposition, the type of discussion I have pursued above has been very rare. The quoted article by Papava and Gegeshidze is an exception. As I have already mentioned, most of the vociferous anti-Saakashvili politicians I have met have almost no alternative policy to offer, either internal or external. What they are virtually telling the voters is, 'The president is a liar and a corrupt criminal; he is

The author interviewing Salome Zurabishvili, former minister of foreign affairs under Saakashvili, now one of the toughest critics of the president and most realistic politicians concerning relations with Russia and the breakaway provinces. After the publication of the EU Tagliavini report on the Ossetia War in September 2009 she declared that a basic prerequisite for the restoration of Georgia's territorial integrity is that Georgia asks for forgiveness for its policies towards Ossetians and Abkhazians.

destroying the democracy just to remain in power. You should trust us, we are honest and democratic and uncorrupted, and if we can only get rid of Saakashvili, we will take over and pursue – exactly the same neoliberal, pro-American and anti-Russian policy. Only we will do it in an honest way!'

A problem is of course that almost every one of these politicians had until quite recently been a close colleague of the president, and until the moment they decided to defect, they were themselves just as scornful and contemptuous about those who had defected a week, a month or a year earlier as the president himself. Why should Georgian voters believe them?

There is no lack of alternative politicians in Georgia, although most are not so alternative that they have never been on board as loyal supporters, not only of Saakashvili but also of Shevardnadze, and in some cases also of Gamsakhurdia, not to mention even earlier personal histories as members of the Communist *nomenklatura*. What is lacking is alternative politics. Among the major parties that have been represented in parliament during the last ten years, only Labour has, in principle, some alternative ideas. This does not mean that I support this party. Even the Greens have of course a very different programme, but for almost two decades now they have not been able to recover from the shock of the defection of their founder, Zurab Zhvania. Most important, however, both Labour and the Greens have understood that NATO is a dead end for Georgia and completely contrary to its geostrategic and economic reality.

There is no doubt that Georgia's future lies in the framework of European cooperation, even as a full member of the European Union. But just as the Finns did after the Second World War and the loss of Karelia, the Georgians must realize that every country with a long common border with Russia must take that reality seriously and cope with it in a rational, unemotional manner. This does not mean that a Finnish model is the unavoidable solution. On the contrary, if the Georgians learn from the Finns how to cope with Russia in an appropriate way, they might find sooner than expected that it is the Cyprus model that becomes possible, which means a nonaligned federation of Georgia, Abkhazia and South Ossetia, as a member of the European Union but not of NATO, and at the same time under some common umbrella with Russia.

Even before the Ossetia War was over, a 'hawkish' US newspaper drew the conclusion that 'Georgia's bid to join NATO is a political casualty of war'.[15] And in September 2009 the very pro-NATO Central Asia-Caucasus Institute estimated that:

the war showed political elites in Georgia that the country's security cannot only revolve around the U.S. and a hypothetical accession to NATO. In Brussels, some political circles have spelt out the possibility of a scenario of 'more EU, less NATO' in order to provide some security guarantees to Georgia without NATO membership.[16]

There were several signs pointing in the direction of closer relations between the European Union and Georgia, such as talks on a comprehensive free trade agreement and moves towards visa facilitation. At the same time reports from the two newly 'independent' separatist states indicated that neither Abkhazians nor Ossetians were completely satisfied with their 'freedom'. The South Ossetians were said to realize that they 'were not ready for independence and may not even want it'.[17] In Abkhazia 'fear of growing Russian influence' is said to have become a major issue of dispute between the government and the opposition.[18] For an imaginative Georgian leadership this should stimulate a long-time strategy of carrots and peaceful methods to make some kind of reunification with Georgia an attractive option for Abkhazians and Ossetians. But as long as Georgia's attitude towards the sincere wishes of these peoples to rule themselves continue to be even more scornful and negative than the attitude of the Kremlin towards the real independence of Georgia, the two regions are inevitably pushed deeper and deeper into the embrace of the Russian bear. If the Georgian opposition wants to challenge the Saakashvili regime it should come up with an alternative strategy towards Abkhazia, South Ossetia – and Russia. Considering the number of former diplomats, government ministers and other experts who have joined the ranks of the opposition, this should not be impossible.

Maybe the reactions to the EU-sponsored Tagliavini report on the Ossetia War, presented on September 30, 2009, heralded a serious political distinction between the regime and the opposition on a crucial issue.[19] While President Saakashvili made contradictory statements, sometimes being dissatisfied with the Tagliavini report because it 'did not name Russia as the aggressor',[20] sometimes declaring the report to be 'a great diplomatic victory of Georgia',[21] the representatives of the opposition rather coherently interpreted the report as a clear rejection of the Georgian policy towards Abkhazia and South Ossetia. 'We believe that the politically irresponsible and indiscreet decision of President Saakashvili to open fire towards Tskhinvali has jeopardized Georgian statehood and its development as a free state,'

said Irakli Alasania, leader of the Alliance for Georgia. Nino Burjanadze, leader of the Democratic Movement-United Georgia party,
said that President Saakashvili should be held responsible for his
decisions.[22] And Salome Zurabishvili made the president 'personally
responsible to his people for having launched the military aggression against Tskhinvali'. She also asserted that 'if in the future we
ever want to renew ties with the populations of Abkhazia and South
Ossetia ... we shall have to ask for forgiveness for the assault upon
Tskhinvali'.[23]

If such statements by people who have a fair chance of becoming the democratic rulers of Georgia in the near future are seriously
meant, the prospects for the future of Sakartvelo, as well as for the
whole Caucasus region, are better than they have been for quite
some time.

NOTES

1   *Georgian Times*, 'Biden's skilful diplomacy leaves Georgians jubilant
    amidst uncertainty', July 27, 2009.
2   The others are Finland, Austria, Ireland, Malta and Cyprus.
3   Gareth Evans and Alain Délétroz, 'NATO and Russia: in need of a bold
    step', International Crisis Group, April 2, 2009.
4   Archil Gegeshidze and Vladimer Papava, 'Post-War Georgia pondering
    new models of development', *CACI-Analyst*, January 14, 2009.
5   Tackade nej till Karelen (Said no thanks to Karelia), *Populär historia*
    no. 5/09, p. 57.
6   This of course meant that there should be no attempt to reconquer
    Finland. The national efforts, instead, should be used for the social and
    economic development of the remaining 'core' Sweden.
7 ' The new threat of the old Cold War', <e.politik.de>, February 18,
    2009.
8   *Caucasus Reporting Service*, no. 485, March 20, 2009.
9   European Council for Foreign Relations, 'Can the EU win the peace in
    Georgia?' August 7, 2008 <www.ecfr.eu>.
10 *RIA Novosti*, August 14, 2008.
11 *Novaya Gazeta* and *Interfax*, February 12, 2009.
12 EU/Georgia ENP Action plan of September 14, 2006.
13 European Union, Presidency Conclusions, Brussels, March 19/20,
    2009.
14 Jurij Luzhkov, *Rossia 2050 – v systeme globalnogo kapitalizma* (Russia
    2050 in the system of global capitalism), Moskovskiye Uchebniki,
    Moscow, 2007.
15 US News and World Report, August 12, 2008.
16 Oscar Pardo Sierra, 'A point of no return? Georgia and the EU one year
    after the August war', *CACI Analyst,* August 19, 2009.

17 *Caucasus Reporting Service*, no. 507, August 21, 2009.
18 *Caucasus Reporting Service*, no. 505, August 7, 2009.
19 Independent International Fact-Finding Mission on the Conflict in Georgia, *Report Vol I–III*, September 2009.
20 N. Kirtzkhalia, 'Georgian President dissatisfied with Tagliavini commission's interpretations', *Trend News*, October 2, 2009.
21 *Civil Georgia,* October 1, 2009.
22 *Civil Georgia,* October 2, 2009.
23 Salome Zurabishvili, 'What lessons should Georgians draw from war probe findings?' Radio Free Europe/Radio Liberty, October 2, 2009.

BIBLIOGRAPHY

Newspaper and other articles and specific website material are not listed here: see the notes to chapters for details.

Anchabadze, George (2005) *History of Georgia: A short sketch*, Caucasian House, Tbilisi.

Babtjenko, Arkadij (2009) *Bilder av ett litet krig* (Pictures of a small war), trans. from Russian by Maxim Grigoriev and Ola Wallin, Ersatz, Stockholm.

Balivet, Thomas (2005) *Géopolitique de la Géorgie, souveraineté et controle des territoires* (Geopolitics of Georgia, sovereignty and control of territories), L'Harmattan, Paris.

Barrington L B (2006) *After Independence: Making and protecting the nation in postcolonial and post-communist states,* University of Michigan Press, Ann Arbor, Mich.

Blijev, Mark (2006) *Juzhnaya Ossetia v kolliziakh rossijsko-gruzinskikh otnosheniakh* (South Ossetia in the confrontation of Russian–Ossetian relations), Evropa, Moscow.

Cassola, Arnold and Gahrton, Per (eds) (2003) *Twenty Years of European Greens 1984–2004*, European Federation of Green Parties, Brussels (Russian version by East European Development Institute, Kiev, 2004).

Central Asia-Caucasus Institute, CACI Forum (2008) *Recent Russian Policies in Georgia: How should the West respond?'* Johns Hopkins University, Md., April 22.

Chervonnaya, Svetlana (1994) *Conflict in the Caucasus*, Gothic Image Publications, London.

Chikvaidze, Alexandr (2006) *Na izlome istori* (At the fracture of history), Mezhdunarodniye Otnosheniya, Moscow.

Coppetier, Bruno and Legvold, Robert (eds) (2005) *Statehood and Security: Georgia after the Rose Revolution*, MIT Press, Cambridge, Mass.

Cornell, Svante (2002) *Autonomy and Conflict: Ethnoterritoriality and separatism in the South Caucasus – cases in Georgia*, Uppsala University, Uppsala.

Cornell, Svante E. and Nilsson, Niklas (eds) (2008) *Europe's Energy Security: Gazprom's dominance and Caspian supply alternatives*, Central Asia-Caucasus Institute and Silk Road Studies Program, Johns Hopkins University, Baltimore, Md.

Cornell, Svante E. and Starr, Frederick S. (eds) (2009) *The Guns of August 2008: Russia's war in Georgia*, M. E. Sharpe, Armonk, N.Y.

236 BIBLIOGRAPHY

Edisherashvili, Sergio (2007) *Georgia*, GAT, Tbilisi.

Ekedahl, Carolyn McGriffith and Goodman, Melvin A. *(2001) The Wars of Eduard Shevardnadze*, 2nd edn, Brassey's, Washington D.C.

Emerson, Michael and Tocci, Nathalie (2000) *A Stability Pact for the Caucasus*, Centre for European Policy Studies (CEPS), Brussels.

Engdahl, William F. (2008) *Mit der Ölwaffe zur Weltmacht: Der Weg zur neuen Weltordnung* (With the oil weapon towards world supremacy: the road to a new world order), 3rd edn, Kopp, Rottenbach.

European Union (2003) Tacis National Indicative Programme 2004–2006, *Georgia, Country Strategy Paper 2003–2006,* adopted by the European Commission on September 23, 2003.

Fähnrick, Heinz (2007) *Kulturland Georgien: Kurzführer für Turisten* (Georgia: country of culture, handbook for tourists), Reichert Verlag, Wiesbaden.

Gahrton, Per (2002) *Report on the Communication from the Commission to the Council and the European Parliament on the European Union's Relations with the South Caucasus, under the Partnership and Cooperation Agreements*, Committee on Foreign Affairs, Human Rights, Common Security and Defence Policy, February 28, A5-0028/2002.

Georgian Young Lawyers Association (GYLA) (2006) *Freedom of Expression in Georgia*, GYLA, Tbilisi.

Goltz, Thomas (2006) *Georgia Diary: A chronicle of war and political chaos in the post-Soviet Caucasus*, M. E. Sharpe, Armonk, N.Y.

Gumppenberg, Marie-Carin von and Steinbach, Udo (eds) (2008) *Der Kaukasus – Geschichte – Kultur – Politik* (The Caucasus – history, culture, politics), Verlag C.H. Beck, Munich.

Hedlund, Stefan (1993) *Hur många Ryssland efter Sovjet?* (How many Russias will there be after the Soviet Union?), T. Fischer, Stockholm.

Hoseli, Eric (2006) *À la conquête du Caucase – épopee géopolitique et guerres d'influence* (Conquering the Caucasus – geopolitical epos and war for influence), Éditions des Syrtes, Paris.

Independent International Fact-Finding Mission on the Conflict in Georgia, *Report, Volume I* < www.ceiig.ch/pdf/IIFFMCG_Volume_I.pdf> (accessed December 8, 2009).

International Centre for Civic Culture (ICCC) (1999) *Political Parties of Georgia, Directory 1999*, ICCC, Tbilisi.

Jawad, Pamela (2006) *Diversity, Conflict, and State Failure: Chances and challenges for democratic consolidation in Georgia after the 'Rose Revolution'*, Cornell University Peace Studies Program, Occasional Paper no. 30-3, December.

Jha, Prem Shankar (2002) *The Perilous Road to the Market*, Pluto Press, London.

Jones, Stephen (2006) 'Georgia – nationalism from under the rubble', in L. B. Barrington, *After Independence: Making and protecting the nation in postcolonial and postcommunist states*, University of Michigan Press, Ann Arbor, Mich.

Jonsson, Anna and Vendil Pallin, Carolina (2009) *Ryssland: Politik, samhälle och ekonomi* (Russia: politics, society and economy), Ersatz, Stockholm.

Kandelaki, Georgi (2006) *Georgia's Rose Revolution: A participant's perspective*, Special Report 167, United States Institute of Peace, July.

Karny, Yo'av (2000) *Highlanders: A journey to the Caucasus*, Farrar, Straus & Giroux, New York.

Karumidze, Zurab and Wertsch, James V. (eds) (2005) *'Enough': The Rose Revolution in the Republic of Georgia 2003*, Nova Science, New York.

Kleinhanss, Silke (2008) *Die Aussenpolitik Georgiens: Ein failing state zwischen internem Teilversagen und externen Chancen* (The foreign policy of Georgia: a failing state between internal part failure and external possibilities), LIT Verlag, Münster.

Kochieva, Inga and Margiev, Aleksej (2005) *Gruzia: etnicheskie chistki v otnoshenie osetin* (Georgia – ethnic cleansing in relation to the Ossetians), Evropa, Moscow.

Kunin, Daniel (ed.) (2006) *Javakheti*, Millennium Challenge Georgia Fund, Tbilisi.

Leontiev, Mikhail and Zhukov, Dmitrij (2008) *'Nezavisimaya' Gruzia: Bandit v tigrovoj shkure* ('Independent' Georgia: a bandit in a tiger's hide), Yauza Press, Moscow.

Luzhkov, Jurij (2007) *Rossia 2050: V systeme globalnogo kapitalizma* (Russia 2050 in the system of global capitalism), Moskovskye Uchebninki, Moscow.

Lövkvist, Amanda (2007) *I väntan på Lenins begravning* (Awaiting the funeral of Lenin), Silc, Stockholm.

Marshania, Lorik (1998) *Pravda o tragedii Abkhazii* (The truth about the Abkhazian tragedy), Samshoblo, Tbilisi.

Metreveli, Roin (1995) *Georgia*, Publishers International, Nashville, Tenn.

Minassian, Gaïdz (2007) *Caucase du Sud, la nouvelle guerrre froide* (South Caucasus, the new cold war), Éditions Autrement, Paris.

Mitchell, Lincoln A. (2009) *Uncertain Democracy: U.S. foreign policy and Georgia's Rose Revolution*, University of Pennsylvania Press, Philadelphia, Pa.

Moroz, Oleg (2006) *1996: Kak Ziuganov ne stal presidentom* (1996: How Ziuganov did not become president), Raduga, Moscow.

Mossberg, Mathias (2009) *I mörka vatten: hur svenska folket fördes bakom ljuset i ubåtsfrågan* (In dark waters: how the Swedish people were decieved about the submarines), Leopard, Stockholm.

Munkhammar, Johnny and Millarp, Jon (2008) *Georgien: den lysande stjärnan på reformhimlen* (Georgia: the shining star on the reform sky), Timbro, Stockholm.

Nasmyth, Peter (2001) *Georgia: In the mountains of poetry*, 2nd rev. edn, Curzon Caucasus World, London.

Naumann, Klaus, Shalikashvili, John, Inge, Lord, Lanxade, Jacques and van den Breemen, Henk (nd) *Towards a Grand Strategy for an Uncertain World: Renewing transatlantic partnership*, World

Security Network, Munich, Germany <www.worldsecuritynetwork. com/.../3eproefGrandStrat(b).pdf> (accessed 23 November 2009).

Nielsen, Fred (2006) *Wind der weht: Georgien im Wandel* (Blowing wind: Georgia under transformation), Wieser Verlag, Vienna.

Nilsson, Niklas, Popjanevski, Johanna, Metreveli, Ekaterine and Yakobash-vili, Temuri (2009) *State Approaches to National Integration in Georgia: Two perspectives*, Central Asia-Caucasus Institute and Silk Road Studies Program, Johns Hopkins University, Baltimore, Md.

Nodia, Ghia and Pinto Scholtbach, Alvaro (2006) *The Political Landscape of Georgia*, Eburan Academic, Delft.

Papava, Vladimer (2005) *Necroeconomics: The political economy of post-communist capitalism*, iUniverse.com, New York.

Papava, Vladimer and Ismailov, Eldar (2006) *Tsentralnyj Kavkaz, ot geopolitike k geoekonomike* (Central Caucasus, from geopolitics to geo-economics), CA & CC Press, Stockholm.

Pavlovskij, G. O. (2005) *Kirgizkij perevorot, mart aprel 2005* (The Kirgizian rebellion March–April 2005), Evropa, Moscow.

Poe, Marshall T. (2005) *Den ryska tiden i världshistorien* (The Russian time in world history), SNS, Stockholm.

Pogrebinskij, M B (2005) *Orenzhevaya revolutsia: losungi i realnost* (The Orange revolution: slogans and reality), Evropa, Moscow.

Politkovskaya, Anna (2003) *Tjetjenien: sanningen om kriget* (Chechnya: the truth about the war), Ordfront, Stockholm.

Politkovskaya, Anna (2004) *Putins Ryssland* (Putin's Russia), Ordfront, Stockholm.

Primakov, Evgenij (1999) *Gody v bolshoi politiki* (The years in big politics), Molodaya Gvardiya, Moscow.

Primakov, Evgenij (2007) *Minnoe pole politiki* (The minefield of politics), Molodaya Gvardiya, Moscow.

Quiring, Manfred (2009) *Pulverfass Kaukasus: Konflikte am Rande der russischen Imperialismus* (Powder keg Caucasus: conflics at the margin of Russian imperialism), Ch. Links Verlag, Berlin.

Regnum (sbornik/anthology) (2006) *Vosstanye menshinstv – Kosovo, Moldaviya, Ukraina, Gruzia, Kyrgystan* (The revolt of the minorities – Kosovo, Moldavia,Ukraine, Georgia, Kirgizia), Evropa, Moscow.

Roelofs, Sandra Elizabeth (2005) *Die first lady of Georgië – het verhal van een idealiste* (The first lady of Georgia, the story of an idealist), Archipel, Amsterdam.

Rotbacher, Albrecht (2008) *Stalins langer Schatten, Medwedjews Russland und der postsowjetische Raum* (The long shadow of Stalin, Medvedev's Russia and the post-Soviet area), Ares Verlag, Graz.

Rudbeck, Olof (1679–1702) *Atland eller Manheim*, Curio, Uppsala.

Russian Orthodox Church (2007) *Rossija i jejo 'kolonii' – o tom kak Gruzia, Ukraina, Pribaltiki i prochiye respupbliki voshli v sostav Rossii* (Russia and its 'colonies' – how Georiga, Ukraine, the Baltic States and other republics entered the Russian realm), Moscow.

Rustaveli, Shota (1984) 'Vitjas v tigrovoj shkure' (The knight in the panther's skin), Merani, Tbilisi.

Schewardnadze, Eduard (Shevardnadze, Edward) (1999) *Die neue Seiden-strasse: Verkehrsweg in die 21. Jahrhundert* (The new Silk Road: a communication route of the 21st century), Econ Verlag, Munich.

Schewardnadze, Eduard (Shevardnadze, Edward) (2007) *Als der Eiserne Vorhang zerriss, Begegnungen und Erinnerungen* (When the Iron Curtain was torn to pieces, meetings and memories) Peter M. Metzler Verlag, Duisburg.

Serrano, Silvia (2007) *Géorgie: sortie d'empire* (Georgia: exit from the empire), CNRS Éditions, Paris. Solzhenitsyn, Alexander (1998) *Rossia v obvale* (Russia at the brink of crumbling), Moscow.

Starr, S. Frederick and Cornell, Svante E. (2005) *The Baku–Tbilisi–Ceyhan pipeline: Oil window to the West*, Central Asia-Caucasus Institute and Silk Road Studies Program, Johns Hopkins University, Baltimore, Md.

Suny, Ronald Grigor (1994) *The Making of the Georgian Nation,* 2nd edn, Indiana University Press, Bloomington, Ind.

Telen, Ludmilla (2004) *Pokolenye Putina* (Putin's generation), Vagrius, Moscow.

Turmanidze, Turnike (2009) *Buffer States: Power policies, foreign policies and concepts*, Nova Science, Hauppauge, N.Y.

United Nations (2008) *Report of the Secretary-General on the situation in Abkhazia, Georgia*, S/2008/480, Security Council, July 23, 2008.

United Nations (2009) *Report of the Secretary-General pursuant to Security Council resolutions 1808 (2008), 1839 (2008) and 1866).*

UN Environment Programme (UNEP) (2002) *Caucasus Environment Outlook,* UNEP, Geneva <http://www.grid.unep.ch/activities/assessment/geo/ceo.php> (accessed 23 November 2009).

Wright, John (2000) *Tbilisi: A guide*, W. & W. Press, Tbilisi.

Yeltsin, Boris (2000) *Presidentskij Marafon* (The presidential marathon), AST, Moscow.

Zaslavskij, Ilja (2005) *Delo truba – Baku–Tbilisi–Ceyhan i kazakhskij vybor na Kaspii* (The issue of the Baku–Tbilisi–Ceyhan pipeline and the Kazakh choice at the Caspian), Evropa, Moscow.

Zhvania, Zurab (2009) *The Privilege of our Generation*, GIPA, Tbilisi.

Zhylina, I. U. (ed.) (2001) *Ekonomicheskiye i sotsialniye problemy Rossii: desyat let rossiskich ekonomicheskikh reform* (Economic and social problems of Russia: ten years of economic reform), Inion RAN, Moscow.

Zhyltsov, S. S. (2002) *Geopolitika Kaspijskogo regiona* (The geopolitics of the Caspian region), Mezhdunarodniye Otnosheniya, Moscow.

WEBSITES WITH NEWS AND COMMENTS ABOUT GEORGIA

www.apsny.ge
www.ca-c.org
www.cacianalyst.org

www.caucaz.info
www.cenn.org
www.civil.ge
www.georgiatoday.ge
www.geotimes.ge
www.ghn.ge
www.gyla.ge
www.kavkazweb.net
www.messenger.com.ge
www.novayagazeta.ru
www.pankisi.info
www.papava.info
www.regnum.ru
www.silkroadstudies.org
www.svobodnaya-gruzia.com

INDEX